SPECIAL PROVISION FOR READING
When will they ever learn?

SPECIAL PROVISION FOR READING
FOR READING
When will they ever learn?

David Moseley

NFER Publishing Company

Published by the NFER Publishing Company Ltd.,
Book Division, 2 Jennings Buildings, Thames Avenue,
Windsor, Berks., SL4 1QS

Registered Office: The Mere, Upton Park, Slough, Berks., SL1 2DQ

First Published 1975

© *David Moseley 1975*

85633 063 9

Printed in Great Britain by
King, Thorne and Stace Ltd., School Road, Hove, Sussex, BN3 5JE

Distributed in the USA by Humanities Press Inc.,
Hillary House-Fernhill House, Atlantic Highlands,
New Jersey 07716, USA

Contents

Acknowledgements

I am grateful to Professor John Merritt for suggesting that I should write this book, and to him and others at the Open University for the example of a rigorous approach to research-based writing.

Colleagues at the Centre for Learning Disabilities were always willing to try out new ideas, to prepare new materials, and to keep records. Without their support and enthusiasm, relatively little would have been achieved at the Centre between 1968 and 1971.

Thanks are due to the LEA officers who completed a questionnaire on remedial provision and who approved the summary statements given in Chapter 4.

David Fairman, Howell Morgan and the National Society for Mentally Handicapped Children kindly supplied some of the photographs. My thanks are also due to the teachers, students and parents who agreed to be photographed for this book.

Veronica Finch, Pat Gillam, Jean Gross and David Hinton wrote drafts for the Activity Sheets in Appendix D. They and other trainee educational psychologists have helped to develop the practice of extended assessment and diagnostic teaching at the Child Guidance Training Centre.

I should like to thank Houghton Mifflin and Penguin Books for permission to quote from Kozol's *Death at an Early Age*.

Caroline Moseley has endured the manuscript's protracted birth pangs and has exercised both menial and intellectual talents in nourishing it.

Chapter One

Approaching the Problem

Special provision for backward readers has steadily expanded since 1945. Many local authorities employ a number of teachers in Child Guidance Clinics. Teams of peripatetic teachers have been recruited, part-timers brought into service, remedial departments set up. Diploma courses in the teaching of reading have been established and in-service training is proceeding apace. New methods and aids have come into use and even the Talking Typewriter has been given a fair trial.

The main impetus for the expansion of special reading services has come from surveys which have shown the extent of reading backwardness and have pointed to the association between illiteracy and antisocial behaviour. In these circumstances one would expect local authorities to keep careful records in order to assess the effectiveness of their services. One might suppose that certain types of organization would prove to have clear advantages, and that expansion would be planned accordingly. In fact, very few authorities seem to have based their decisions on internal action research. The diversity in the scope and nature of special educational provision shows that development has been almost entirely on an *ad hoc* basis. From time to time doubts have been expressed regarding the effectiveness of remedial teaching and other forms of special provision for slow learners. There are now a number of small-scale studies showing that improved scores after remedial work are at best short-term gains. Those in charge of remedial services like to think that they have overcome problems of this kind, but are unable to produce evidence to prove the point.

Despite the increase in special provision, there are still large numbers of children who cannot or will not read. In fact, the evidence (Start and Wells, 1972) suggests that there are now more backward readers in ordinary schools than there were ten years ago. Is something seriously wrong with teacher-training or perhaps with classroom practice? Are we spending enough on giving individual help to children with learning problems? Is more research needed? Do we make proper use of medical and psychological expertise ? Have the linguists or sociologists something to offer ? Or should we admit that no more can, or nowadays need, be achieved, and try to equip non-readers with other useful skills ?

This book is concerned with various possible ways of using additional personnel and equipment in order to reduce the incidence of poor attainment in reading. Value judgements are inevitable in a work of this kind. The writer believes that maximum effort should be directed towards achieving minimum standards of literacy in all children, except the most severely subnormal. There are far too many children, in both junior and secondary schools, who are unable to read more than a few hundred words and who have the greatest difficulty in writing intelligible sentences. Some of these children are alert and creative in other ways, but the majority appear to be untalented, deprived, unhappy, lazy, poorly or wrongly motivated. If their learning difficulties and their emotional needs are neglected, backward readers typically become increasingly discouraged and disturbed. The personal and social consequences of illiteracy are difficult to assess at all objectively, but in extreme form can involve a total rejection of school and society.

There is reason to believe that with skilled individualized teaching, almost all children can achieve at least a minimum standard of literacy (i.e. a reading vocabulary of approximately 1000 words and writing skills adequate for regular correspondence). Moreover, it is not only the apparently bright retarded reader who responds to special provision: the dull child is known to benefit almost as much from extra help if he is a non-starter (Lytton, 1961; Cashdan and others, 1971).

Backwardness and retardation

'Remedial' education is one form of special educational treatment, and is provided in terms of the 1944 Education Act for children whose attainments in basic subjects are well below average. In practice, remedial teaching is normally offered to children whose attainments fall below the standard expected for their age and ability by more than 20 per cent. In the Department of Education and Science (1964) pamphlet *Slow Learners at School*, it is estimated that approximately ten per cent of the total school population is significantly backward in language and in number. Some of these children attend special schools, but the majority attend ordinary schools. The authors of the pamphlet suggest that special classes should be set up for slow learners (at least two per school at junior level), and that remedial help should also be available. 'The head teacher can often withdraw those who need help and teach them in small groups in his room. Part-time and peripatetic teachers can also be useful. . . . In this way groups of up to five or six children can receive short, preferably daily, periods of help. . . .' The distinction between 'slow learners' and children in need of remedial help is based on the distinction between general *backwardness* and specific *retardation*. The argument is that it is unreasonable to expect much progress in the basic subjects from children who are both dull and backward. These children should therefore be taught in relatively large groups called special classes. On the other hand, there may well be untapped talent in those who are of average intelligence or above and yet are backward in one of the three Rs, so they should be given intensive help in small groups.

The classical 'remedial' child, as described by Schonell (1948), is one who has not realized his educational potential, who 'could do better'. Remedial teaching (if one interprets the term strictly) is based on the assumption that there are certain kinds of specific learning difficulty which can be overcome by appropriate educational methods. Remedial teaching (in the narrow sense) is not suitable for those dull children who have no particular strengths or weaknesses, nor for those children whose handicaps cannot be remedied in the short term. This concept of remedial education depends, however, on the validity of the procedures whereby one tries to measure educational potential as well as on empirical evidence regarding the efficacy of special teaching methods and therapeutic practices.

Current doubts about the value of intelligence tests in general, together with a growing body of research concerning the poor predictive value of IQs in remedial settings, lead one to question the value of making a distinction between backward readers and retarded readers. When the distinction is made it invariably works against the much larger body of slow learners and favours the retarded, who usually have higher IQs and certainly include a large proportion of middle-class children than those who are both dull and backward. In practice it is the remedial services having close links with Child Guidance Clinics that have tended to confine their interest to the Schonellian 'retarded' child. Elsewhere, particularly in secondary schools, the distinction between remedial provision for the retarded as opposed to special provision for the dull and backward has become increasingly blurred. In their survey of remedial education at secondary level, Sampson and Pumfrey (1970) have found that little distinction was made between 'slow learners', 'backward' and 'remedial' types.

Teachers understandably feel that individualized instruction and other special help (such as psychotherapy or counselling) should be available for all children with learning difficulties. Those who have to teach 'special' classes of 20 or more children know that much more could be achieved if extra help and suitable individualized programmes of work were available. Teachers have to spend too much of their time dealing with behaviour problems. These would be much less likely to arise if 'special' education became a reality (Moseley, 1972a).

The clinical approach

The word 'remedial' suggests a medical model and implies that there is something wrong with the child which can be put right by 'treatment'. Historically, many remedial services have had a clinical origin. Until the late 50s the usual Child Guidance approach to a backward reader was to assume that no real progress was possible unless an emotional block were removed. There has since been a gradual (but not universal) change of emphasis. Pringle (1962) advocated a concurrent approach in which the teaching of reading was accompanied by 'emotional re-education'. While no remedial teachers would underestimate the importance of creative and expressive work, there are now many for whom the aspect of skill-acquisition is primary. In fact, psychiatrists sometimes recommend remedial teaching as a therapeutic measure because of the increased self-confidence which develops once a pupil begins to make progress. In a substantial proportion of cases, emotional disturbance is now thought to be a consequence rather than a cause of reading failure.

While psychiatrists have been concerned mainly with emotional con-comitants of learning difficulties, neurologists have approached the subject by looking at cognitive, perceptual and motor development. In a very few cases there is some evidence of damage to the nervous system, but in the absence of this, neurologists tend to think in terms of slow maturation and genetic abnormalities. Critchley (1970) reports that a group of neurologists has defined 'specific developmental dyslexia' as 'a disorder manifested by difficulty in learning to read despite conventional instruction, adequate intelligence, and socio-cultural opportunity. It is dependent upon fundamental cognitive disabilities which are frequently of constitutional origin.'

Groups of parents have played an important part in the 'dyslexia' controversy. They have criticized LEA provision which does not include individual teaching for those diagnosed by neurologists as dyslexic, and have pressed for government recognition of 'dyslexia' as a handicapping condition. Charities have provided additional services in the hope that local authorities would follow suit. As a consequence, Section 27 of the Chronically Sick and Disabled Persons Act, 1970, came to be formulated. This requires local authorities to report on their provision (if any) for 'dyslexics'. It does not enjoin authorities to make special provision either for the diagnosis or for the treatment of such persons. In fact, in the opinion of an expert sub-committee of the Department of

Education and Science (1972), no reliable means of diagnosing 'dyslexia' has yet been found. This committee preferred to use the term
'specific reading difficulties' to describe 'the small group of children
whose reading abilities are significantly below the standards which their
abilities in other spheres would lead one to expect'. These children
require the same kind of teaching as other backward readers, namely 'an
approach tailor-made to the needs of the individual child'. The committee drew attention to the danger that children with specific reading
difficulties might be specially favoured at the expense of other backward
readers if they were diagnosed as suffering from 'specific developmental
dyslexia'. This danger is certainly not an imaginary one. Of 98 'specific
dyslexics' described by Naidoo (1972), 75 (77 per cent) belonged to
social classes 1 and 2. Moreover, Critchley's concept of 'specific developmental dyslexia' excludes those who have had inadequate 'socio-
cultural opportunity' to learn to read.

The psycho-educational approach

In the USA parents (and professionals) have been more successful
than in the UK in campaigning for special provision for retarded (as
opposed to backward) children. The diagnostic label which has gained
acceptance in the USA is the term 'learning disabilities'. In 1968, the
US National Advisory Committee to the Bureau of Education for the
Handicapped, Office of Education, put forward the following definition:

> Children with special learning disabilities exhibit a disorder in
> one or more of the basic psychological processes involved in under-
> standing or in using spoken or written language. These may be
> listed as disorders of listening, thinking, talking, reading, writing,
> spelling or arithmetic. They include conditions which have been
> referred to as perceptual handicaps, brain injury, minimal brain
> dysfunction, dyslexia, developmental aphasia, etc. They do not
> include learning problems which are due primarily to visual, hearing
> or motor handicaps, to mental retardation, emotional disturbance
> or to environmental deprivation.

Here again we have a category of handicap which is distinct from the
general problem of backwardness and which excludes those who suffer
from 'environmental deprivation'. A sceptic might feel that the professionals concerned have selected a subgroup of slow-learning children
upon whom to practise their expensive diagnostic expertise. In practice
however, the term 'learning disability' is often interpreted more
flexibly than the above definition might suggest.

In America 'learning disabilities' is rapidly becoming a high-
prestige branch of special education. School systems receive govern-

ment subsidies if they set up special classes and other services for children so diagnosed.[1] Many universities now offer courses leading to a master's degree or to a doctorate in learning disabilities. The 'diagnostic-remedial specialist' is emerging from such courses, as described by Kirk (1969). 'In the past we have relied on the doctor to make a medical examination, the psychologist to administer the mental or other tests, the social worker to give a history, and then when the team has determined that a learning disability in a child does exist, the child is referred to a remedial teacher to organize a programme for him. This procedure has not worked too well, since the individuals who assess the child and determine his eligibility for a programme have few specific suggestions for the teacher who is going to conduct his remediation. What we really need are people with interdisciplinary training who can give the psycho-educational diagnosis, evolve the remedial hypotheses, and organize the remedial programme for the child.'

There is general agreement in this country that the majority of children with specific learning difficulties should be given extra help in their ordinary schools, either in withdrawal groups or in the ordinary classroom. Because of this, it is unlikely that we shall see special classes for children with learning disabilities set up in our schools. The resource-room approach, however, has considerable potential, and most class teachers welcome practical support from specialists. In many areas, there is a desperate need for improved screening, diagnostic, advisory and teaching services for children who cannot easily adapt to a normal curriculum.

This point was forcibly made by Rutter and others (1970) in their postscript to the Isle of Wight study: 'The ordinary classroom teacher will be responsible for the education of most handicapped children. But just as in medicine the general practitioner requires to be able to turn for advice to a medical consultant, so also the classroom teacher should be able to turn to educational consultants for advice about teaching methods'. They go on to say that 'many of the children requiring special educational help for their reading difficulties are also those whose behaviour presents many problems in the classroom. Poor concentration, restlessness, mischief-making, and poor relationships with other children are likely to be prominent features. The anti-social disorder may require treatment at the clinic or elsewhere outside the school but

---

[1]The Education of all Handicapped Children Bill (1973) would provide for Federal payments of 75 per cent of the average additional costs required to provide public education for handicapped children. The terms of the Bill include learning disabilities and require (a) that an individualized written programme should be devised for each child, and (b) that handicapped children should be educated, at least partly, with their normal peers.

recent studies have also suggested that modification of the classroom situation itself may have a most important part to play in treatment'.

This view implies a move away from the medical model of disease, diagnosis and treatment towards a psycho-educational model which emphasizes the modification of behaviour in the learning situation. An explicit recommendation on this point was made by the Canadian Committee of the Council for Exceptional Children (1971):

> It is recommended that for educational purposes, exceptional children should be classified according to learning characteristics rather than according to medical aetiology.

The socio-linguistic approach

A learning situation in school and a test situation in a clinic are both social situations involving the use of language. Children from financially and emotionally impoverished families are much more likely to fail in school than those who are secure, creative and confident. The failing child may be rejected by other children and even by his teacher, particularly if his behaviour is immature or disruptive, or if he has 'dirty' habits. If his language development is retarded he may have difficulty in understanding and in making himself understood. Disadvantaged children from working-class families, as well as those with foreign-born parents, may also find themselves on the receiving end of class and racial prejudice. The attitudes of most schools are middle-class, and the vocabulary of a typical reading test suggests that teachers are aiming to turn out academic gentlefolk well-versed in the classics.

The National Child Development Study (Davie and others, 1972) is the latest in a series of surveys which have shown that working-class children tend to perform rather badly on tests of intelligence and attainment and are more likely than others to be considered maladjusted by their teachers. Davie and others found that 70 per cent of the national sample of 14,128 children had fathers in manual occupations. One can infer from this statistic that the majority of children in this country respect and love adults who show indifference if not disdain for 'book-learning'. We do not really know just how much the presence of a teacher or tester of higher socio-economic status limits the educational performance of working-class children, but evidence that this does happen is beginning to accumulate. It is perhaps for similar reasons that immigrant children perform better if their teachers are able to bridge the culture-gap, and negroes in New York perform better when tested by computer than when tested by a researcher (Johnson and Mihal, 1973).

Bernstein (1958) was one of the first to focus attention on the different patterns of language to be found in working-class and middle-class groups. There can be little doubt that these language differences are socially divisive, and that the 'restricted code' of many children from working-class families handicaps them in school. Yet it is naïve to assume that teachers can redress the balance of social and economic disadvantage by simply 'teaching them to speak'. To attempt to change a child's language by giving him the vocabulary, sentence-structure and accent of his middle-class peers is not only quite unrealistic, but may be positively harmful. One the other hand, much can be achieved by teachers who honestly value the experiences and the language of *all* children, however deprived.

Language development is one of the central themes in what is variously called 'compensatory education' or 'education for equality'. Both in the USA and in this country the language abilities of poor children fall more and more below national norms from the beginning to the end of compulsory schooling. The effects of poverty and deprivation are self-perpetuating, from one generation to the next, and it was 'to secure for every child increasing opportunities of contributing to the nation's progress' that the idea of 'positive discrimination' in educational priority areas was put forward in the Plowden report (Department of Education and Science, 1967).

Halsey (1972) outlines three basic educational approaches to the problems of poverty, focusing (a) on the home, (b) on the school and (c) on the relationships between the school and the community. All three approaches feature in the Plowden recommendations, the aim of which was 'to make schools in the most deprived areas as good as the best of the country'. This was to be done by applying the principle of positive discrimination in favour of such schools, 'going well beyond an attempt to equalize resources'. It was hoped that within five years 10 per cent of all pupils would benefit from the measures suggested, and that in the longer term 'the programme may be expanded to cover a larger proportion of the population'.

In the event, the extra resources that have been allocated to priority schools either by central or by local government have been so meagre that no-one has been able to point to any marked improvements in pupil attitudes or attainments. The financial deprivation which besets British action-research in compensatory and special education is such that no-one is able to say whether or not it is possible to reach the Plowden goal of equality of access to (higher) education. In the words of the Plowden report, the attempts so far made 'have not been sufficiently generous or sustained, because the handicaps imposed by the environment have not been explicitly and sufficiently allowed for'.

Many sociologists would subscribe to the view that equal *access* to education is not enough, and that suppressed and minority groups should be enabled to *achieve* the same educational standards as everyone else. It is doubtful whether this goal could ever be attained by purely educational intervention, since job opportunities and prospects depend not only upon academic attainments, but upon social and racial 'background' characteristics. It is as unrealistic to expect that major social and political problems can be solved by educational means as it is to expect that those who learn to observe the rules of cricket will later in life always 'play the game'. Indeed, there are some who believe that compensatory education and social service programmes are at best palliatives which draw attention away from more urgent social and political problems.

In Chapter 3 the rationale for compensatory education is considered in greater depth. Much more work has been done in the USA than in this country, and there is much to learn from the mistakes that have been made as well as for the positive findings. In some ways we are about ten years behind the Americans in educational research and innovation, and yet seem to be blindly following the same paths.

The organization and cost of special provision

There is no legal necessity for a local education authority to provide any particular form of special education for slow learners or for children with specific difficulties, nor is a given level of provision required by law. This is also true of special services for immigrant pupils. It is for this reason that there are considerable inequalities in present provision throughout the country.

Statistics relating to special schools are published annually by HMSO and may be found in the Education Committees' Year Book. There is no equivalent source of information about provision for slow learners in ordinary schools, but surveys of remedial education have been carried out by Sampson (1969) by Sampson and Pumfrey (1970) and by Goodacre (1971). A further survey was carried out by the author in order to obtain a more detailed picture of selected remedial services to be described in this book. The organization of special language teaching for immigrant children has been described by Townsend and Brittan (1972).

The number of different professional workers in remedial and compensatory education is so large that administrative problems are bound to arise unless a well-defined structure exists. Many local authorities have set up a centrally organized remedial service which is quite distinct from special classes or special school provision. In some areas this service is extensive and may be concerned with various kinds of special provision or even with various categories of handicap. However, in most areas the centrally organized service can cope only with limited numbers, with the result that the organization of remedial work is left largely to individual headteachers. Such arrangements may work extremely well in individual cases, but it happens all too often that other problems take precedence and that the children who need extra help with their reading do not get regular and skilled instruction.

The allocation of extra rooms, teachers, teaching aids and other resources for reading often leaves much to be desired. At present there are very few schools in which present provision can be said to be adequate. Most remedial services have developed in an *ad hoc* fashion, calling in the odd part-timer, buying the odd tape-recorder or teaching machine, button-holing the odd educational psychologist, and laying on the occasional short course. The end result may be that it is possible to say on paper that a given number of children are receiving remedial teaching, but the extra attention they get is probably quite insufficient. The first aim of remedial teaching is to enable a child to learn more efficiently, so that he can make good a deficit of anything from two to five years of reading age. This is asking a great deal of any child, particularly of those who have previously been unable to learn independently, and who may have developed negative attitudes. An hour a week in a group of six is almost derisory, and yet this is the normal ration for the backward reader.

All class-teachers recognize the need to give individual help to backward readers, but most find in practice that they do not have enough time for this. A relatively new form of special provision for backward readers is classroom-based. Instead of taking withdrawal groups, additional and specialist teachers are going into ordinary classrooms. Of course, this arrangement can work only if the teachers concerned are capable of working together and if they are experienced in the organization of group work.

Another important trend in special education is the increasing use of technical aids which help to develop independent work habits and efficient learning strategies. Self-corrective programmes, whether on cards, slides, film or tape, can be used in a variety of teaching-learning situations. Many audio-visual aids and teaching machines are suitable for classroom use as well as for smaller groups in special units. They are clearly used to best advantage as part of a total reading programme in which follow-up work and other activities are carefully planned. This has implications both for specialists and for class teachers, and as more sophisticated equipment becomes available, new ways of working will be found.

Many of the arguments for improved services do not hold good when it comes to finance. The context to be remembered here is the overall cost of education today. In 1972–3 the total annual cost of educating pupils under 11 years was in the region of £136 per pupil per year, compared with £244 for pupils between the ages of 11 and 16 (Chart. Inst. Pub. Fin. and Acc. and Soc. County Treas. 1974). Assuming a working year of 1000 hours, this is equivalent to 13·6p and 24·4p per pupil per hour respectively. The cost of special schooling is considerably higher than this: 64·6p per pupil per hour in 1972–3, according to an answer given in the House of Commons (Hansard, 1973). This is due more than anything else to the lower pupil: teacher ratio in special schools. Individual teaching, which is sometimes advocated for backward readers, can cost £2 per pupil/hour for the salary of an experienced teacher, plus at least 50p for overheads and equipment. A remedial group of six children will cost approximately 50p per pupil/hour. In fact, the cost of remedial education is almost exactly proportional to the size of the group (assuming current low rates of expenditure on premises and equipment). As the most expensive item is the teacher's salary, it is important to determine the most effective way of deploying remedial teachers. At the same time, the professional and financial status of such teachers is unlikely to rise until it can be clearly shown that they are worth the money.

Chapter Two

Deciding which Children to Help

The question 'What constitutes a reading difficulty?' does not have a simple answer. Different answers can and should be given in general terms for each year-group from the age of five upwards. In addition, the performance of individuals has to be considered in terms of their social and educational background, their behavioural reactions, and in the context of their other skills and abilities.

Backwardness in reading is normally measured either by standardized tests or by a 'book criterion'. A child is said to be backward if he is performing at a level appropriate for a younger child. Some backwardness is remediable, and some is not: the term 'backward' does not imply that the pupil concerned either could or should do better.

Retardation in reading is a more elusive concept. The word 're-tarded' implies that something had held the pupil back. It suggests that it is possible to tell how much progress an individual would have made if it had not been for certain adverse factors; in other words, that one can measure educational potential. This is a questionable claim, since all children are exposed to adverse factors of one kind or another, and since all test results and ratings are affected by environmental pressures. It is, of course, impossible to measure 'pure' potential. The best one can do is to make rather fallible predictions on the basis of the skills and knowledge which an individual has managed to acquire.

To assume that a child's performance on an intelligence test indicates his capacity for learning to read is to make more than one mistake. Intelligence tests measure a broad range of attainments rather than learning capacity as such (Vernon, 1968). Moreover, the attainments which are sampled by an intelligence test overlap with, but are in some ways quite different from, those measured by a reading test. It is certainly possible for children with low IQs to learn to read at their age level, just as it is possible for children with high IQs to be handicapped in learning to read by specific genetic or environmental factors. Further-more, it is a mistake to assume that the relationship between IQ and reading ability which exists in normal children is also to be found in handicapped and disadvantaged groups.

Intelligence tests are designed to sample a wide range of cognitive processes, especially those involving verbal reasoning. They are not designed to predict the rate at which word-recognition skills are likely to be acquired, any more than to predict rates of learning foreign languages or the Morse Code. An IQ will give us a good idea of a child's ability to solve verbal reasoning problems presented in print if one can assume that the child can decode the print. However, many of the skills involved in decoding print are specific to the task, and are not a function of general intellectual ability. Most individually administered intelligence tests, such as the Stanford-Binet and the Wechsler tests, involve either a minimal amount of reading or no reading at all. They include some tasks which are quite unlike reading (such as assembling jigsaws) and do not measure some of the specific skills which are involved in reading (such as the rapid processing of over-learned sound-symbol associations).

It is because reading attainment and IQ are two different (although related) areas of skill that some children are relatively better at IQ tests that at reading tests, whereas others are relatively better at reading tests than at IQ tests. It does not make sense to say that a pupil whose reading is above the average for his age, but whose IQ is below average, has exceeded his reading capacity. The fact is that IQ is not a measure of capacity at all: it is a measure of achievement.

Psychologists are unable to measure the constraints placed on the development of intelligence by genetic and other constitutional factors. They can, however, sample a wide range of mental skills with intelligence tests. Yet they are still far from an objective measurement of intelligence in the sense in which the word is normally used. Vernon defines intelligence as 'the totality of mental skills or ideas which a person has built up during his lifetime and with which he copes with life's problems: it is the all-round effectiveness with which he perceives and comprehends, manipulates things mentally, grasps their relations and reasons out solutions'. Conventional intelligence test sample ways of thinking which are familiar to those who have climbed to the top of the western academic tree, but which may be foreign to many children, particularly to those from developing countries. There are no truly culture-fair tests, and yet intelligence is culturally conditioned 'in the sense that ethnic groups favour, and provide stimulus for, many different ideas and skills'. Vernon reported that the longer immigrant children had lived in the UK, the higher their IQs. The effects of environmental factors of various kinds on the development of intelligence have been evaluated by Clarke (1969). This author reviewed several studies showing that children from deprived homes can make substantial gains in IQ and that these gains are often maintained into adulthood.

If gains in general intellectual ability can be made by both immigrant and deprived groups, there is reason to believe that even greater gains are possible in specific areas of achievement such as reading. The fact that a child has a low IQ does not mean that he will not learn to read. Indeed, if his low IQ is the product of socio-cultural deprivation, it is probable that he will respond more quickly to an intensive reading programme than to a programme designed to accelerate cognitive development on all fronts. Children with low IQs are often surprisingly good at learning facts and acquiring skills which they know to be useful or which give them prestige. Jensen (1968) found that the ability of dull children of low socioeconomic status to learn associations by rote was not related to IQ, as was the case in other ability and socioeconomic groups. It is possible, therefore, that IQs are least reliable as indices of expected reading standards in dull, deprived children, for rote-learning plays an important part in the early stages of learning to read.

Our present understanding of the ways in which various constitutional and psychological factors can facilitate or impede progress in learning to read is remarkably limited. In clinical practice one can sometimes speculate, but can very rarely be sure how far a backward reader is handicapped by genetic as opposed to traumatic or other environmental factors. Individuals compensate for their deficiencies in many different ways, and it is only in cases of obvious handicap that the causes of learning difficulties can be easily established. In handicapped children mental skills are likely to be grouped and organized in unusual and idiosyncratic ways. There is some evidence of different patterns of ability in children diagnosed as neurologically abnormal (Boshes and Myklebust, 1964), as well as in children with EEG abnormalities (Hughes, 1967) and in those with ophthalmological disorders (Lawson, 1967). Sabatino and Hayden (1970) were able to identify a specific perceptual-motor factor which was associated with word-recognition skills in backward readers with IQs above 85, but found no evidence of a similar factor in children who were both dull and backward.

Large-scale factorial studies like that of Sabatino and Hayden have clearly established the main test correlates of reading disability. The results of such studies suggest that if we wish to predict reading levels there are better ways of going about it than measuring intelligence. Klasen (1972) summarizes and adds to the overwhelming evidence that basic reading skills depend much more on the ability to process information rapidly than on verbal reasoning ability. It would perhaps be better to define retardation in relation to information-processing and sequencing skills rather than by reference to global IQ. However, even if this were done, many of the problems described in this chapter would remain. We should also have additional worries, for information-processing and sequencing skills are to a considerable extent task-specific. These skills are impaired by poor concentration, and sometimes develop slowly as a result of reading failure. It would certainly be invalid to suppose that tests of sequencing skills can indicate a child's capacity for learning to read. They throw light on the nature of a child's learning difficulties, but do little more than indicate a starting-point for remedial work.

Backwardness in infant schools

It is not easy to define backwardness at the infant stage, because practices vary so widely, not only in terms of method, but also as to the time at which books and formal instruction are introduced. This makes it very difficult to make objective statements about standards of attainment. However, within a particular class or school it is possible to tell which children are having difficulty in acquiring basic skills by the age of six. A six-year-old who can identify no more than a single letter by name or sound and who cannot read a single sentence is certainly backward. Similarly, if a seven-year-old cannot read a book containing more than 50 different words, he must be considered backward when compared with the average child who can read books containing 200 words at the same age (Latham, 1971).

The range of possible attainments in the early stages of learning to read is to some extent limited by the books and materials available in school. The vocabulary of most early 'reading scheme books' is very tightly controlled, and the range of linguistic structures is to some extent limited because sentences are kept short. Table 1 summarizes some of the data presented by Latham.

Many children read very little outside the classroom, often because they receive insufficient stimulus from their parents. There are large numbers of slow-learning children who never look at a book unless they have to, and who may take a week or longer to 'read' a single page. This

TABLE 1: *Vocabulary load and sentence length in selected reading schemes*

APPROX. READING AGE	NO. BOOKS ANALYSED	AVERAGE NO. DIFFERENT WORDS	AVERAGE SENTENCE LENGTH
6½	10	58	3·9
7	16	205	6·3
7½	16	427	8·3
8	6	1108	10·2

situation is not as infrequent as many teachers would like to believe, according to Pitman (1970), who analysed the survey data of Morris (1966) in terms of the average time taken to progress from one double page of the *Janet and John* readers to the next. Some schools still use only one reading scheme, and if a backward child is not able to read a particular book he may have to stick with it until he has mastered it. Although almost all infant classes have their own stocks of library books for supplementary reading, the backward reader is likely to use them least. Even when the slow-learner does begin to read, he is likely to regress during school holidays if his reading habits are not reinforced at home (Turner, 1972).

Most parents are content to leave the teaching of reading to teachers, so most children are largely dependent on the reading experience provided in school until they reach the stage at which they can read independently.[1] Nicholson (1958) carried out a massive study of 2188 American children entering first grade at the age of six-plus. The children were tested during the first term, and Nicholson found that none of her measures of early reading skills were related to chronological age (the highest correlation coefficient being 0·17). This result suggests that school experience and instruction almost completely outweigh maturational factors in determining early reading performance in six-year-olds. Nicholson's study also showed that experience counts for more than intelligence at this stage. As shown in table 2, even the most intelligent children were quite limited in their knowledge of letter names and sounds. Their performance certainly did not begin to approach the level one would expect from older children of the same mental age (seven years, nine months).

Of course, most intelligent children do learn to read more quickly than most dull children, but a high IQ is no guarantee of success. There are

TABLE 2: *Median scores of average and highly intelligent six-year-olds in naming and sounding letters (from Nicholson)*

	AVERAGE IQ GROUP (n=546)	HIGH IQ GROUP (n=546)
Mental age	6y. 0m.	7y. 9m.
Chronological Age	6y. 2m.	6y. 5m.
Naming capitals	5/26	19/26
Naming lower case	3/26	13/26
Giving sounds of capitals	0/24	4/24

[1]See Chapter 3 for evidence that school variables are important, as well as home circumstances.

some bright children (usually boys) who are slow starters, even among those from privileged homes. Cane and Smithers (1971) found that verbal IQ was a relatively poor predictor of the amount of progress made during the infant stage of schooling by children who were slow starters (r=0·39). Performance IQ yielded an even lower correlation (r=0·26). Cane and Smithers concluded that 'we should see learning to read – as distinct from the later problem of learning how to develop good reading habits – as a skill with specific characteristics of its own, which cannot be included in some general category of intelligence, and which therefore needs deliberate and well-thought-out teaching specifically geared to it'.

If we view learning to read as a matter of acquiring specific skills, it makes sense to check from time to time to find out which skills have been learned and which have not. Informal measures which are closely related to the materials in use are better for this purpose than standardized tests. In the first two years of infant schooling (as well as with older backward readers performing below the seven year level) it is a good idea to monitor progress by finding out how well children understand the function of letters in words, and by estimating the number of words they know at sight. It is also useful to measure the rate at which the slower children can acquire certain skills and learn new words. It would be pointless to attempt to standardize tests of this kind, since performance depends so much on the nature and timing of the instruction given. However, each teacher can use her own informal tests to find out which children are most in need of extra help.

Some reading tests, such as those of Daniels and Diack (1958), Carver (1970), Williams (1970), Jackson (1971a) and McLeod and Atkinson (1972) have a strong phonic bias. They are concerned primarily with the structural aspects of word-recognition (i.e. the number and sequence of letters and sounds, and the patterns of correspondence between letters and sounds). Children taught exclusively by a 'look and say' method may be at a disadvantage when given tests designed to measure their grasp of word-structure, especially if they are slow to acquire a sight vocabulary. Young and Stirton (1971) found that after the introduction of 100 words in a reading scheme, 354 children who had received very little help with phonics were able to read 70 per cent of their scheme words, but only 11 per cent of non-scheme words when these appeared in the Burt test of word-recognition. Nevertheless, all children have to learn to generalize from known to unknown words of similar structure. Without this ability a child is likely to remain at the five-to-six year level, unable to extend his reading vocabulary beyond a limited number of sight words.

As shown in table 1, there is a rapid increase in the vocabulary load of reading schemes between the six- and eight-year-levels. It is during this period that most children show a 'growth spurt', not only in the number of words they can read, but also in phonic skills (Davies and Williams, 1975). Williams (1961) devised a word-recognition test consisting of a random sample of 100 words from *The Concise Oxford Dictionary*. He found that the rate of acquisition of word-recognition skills was at its maximum between the ages of six and a half and eight years (see fig. 1). In a later study, Davies and Williams found that individual children did not achieve a growth spurt in word-recognition skills unless they had first shown a spurt in phonic skills.

FIGURE 1: *The growth of word-recognition skills (from Williams)*

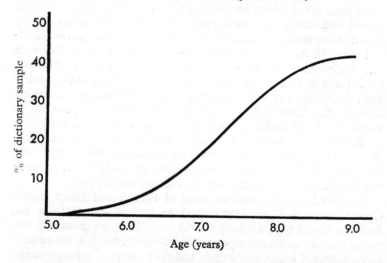

Diagnostic tests of phonic skills are therefore useful in showing how far a pupil has developed the ability to generalize from known to unknown words, and in finding out which children are in greatest need of explicit phonic instruction. When we consider that there are more than 100 patterns of correspondence between sounds and letters in most books written for infants, it is not surprising that some children have great difficulty in learning to decode unfamiliar words.

Measures of learning rate are particularly useful in identifying the slow learners and in giving the teacher a good idea of the amount of information these children can absorb at once. A test of learning rate for sight vocabulary, using a standard flash-card procedure, was used by Nicholson in her survey of reading skills in first-grade children. The words were first of all taught in a systematic fashion, then checked twice during the day, and finally tested at the end of the day. The number of words correctly identified was taken as the measure of learning rate, and was found to be related to attainments in letter and word-recognition. Nicholson found that learning rate showed only a moderate correlation with mental age (r=0·37), and none at all with chronological age (r=0·02).

Learning rate is partly a function of previous learning, and can certainly be increased by teacher intervention. Durrell and Murphy (1953) reported that special exercises which involved auditory and visual discrimination of word elements led to an increase in learning rate as well as in attainment, compared with exercises from normal reading schemes. One wonders whether certain phonically graded schemes might similarly produce an acceleration in the rate at which phonic skills are acquired.

Most diagnostic and attainment tests have been criticized at one time or another because they appear to be slanted towards particular teaching methods. These criticisms are in many cases valid, particularly as applied to tests designed for children below the age of seven. However, once children reach the stage at which they have the means of attacking new words, they rely much less on what their teacher tells them to do and much more on their own learning strategies. As Bond (1935) found, the performance of eight- to nine-year-olds on tests of phonic skills bore little relation to the teaching methods which had been used. We can therefore be confident that standardized tests of word, sentence, or paragraph reading sample these skills without undue bias once a child has developed some awareness of word structure, and is making intelligent use of context cues. The average child reaches this stage in the last year of infant school.

Standardized reading tests are frequently administered at seven-plus, during the summer term before children move on to junior school. In many cases the selection of a suitable test is left to individual schools, but in an increasing number of LEAs a uniform survey procedure is used. This means that not only the junior school teachers but the LEA advisers obtain reliable information about the need for special provision for children with reading difficulties.

Standardized tests allow one to compare a child's performance with norms based on the performance of large numbers of children of the same age. However, different tests sometimes yield different results since they were standardized at different times and not always on populations representative of the country as a whole. For example, the Neale Analysis of Reading Ability was standardized (very inadequately) in Birmingham, and is known to over-estimate performance at the lower end of the scale. Again, the Southgate Group Reading Tests, which were standardized in Worcester, were found to over-estimate national mean scores at seven-plus by six to nine months in the large-scale survey by Pringle and others (1966).

It is of course unlikely that different tests will be used in a single school, and provided that it is administered and marked in a consistent fashion, a standardized reading test is preferable to informal means of assessment if the results are to be passed on to other teachers. Informal measures are of unknown reliability, and different standards are likely to be applied by each teacher involved. It is also likely that with informal assessment some children will be incorrectly assessed owing to bias on the part of the class teacher. Although some teachers are able to predict the reading progress of their pupils fairly accurately (Hirst, 1970), a change of teacher can sometimes throw predictions awry, since children react differently to different teachers and since teachers have different expectations of the same children.

If an attainment test has been consistently administered to a class or year-group, it is possible to place pupils in rank order in terms of the skills and knowledge measured by the test. Another way of expressing rank order is in the form of *percentiles*, from 0 (low) to 100 (high), with the middle rank at the 50th percentile. One might therefore give a word-recognition test to a year group of, say, 100 children with the aim of identifying, say, 25 who are making slow progress (i.e. percentiles 0–25). This would not be done simply by picking out the 25 children with the lowest scores (since this would not take account of chronological age and length of schooling), but by ranking the children in terms of (a) reading quotient or (b) standard score.

a Reading quotient

$$\text{Reading quotient} = \frac{\text{Reading age} \times 100}{\text{Chronological age}}$$

A child whose test performance is average for his age-group has a reading quotient (RQ) of 100. A Ministry of Education pamphlet (1950) suggested that the term 'backward' should be applied to children with RQs below 80. This is a somewhat arbitrary cutting point, and is in any case not very useful at infant level. A seven-year-old with an RQ of 80 has a reading age (RA) of five years, seven months, and at such a low point on the scale reading tests are not very reliable. It is much more practical to consider all children with RQs of 95 or less (alternatively 90 or even 85) as being at risk, and to arrange for further assessment[1] of

---

[1]This should involve further testing (see Appendix D) as well as the gathering of precise information from teachers, parents, and sometimes from other professionals such as social workers, speech therapists, psychologists and doctors.

their learning difficulties before arranging special provision for some of them. The choice of a cutting point for screening purposes will depend on local standards and resources. In one school a cutting point of RQ 90 may classify 20 per cent of an age-group as being at risk, and in another school 60 per cent may fall below the same point. Differences of the same order are also known to obtain between different residential districts and between different LEAs. Three suggested cutting points are given in table 3, which are applicable to the age-range normally to be found in any class during the last term of infant schooling.

TABLE 3: *RQ cutting points for identifying children 'at risk' at 7+*

CHRONOLOGICAL AGE (CA)	RA EQUIVALENTS OF RQ		
	RQ 85	RQ 90	RQ 95
6y. 6m.	5y. 6m.	5y. 10m.	6y. 2m.
6y. 9m.	5y. 9m.	6y. 1m.	6y. 5m.
7y. 0m.	5y. 11m.	6y. 4m.	6y. 8m.
7y. 3m.	6y. 2m.	6y. 6m.	6y. 11m.
7y. 6m.	6y. 5m.	6y. 9m.	7y. 2m.
7y. 9m.	6y. 7m.	7y. 0m.	7y. 4m.

b *Standard score*

A standard score, unlike an RQ, corresponds to a fixed point on a percentile scale. There are different forms of standard score, but the one which is most often used has a mean of 100 (the 50th percentile) and a standard deviation of 15. As shown in fig. 2, a standard score of this kind is equivalent (by definition) to a certain percentile point in the standardization population (*not* in the local sample, of course).

FIGURE 2: *Standard scores and percentile equivalents*

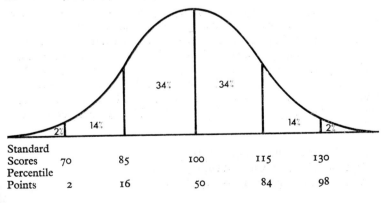

Standard Scores	70	85	100	115	130
Percentile Points	2	16	50	84	98

Thus, a given cutting point will by definition give us the same proportion of children at each age level. At all ages, for example, 25 per cent of children in the standardization population have (by definition) standard scores of 90 or less. However, because of local variations in reading standards, we may find different proportions of children in each school falling below a particular cutting point. A complete table of percentile points and equivalent standard scores may be found in Appendix E.

If standard scores are used instead of RQs to determine which children should be considered at risk at seven-plus, it is suggested that a cutting point somewhere between 93 and 100 should be used. A cutting point of 93 would place about one-third of the population under surveillance. According to a recent survey by Barnett (1972), an RQ of 90 on the Schonell Graded Word Reading Test is equivalent to a standard score of 94 on the same test at this age level.

Both RQs and standard scores are ways of measuring backwardness, pure and simple. They take no direct account of skills and abilities other than reading, such as auditory and visual discrimination, sequencing skills, vocabulary, verbal reasoning, and so on. Yet skills and abilities of this kind are certainly involved in reading, indeed some would say that they are essential preconditions for learning to read. They should certainly not be ignored by the diagnostician, nor by the remedial teacher. These skills and abilities are among the factors to be considered when estimating the severity of a learning problem, and in deciding whether specific remedial techniques should be applied.

As we have already seen, general intellectual ability is a relatively poor predictor of progress in the early stages of learning to read. Very few correlations between IQ and RQ exceeding 0·5 have been reported in the literature. It does not make sense to derive expected reading levels from a single measure such as IQ when better predictors are available. Hirshoren (1969) was able to show that various subtests in the Illinois Test of Psycholinguistic Abilities (given in kindergarten) gave better prediction of reading scores two years later than did Stanford-Binet IQs. The best single predictor of subsequent performance in reading, spelling and arithmetic was the visual-motor sequential subtest. However, this is not the only diagnostic test that is worth considering. Some of the skills which are related to reading and yet which have only low or moderate correlations with IQ are listed below, together with key references:

Associative learning (Evans, 1972)
Auditory blending (Chall and others, 1963)
Auditory discrimination (Dykstra, 1966)

Auditory-visual association (Muehl and Kremenak, 1966)
Letter sequence matching (de Hirsch and others, 1966)
Memory for digits (Hirst, 1970)
Perception of orientation (Weiner and others, 1965)
Spelling (Russell, 1943)
Visual sequential memory (Hirshoren, 1969)

The value of diagnostic testing is discussed in some detail in Appendix D.

We could undoubtedly improve the accuracy of diagnosis and prediction by developing more refined diagnostic and readiness tests than those currently available. If this were done we could be reasonably sure that specific difficulties were properly diagnosed and that appropriate remedial programmes were recommended. The diagnostician would be on firmer ground in setting goals for individual children and in guiding parents. As things are, he has to hedge his bets with so many qualifications that it is sometimes hard to tell whether he is betting at all.

Yet, however good our tests, there would still be a place for intuitive judgement. There are some children of exceptionally high ability, lacking none of the perceptual-motor skills normally associated with reading, who nonetheless find reading difficult and who produce inadequate written work. Some of these children are deliberately avoiding academic success and may have deep-seated emotional problems. Others may simply not be interested, or may have conflicting interests. In cases of this sort one has to rely on intuitive judgement or on clinical experience when making recommendations. This applies not only when there is an obvious emotional problem or behaviour disorder, but also when one tries to weigh up the effects of constitutional factors or of environmental disadvantage. No statistical formula can tell us whether remedial teaching should be given to an apparently dull non-reader from a large family in Liverpool 7, and neither can it tell us how the child would have performed if he had been given extra help earlier. If it seems that a child's backwardness is entirely due to environmental disadvantage, test results will reflect this, and should not be interpreted as indicating his potential. With remedial teaching the entire test profile may change, and both IQ and attainments may increase.

In deciding whether to make special educational provision for a particular child, one must attempt to assess the social, emotional, and educational consequences of his failure to learn to read. Ultimately, this is a political, not a statistical decision. If no special provision is made, some are bound to become educational 'casualties' and may eventually require custodial or institutional care.

It is obviously unrealistic to work out regression equations to take account of every possible factor from shared bathrooms to private tutors before deciding whether or not to admit a particular child to a special reading group. It is much more practical to make some small-group and individual provision for *all* severely backward readers, and at the same time to provide help for pupils who are particularly talented in some ways and yet find reading rather difficult, or are unable to express themselves adequately in writing. It is important to remember that an intelligence test is one means whereby a teacher can become aware of unsuspected hidden talent.

Summary

It is not possible to talk about backwardness in reading in children younger than six. Backwardness in six- and seven-year-olds can be measured in terms of letter knowledge, sight vocabulary and phonic skills. However, even before the age of six it is possible to identify children who are likely to be slow in learning to read by giving informal tests of learning rate, supplemented by tests which measure relevant cognitive, perceptual and memory processes.

The concept of retardation is almost meaningless at infant level, since in the early stages of learning to read, experience counts for much more than intelligence. Children who come to school prepared for reading or already able to read have a great advantage. Those who learn quickly invariably spend a good part of their leisure time with books, whereas the slow learning child may pick up a book only when his teacher tells him to. Some children get insufficient practice in reading, so that they never reach the point at which a growth spurt, first in phonic skills and then in word-recognition skills, takes place.

By the end of the infant stage, most children have started to generalize from known to unknown words. They can decode unfamiliar words if they conform to known patterns of word-structure. However, backward readers often have very limited knowledge of word-structure. In the final year of infant schooling, standardized reading tests are a reliable means of distinguishing between advanced, average and backward readers. The severity of backwardness can be assessed by comparing reading quotients or by ranking in terms of standardized score. If group tests are used for screening at seven-plus, between one-quarter and one-third of an LEA population should be considered 'at risk'. Diagnostic tests should be used to provide additional information about an individual's strengths and weaknesses. Before deciding which children to help, the observations of teachers and parents, and sometimes the views of other social, medical or educational agencies, should be sought.

In selecting children for extra help with reading, one should choose not only the most backward (irrespective of any other factors) but also a few of those who are doing *relatively* badly in reading and writing and very well in other respects. Statistical techniques do not make human judgement redundant when it is a matter of estimating the severity of a learning problem.

Backwardness in junior schools

First year

At the beginning of the first year in the junior school, the youngest child in a class is likely to be just seven years and the oldest seven years, eleven months. A typical class is bound to contain several children who have not yet mastered a reading book like *Happy Venture, Book 1* which is designed for children who are just seven. Morris' 'book criterion' was based primarily on the *Happy Venture* series, so it will be as well to look at the vocabulary and sentence length of the first four books of this series. The data in table 4 is taken from Latham (1971).

TABLE 4: *The grading of the Happy Venture series*

BOOK	RA (SPACHE FORMULA)	NO. OF DIFFERENT WORDS (CUMULATIVE)	AVERAGE SENTENCE LENGTH
1	6·9	138	6·4
2	7·4	299	9·2
3	7·5	551	8·2
4	8·0	1004	10·8

Morris found that in 1954 19 per cent of 3022 children entering Kent junior schools were still on Book 1 of a reading scheme, while a further 26 per cent were on Books 2 or 3. This is fully consistent with her finding that reading standards in Kent were slightly above the national average according to standardized tests. There is no inconsistency between this result and that obtained by Pringle and others (1966) for infant children (ten per cent, on Book 1 or below), because the 'book criterion' is not an absolute scale. The 'book criterion' in terms of *Janet and John* (which was the most popular scheme at the time of Pringle's survey) represents a lower standard of achievement than its equivalent in terms of *Happy Venture*.

The tremendous growth in reading vocabulary that takes place between RA 7 and RA 8 (see fig. 1) is inadequately reflected by the number of words included in any given scheme written for this age-group. However, we can use figures like those in table 4 in order to arrive at a minimum estimate of the rate at which new words come to be recognized. This gives us a basic minimum of three words per day during this growth period, which should be compared with one word per week during the infant stage. A new kind of learning is going on,

B

whereby new words are more easily assimilated because they have structural characteristics which are already familiar. The teaching skills required to facilitate this process are quite different from those normally exercised by infant teachers. While it is true that some children reach and pass this stage while in their last year in the infant school, these are mainly the older and brighter children, many of whom learn to read without a great deal of help from teachers. Up to 50 per cent of all pupils reach junior school with very little understanding of word-structure in terms of phoneme-grapheme correspondence. A knowledge of the sounds of single letters is insufficient. Immediate recognition of digraphs and a degree of flexibility in assigning sound-values to letters is needed as a basis for generalization.

Carver (1970) studied the development of word-recognition skills in children up to the age of eight years, seven months. His description of average performance at the seven- and eight-year levels illustrate the rapid development of decoding skills during this period, and are consistent with the observations of Davies and Williams (1975). Carver summarizes his findings as follows:

$6\frac{1}{2}$–7 yrs. Beginning to discriminate aurally initial multiple consonants (e.g. cl, gr, fl); probably recognizes simpler ones (such as pl, fr) in words; could still be confusing b and d; strong knowledge of the initial sound, its equivalent letter symbol and its serial position at the left of a word; could still have a specific vowel discrimination difficulty, especially with short i and e and possibly u; most single letter endings identified.

$7\frac{1}{2}$–8 yrs. More sophisticated learning, e.g. of the combined vowel sounds or, aw; generally knows and hears initial consonants ch, and th, though may be having difficulty in discriminating between ch and sh; initial multiple consonants well established, including sw, ch, gl, cr, th, dr, gr; but complex initial groups yet to be conquered (spr, str, thr).

It can be seen that at the seven-year level most children are able to read three-letter words such as 'big', 'red', and 'bus', whether or not they are known as sight words, whereas at the eight-year level (a) separate sounds in consonant clusters are discriminated and (b) digraphs are correctly decoded as representing single sounds. The author has analysed a composite word list of more than 5000 words, and finds that there are only about 180 'regular' two- and three-letter words containing short vowel sounds. However, there are a further 500 short-vowel monosyllables containing consonant digraphs and clusters; and once a child becomes familiar with vowel digraphs he has the key to an additional 1500 words at least (not including polysyllabic words).

There can be little doubt that the first year of junior school is also a critical period in the development of written work. The words that children can write are always fewer in number than those they can read, but word-recognition and spelling are highly correlated sets of skills (e.g. Russell (1943) obtained a correlation coefficient of 0·88 between word-recognition and spelling in 116 seven-year-olds). It is at the age of seven-plus that most children become able to put their thoughts on paper by writing a few connected sentences. This means that they can participate in written work no matter what is the subject. Those who remain unable to do this become severely handicapped educationally.

To what extent do the teachers of first-year junior classes succeed in teaching the requisite skills? The most appropriate index here is the number of children performing below the seven-year level. Morris found that the percentage of children below the seven-year level according to the book criterion fell from 45 per cent to 12 per cent during the first year in junior school. This statistic may, however, give an over-optimistic impression. Teachers sometimes give books which are really too difficult to backward readers, because the children refuse to accept 'baby food'. Hammond's (1967) study gives us percentages of backward readers according to the Burt Word Recognition Test, and these figures are probably more reliable. Her study involved more than 800 children at each age-level, and was carried out in Brighton. She found that the proportion of pupils with word recognition scores below the seven-year level was halved in the course of the first year in the junior school. Towards the end of their first year, 25 per cent of the boys and 15 per cent of the girls were still performing below the seven-year level. Crawford (1968) was able to demonstrate a similar trend in Liverpool, but the incidence of backwardness was considerably greater than in Brighton. At the same age the corresponding percentages were 38 per cent of boys and 24 per cent of girls below the seven-year level. Reading standards were lowest in the dockland area and highest in the southern suburban area.

It is instructive to compare the poor reading standards in Liverpool with those in Dunbarton. Clark's survey (1970) shows that good reading standards can be maintained in a highly industrialized area which is in some ways not unlike parts of Liverpool. About 70 per cent of the population of Dunbarton live in urban areas, the largest of which is Clydebank. Yet the mean RA of 1544 children at the average CA of seven years, six months[1] was eight years, one month on the Schonell Graded Word Reading Test. This impressive performance could not be attributed to superior verbal intelligence, as the mean standardized score on the English Picture Vocabulary Test was only 98. Nor can it be explained in terms of differences between the Burt and Schonell tests, since these are

[1] NB: the age-group tested was the younger half of a school year.

minimal at this level (Ministry of Education, 1950; Young and Stirton, 1971).

Clark's study was a longitudinal one, and her findings certainly suggest that good initial standards mean that only a small proportion of children have continuing difficulties in reading and spelling. At the average age of eight years she found that only eight per cent (nine per cent of boys and seven per cent of girls) scored below the seven-year level on Southgate's Reading Test 1, and nine per cent (eleven per cent of boys and seven per cent of girls) scored below the seven-year level on Daniels and Diack's Spelling Test. Even if we make generous allowances for inequalities in the published norms of the tests concerned, this proportion of backward children is about half of that found in Brighton, and one-third of that found in Liverpool. Socioeconomic factors alone could not explain a difference of this order. The place of the school in the community, and the practice of teachers within the school must also be relevant.

Second year

The only study among those mentioned so far to give us the incidence of backwardness in all four junior year-groups is that of Hammond. Fig. 3 shows the proportion of boys and girls with reading ages of less than seven years on the Burt test at each age.

FIGURE 3: *Incidence of severe backwardness in the Brighton junior schools (from Hammond)*

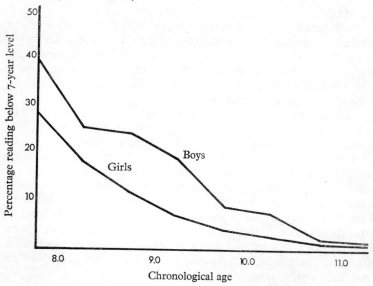

There is a striking difference between the two curves; while the girls' curve is a smooth one, there is a definite hump in the boys' curve. This shows that many of the 25 per cent of boys who score below the seven-year level after nine months in the first year of junior school get stuck for a year or more. The proportion of boys to girls among the backward group is 2:1 during the second and third years, but only 3:2 in the first and fourth years.

Hammond's survey showed that in Brighton between a quarter and a fifth of boys in a typical second-year class were to all intents and purposes unable to read. This is a sizeable problem, and difficult if not impossible for most class teachers to cope with single-handed. Perhaps this high incidence of failure could have been avoided by more effective teaching and special intervention in the preceding years for, as we have seen, Clark's Dumbartonshire survey does show that better results can be achieved. At the same time, remedial measures are needed in the second year of junior school. Children of this age are capable of a good deal of independent learning, and backward readers should be encouraged to work by themselves for short periods so that they do not become totally dependent on their teachers.

Second-year children who are backward in reading have a considerable history of failure, dating back as much as four years. Crawford found that 86 per cent of her nine-year-olds with reading quotients of 80 or less had remained in the same category for at least two years. Morris followed up a sample who obtained standard scores of 85 or less on NFER Reading Test AD in the second-year juniors. She found that 70 per cent of the original poor readers were in the same category two years later. However, by the end of the secondary school only 42 per cent of the original backward group still showed scores of 85 or less. It seems that older children are more likely to improve without special help, whereas seven- to nine-year-olds are more dependent on teacher intervention.

Morris' survey is frequently quoted in support of arguments for preventive measures intended to reduce the initial incidence of reading failure. The discouragement which results from continued failure is certainly massive, and comparatively few children with severe reading difficulties have the courage to tackle the learning task unaided. Backward readers often appear ambivalent or resistant towards learning to read, and some of them develop emotional problems which may or may not be manifested in disruptive behaviour. All kinds of unproductive ways of 'getting by' may be learned, together with habits of word-attack which actually impede progress. It is scarcely surprising that so many backward readers remain backward year after year, and the arguments for a more intensive and systematic approach to the teaching of reading in infant schools carry much weight.

At the same time, one has to ask whether the tendency for backward readers to remain backward throughout junior school should be taken as evidence that their needs tend to be neglected. Very few of the children studied by Crawford in Liverpool and by Morris in Kent were receiving specialized remedial teaching. Morris found that of 101 poor readers, 53 in the 2nd year 38 in the 3rd year; 22 in the 4th year, never read by themselves to a teacher. Moreover, those who did read to their teacher did so on average only once a week. Apart from this, most children received no help, either in the form of games, personalized language-experience work, techniques for learning new words, or systematic phonic instruction. Class teachers had insufficient time to ensure a high success rate on simple tasks or to help the children to work independently. The emotional needs and behaviour disorders of the slow-learners for the most part were disregarded. All this reflects quite inadequate standards of provision in the county of Kent in the years 1954–7. There has been a considerable improvement since that time, both in Kent and elsewhere, but it is still not uncommon for the only form of extra help to consist of 'hearing children read'.

Third year

Referring to Hammond's data (fig. 3) we see that approximately eight per cent of the boys and four per cent of the girls in third-year junior classes were performing below the seven-year level. This was in Brighton in 1962, but the median scores reported by Hammond were close to the age-norms for the test, so we can assume that the results are fairly typical. Experience confirms that there are frequently at least two pupils in a third-year class who can read only with great difficulty, and who are virtually unable to produce any original writing. Morris (1966) found that 24 per cent of poor readers in the third year of junior school did not know all the letter names and that the average number of lower case letters correctly sounded by this group was 20/26. Their phonic blending skills were in many cases rudimentary.

In addition to the non-starters and very slow starters, there are other backward readers who get stuck at the seven- to eight-year level of attainment. Some of these have difficulty in mastering the full range of phonic skills, often because they do not get enough practice. Many of them prefer less arduous ways of obtaining information, and probably watch television rather than read books at home. Some read accurately, but very slowly, and others are fast and inaccurate. Some read mechanically, making little effort to understand what they are reading, and others absorb the gist of a passage but pay no attention to details. Some children are able to read quite well, but have great difficulty with spelling.

An informal comparison of the words included in standardized reading and spelling tests shows that on average children can read words accurately about one year before they can spell them accurately, but sometimes this gap is much greater. Children with specific spelling problems often avoid using words they do not know, with the result that their written vocabulary is artificially restricted. In extreme cases it is difficult to decode what the child has put down, whereas in mild cases there may be nothing more serious than an unconventional but none-theless phonetically accurate orthography.

Somewhat rarer are those children who produce very little written work because they agonize over every word. This is neither a spelling problem nor a handwriting problem, and it is not always obvious to the teacher that there is something wrong. Fluency and organization may be lacking in writing and yet present in speech, or perhaps lacking in both writing and public speech but present in imagination and intimate speech. It is particularly in the third and fourth years of junior school that problems of this kind can become serious, since it is at this time that children are expected to produce more extended written work, consisting of paragraphs describing their personal reactions as well as factual description and narrative.

Fourth year

A great many backward readers make comparatively rapid progress during their last year in junior school. This can be seen from Hammond's data (fig. 3) and was also reported by Morris. In her longitudinal study of 101 poor readers in the last three years of junior school, Morris found that average progress in reading age during the fourth year was 12 months. Boys progressed more than girls during this period, which is also what Hammond found. The proportion of backward boys to girls (with NFER Reading Test AD standardized scores of 85 and below) was 1·3:1 at 11-plus according to Morris (n=1848).

Reliable estimates of the percentage of children at 11-plus with reading scores of seven years or less are hard to obtain, but (if Brighton can be considered at all typical) the national average is likely to be be-tween two and four per cent. This estimate is consistent with Sampson and Pumfrey's (1970) finding that 25 per cent of pupils in the remedial departments of 242 secondary schools were said to have reading ages of seven years or less.

According to some studies it would seem that there are fewer children than this who are virtually or completely unable to read by the age of 11. One local education authority (Staffordshire, personal communication) recently found that only 50 (0·45 per cent) out of 11,085 children at 11-plus scored below the seven-year level on the Southgate test. However, as we have seen (page 28), Southgate's norms over-estimate national performance at this level by six to nine months. In addition, Staffordshire has one of the best remedial services in the country. Another study which should be interpreted with caution is the NFER national survey (Start and Wells, 1972). Here it is stated that only 0·42 per cent of 11-year-olds in ordinary schools scored below the seven-year level. This statement is misleading, because it is based on a comparison of the performance of 11-year-olds in 1970 with that of seven-year-olds in 1938. The average score of seven-year-olds on the Watts-Vernon test in 1938 was three points, which is very near the floor of the test. This adds to the unreliability of the 1938/1971 comparison. Moreover, we do not know whether the performance of seven-year-olds in 1971 is better or worse than in 1938. If it is better, the percentage of 11-year-olds scoring below the (present-day) seven-year level is bound to be higher than 0·42.

Apart from the virtual or complete non-starters, there are in the fourth year perhaps two or three children in the average class who are reading only at the seven- to eight-year level. These children have an incomplete grasp of phonic skills, and their backwardness is largely a function of poor decoding rather than of limited understanding of content or restricted vocabulary.

In general, the higher his reading age, the more likely it is that a child's oral and receptive language skills will set a limit on the level of his reading competence. This effect becomes an important one among duller children who reach levels of reading attainment above eight years. According to Gates and others (1938) the average growth rate of reading vocabulary between the ages of eight and 12 is 2500 words per year, and if this is so there are bound to be some children who reach a ceiling level of word-recognition because their oral and listening vocabularies include only a few thousand words.

This means that some fourth-year junior children with reading ages between eight and nine years are unlikely to make further progress unless something is also done to improve their understanding and use of language, whereas others may be backward for other reasons and may simply need more reading practice. All children who can read at this level have some degree of independent reading skill and are able to work from written texts expressed in simple language. Although backward when compared with the average child, they do not necessarily need remedial teaching.

In the NFER national survey it was found that 15·1 per cent of 11-year-olds scored below what had been the average for nine-year-olds in 1938. This figure is almost certainly too low by today's standards, and should be compared with the figure of 27.5 per cent which was arrived at by extrapolation from the 1970 data. The fact is that we do not know exactly how many 11-year-olds are reading below the nine-year level. This does not matter very much in practice because it is neither necessary nor desirable to arrange remedial teaching for all of them.

The discrepancy between actual and predicted reading scores

In the first two sections of this chapter it has been argued that it is theoretically unsound to derive expected reading levels from IQs alone and to select for remedial help those children with the biggest discrepancies between 'potential' and actual performance. Yet this is the very procedure advocated by some writers. For example, in the Isle of Wight survey, retardation in reading was defined as 'an attainment on either reading accuracy or reading comprehension which was 28 months or more below the level predicted on the basis of the child's age and short WISC IQ' (Yule and Rutter, 1970). It is therefore worth looking more closely at the relationship between reading and IQ in children of junior school age, and considering the practical implications of the type of selection procedure which depends on measuring the differences between actual and predicted reading scores.

If IQ is used as one of the variables in selecting children for remedial teaching, it is more often with the aim of excluding those who obtain low scores, than with the aim of identifying skill deficiencies. Thus Cheshire Education Committee (1956) published a most unscientific table of 'reading expectancy' as a guide to primary school teachers in dealing with slow-learners. Quoting chapter and verse in Schonell and Schonell (1950), it was stated that children are ready to read when they reach a mental age of six years, six months. Making no distinction between quotient and standardized score, and assuming a perfect correlation between IQ and reading levels, it was then worked out that children with IQ 85 were not ready for reading before the age of seven years, seven months, and that teachers should not be concerned if those with IQs of 70 were not reading at the age of nine years three months, etc. If these recommendations were taken seriously, up to two-thirds of all backward readers would be considered to be working to capacity and to need no extra help.

Yule's regression method is more sophisticated (in statistical terms) than Schonell's ill-conceived achievement quotient, but it has the same kind of practical consequences. Thus, when Barnett (1972) used a regression method to select the most retarded readers from a population of 459 first-year junior boys, only two out of the 60 selected had IQs of 95 or less. To some extent, this was due to the fact that dull children would have had to score below the threshold of the test (five-year level) to have been included in the 60. This in itself rules out the use of a regression method with first-year children. The practical consequences of using the method with second- and third-year children are less extreme but certainly unjust. Yule found 86 children (3·7 per cent) 28 months below predicted level, but almost twice as many 6.6 per cent) with reading scores 28 months or more below chronological age. In other words, the regression formula had the effect of reducing the apparent size of the problem by 50 per cent. Among the duller children excluded from help were many whose low performance on all tests, including intelligence tests, could be explained in terms of their daily surroundings. A social-class bias was undoubtedly introduced in this way. Table 5 gives the expected reading accuracy scores on the Neale test according to Yule's formula for nine-year-olds.

TABLE 5: *Predicted reading ages for nine-year-olds of different WISC IQs*

IQ	RA	IQ	RA
65	7y. 3m.	105	9y. 3m.
70	7y. 6m.	110	9y. 6m.
75	7y. 9m.	115	9y. 9m.
80	8y. 0m.	120	10y. 0m.
85	8y. 3m.	125	10y. 3m.
90	8y. 6m.	130	10y. 6m.
95	8y. 9m.	135	10y. 9m.
100	9y. 0m.	140	11y. 0m.

If we were to apply cutting points two years below the predicted RAs given in table 5, we should exclude from remedial groups large numbers of children of below average IQ who when aged nine were still reading at between the six- and seven-year level. Yule's own cutting point was 28 months below predicted RA, and this excluded most of the duller children whose scores were at or below the threshold of the Neale test (RA six years). The use of this regression formula discriminates against the dull child. There is little to be said in favour of doing nothing for a nine-year-old with an IQ of 85 and a RA of only six years. There are massive numbers of such children in ordinary schools today, particularly in large cities. Berger *et. al.* (1972) found that the average non-verbal IQ of indigenous children in an Inner London District was only 92, and Moseley (1971a) reported a mean EPVT[1] vocabulary score of 94 for an indigenou ssample in a similar area.

This is not to say that there is no relation between intelligence and reading or that we should expect as much from dull as from bright children. There certainly are more backward readers with low IQs

---

[1] English Picture Vocabulary Test by Brimer and Dunn (1962).

than with high IQs. Crawford (1968) found that whereas the average Terman-Merrill IQ of a random sample of Liverpool children was 104, the average IQ of 207 poor readers (defined as having an RQ of 80 or less) was only 91. The proportion with IQs of 100 or above was 25 per cent. The majority had IQs in the range 80–100, and 17 per cent scored below 80. This agrees closely with results obtained by Lovell and others (1964). Of 253 children with RQs of less than 80, 19 per cent scored 100 or above on a picture test of intelligence. More boys (37) than girls (10) were in this category. Clark (1970) found that the average EPVT standardized score of 236 backward readers (defined as having an RQ of 85 or less) was 88. The proportion with EPVT scores of 100 or above was 16 per cent. Clark also reported that the backward girls constituted not only a smaller, but a duller group than the backward boys. The relevant IQ data is presented in table 6.

TABLE 6: *Wechsler intelligence test results of eight-year-olds in Dunbarton with RA below 7 years*

	BOYS (n=138)	GIRLS (n=92)
Mean Verbal IQ	92·5	85·0
% with Verbal IQ of 100 or above	8·0	4·3
Mean Performance IQ	96·0	89·5
% with Performance IQ of 100 or above	13·0	7·6

Many researchers have reported correlations between IQ and reading of the order of 0·5, which indicates only a moderate degree of association between two variables. For a concrete illustration of this, see table 7, which is based on Crawford's data for 790 children in the age-range six years, ten months to eight years, nine months. It can be seen that there were some highly intelligent children who were backward readers, and in this case a substantial proportion of dull children who were not backward readers.

TABLE 7: *Proportion of poor readers to others at different levels of IQ*

IQ	BACKWARD (%)	NOT BACKWARD (%)
120–129	8	92
110–119	8	92
100–109	12	88
90–99	31	69
80–89	48	52
70–79	78	22

One can infer from table 7 that the relationship between IQ and backwardness in reading is much closer in the lower half of the IQ scale than in the upper half. This observation is consistent with the different levels of correlation reported by Cane and Smithers (1971) for ready and unready infant children. We are not, of course, justified in concluding from a correlation coefficient which has been calculated from a full range of scores that there is or should be a substantial relationship between IQ and reading at IQ levels above 100. According to Crawford's data, there is very little relationship here up to the age of eight-plus.

We may interpret this point in a number of ways. We may feel that if highly intelligent children do not read very much better than those of average intelligence, the fault lies with the teachers. The gifted pupil may indeed be under-stimulated in many classes. He or she may develop negative attitudes to a learning situation which he finds trite, boring or trivial. This is particularly likely to happen with intelligent boys, for at this age boys are normally establishing a degree of independence from their mothers. They learn best by discovery and have strong needs for independent achievement. They are likely to react badly to teachers who require conformity and obedience before all else. Of course, not all intelligent children are particularly interested in reading. Some devote their energies to other things because they have never learned how to enjoy books and stories, and others because they genuinely prefer real-life adventures to fictional ones. However, this may not be the whole story. Some would say that a genetically determined syndrome called 'specific development dyslexia' accounts for a high proportion of anomalous reading results among intelligent boys, and hence for the low correlation. The 'dyslexia issue' would be resolved if it were possible to point to a pattern or patterns of impairment either among the subskills of reading or among the abilities underlying those skills, which could be established as causes rather than mere concomitants of poor reading. It would then be necessary to settle the question of genetic determination, but there is little chance of this when opinions are divided about a fundamental issue like the genetic contribution to general intelligence. In any case, it seems unlikely that 'specific developmental dyslexia' should be linked with general intelligence in such a way that it would occur most frequently among the highly intelligent.

So far (see table 7), we have considered backwardness in reading in relation to IQ, but have not considered the relationship between IQ and the reading performance of children who have no difficulties or handicaps and read very well for their age and ability. It is important to do this because intelligence can impose an upper limit on a child's performance in reading, and it is possible that this largely accounts for the commonly reported correlation coefficients of about 0·5 between

IQ and RQ. It is likely that the upper limit is determined not so much by mechanical decoding skills (since many children can pronounce written or printed words they have never heard of), as by vocabulary, verbal comprehension and other language skills. The grading of all reading tests in common use bears this out, particularly above the eight-year level. Compare, for example, the following sentences from the Neale *Analysis of Reading Ability:*

(a) Seven-year level (requiring a basic sight vocabulary and elementary decoding skills)
'She looked in the box for a doll.'

(b) Ten-year level (requiring an advanced spoken vocabulary and level of comprehension)
'Then fatigued but undaunted by this unpleasant accident, he proceeded to provide an escape exit for the submarine's captives.'

It would, of course, be possible to devise a word-recognition test which ten-year-olds would find difficult, even though no comprehension were required and even though only very common words were used. This would be very different from the conventional reading test as it would consist of 'tricky' words to decode like 'brooch', 'christen' and 'pheasant'. One would expect such a test to show a much lower correlation with IQ than conventional word-recognition tests. Experimental evidence on this point is lacking, but Moseley (1969a) obtained relevant results by using spelling tests. In a survey of 1254 second-year juniors a correlation coefficient of 0·48 was obtained between spelling (Schonell) and receptive vocabulary (EPVT). Schonell's spelling test has a steep vocabulary gradient, so that at the upper end of the scale children are likely to fail because the words are totally unfamiliar to them. In other words, the spelling test is (among other things) a test of vocabulary knowledge as well as of spelling. However, when a specially-devised spelling test was given, in which some of the words were difficult to spell although taken from basic word-lists the correlation between spelling and EPVT vocabulary was much lower (0·18).

Both reading and spelling are complex skills which in the early stages of development are largely independent of vocabulary level and which can be acquired by almost all children, however dull. Intelligence is only one of the many factors which determine progress during the period in which basic word-recognition and phonic skills are acquired, and up to a reading level of approximately eight years there is no question of vocabulary or verbal comprehension setting a limit on attainment (except in the severely subnormal). However, above this level it is by no means uncommon for vocabulary, verbal reasoning and other language skills to impose limits on the development of competence in reading, spelling and written English.

We have to conclude that, because most backward readers in junior schools are still at the stage of acquiring fluent and flexible decoding skills, it is unwise to consider IQ as an index of such a child's capacity for learning to read. This means that IQ should not be taken into account (except in extreme cases) when selecting children for special help with their reading. It does not mean that IQ is of no concern to the remedial teacher. As we have seen, IQ is more relevant in setting upper limits to reading achievement, once word-recognition and phonic skills have been acquired. The remedial teacher can make good use of IQs at the point of discharge from a remedial group, that is when he has to decide whether a given pupil has reached his limit. He may well decide to discharge a dull child at a RA of, say eight years, whereas he would not normally discharge a bright child below a RA of, say ten years.

Perhaps the most convincing evidence that it is unsound to derive expected reading levels from the IQs of backward readers comes from predictive studies.

Morris reported a correlation of 0·56 for 1848 second-year children in 52 Kent schools between reading (NFER Reading Test AD) and non-verbal ability (NFER Non-Verbal Test 5). In order to determine to what extent non-verbal ability could be used to predict progress in reading over the subsequent two years, a correlation coefficient was calculated which turned out to be completely insignificant (−0·06). Morris concluded that both reading and non-verbal ability are 'facets of attainment which can be developed'.

There have been a number of studies in which both verbal and non-verbal ability have been used to predict the reading gains of backward readers, but in every case the prediction has been highly inaccurate. Dunham (1960) reported a correlation of 0·21, Lovell and others (1962) 0·19, and Cashdan and others (1971) 0·10. This study covered the full range of ability in junior schools, and showed conclusively that the dullest children (IQ 70–84) respond almost as well as the brightest during the first year of regular remedial teaching. Yule (1973) reported on a five-year follow up of retarded and backward readers on the Isle of Wight, and found that the more intelligent retarded group had made slightly *less* progress than those who were backward but not retarded.

Measuring backwardness

Backwardness in reading can be defined in terms of (a) a given number of months below CA; (b) reading quotient; (c) standardized score or equivalent percentile point. A fixed discrepancy in months of reading age is the least satisfactory of these types of criteria, as it means different things at different ages. Children in the first year of junior school may be of any age between just seven years and eight years, ten months, and a fixed discrepancy of, say 18 months will almost certainly identify different proportions of children at the extremes of this age-range. A reading quotient is a better index of backwardness. Table 8 gives the cut-off points determined by an RQ of 85 for the age-range of first-year juniors. In most schools and LEAs an RQ cutting point of 85 will provide us with a good estimate of the need for special reading provision for seven- and eight-year-olds.

TABLE 8: *RA equivalents of RQ 85 for first-year juniors*

CA	RA (TENTHS)
7y. 0m.	6·0
7y. 3m.	6·2
7y. 6m.	6·4
7y. 9m.	6·6
8y. 0m.	6·8
8y. 3m.	7·0
8y. 6m.	7·2
8y. 9m.	7·4

There is, of course, no guarantee that the same percentage of children will fall below a given RQ at different CAs, but the differences are not likely to be great. Only if standardized scores are available can we be sure of identifying a constant percentage of children, since standardized scores are directly equivalent to percentile points (see page 29 and Appendix E). There is no absolute scale of correspondence between quotients and standardized scores, although they are broadly similar. On the basis of Hammond's data, for example, a reading quotient of 85 gives us a cutting point at the 20th percentile, whereas a standardized score of 85 is by definition equivalent to the 16th percentile (assuming a mean of 100 and a standard deviation of 15).

It has been argued that all children falling below a given cutting point should be regarded as in need of special reading provision, and that we should not set lower cutting points for children with low IQs. These arguments do not, however, mean that we should not set higher cutting points for highly intelligent children. This can be done by the regression method if local norms are available (since there are no published equations based on national norms for British children), or by a variety of *ad hoc* procedures. Two suggestions are given in Table 9, which raise the cutting points for brighter children, but by a smaller amount than would result from a regression method.

TABLE 9: *Suggested RQ cutting points for special provision at different levels of IQ for children aged 7–9 years*

IQ	RQ CUTTING POINTS	
	(a)	(b)
Below 100	85	85
100–109	86	86
110–119	87	88
120–129	88	91
130–139	89	95
140–149	90	100

The effect of raising the cutting points in this way is to increase the numbers of children identified as being in need of special provision, but only by a very small percentage. Thus, if an RQ of 85 picks out 20 per cent of an age-group, only a further one or two per cent will be added by using either method (a) or method (b). The number of highly intelligent backward readers is very small indeed.

In the first two years of junior school, class teachers aim to help as many children as possible to reach the stage when their word-recognition and spelling skills do not limit their ability to comprehend texts and to express themselves in writing. As we have seen, a reading age of seven years corresponds to the stage at which children first become able to participate in a range of classroom activities involving reading and writing. As shown in table 8, a child of eight years, three months with a reading age of seven years has an RQ of 85. For practical purposes, an RQ of 85 can be used up to the age of nine to identify children who need more help in learning to read than class teachers are normally able to provide.

In the third and fourth years of junior school the priority candidates for remedial and special tuition are those whose reading and writing still remains at or below the seven-year level. In addition there are those children whose grasp of phonic skills is incomplete. Both categories of backward reader need some kind of special help.

If a uniform cutting point of, say, 85 were applied in all four years of junior school, there would be too many older children classified as backward when in fact they were able to read quite well. In order to avoid this, some LEAs use different criteria for backwardness at different ages. For example, Goodacre (1971b) found that one LEA used a Reading Age of 7·0 for the under-eight group; RA 7·5 for under nines; RA 8·0 for under tens; RA 8·5 for under elevens; RA 9·0 in the secondary school. This kind of sliding scale has the advantage that more children can be provided with help in the crucial early years. A slightly more precise sliding scale which achieves a very similar result is suggested in table 10.

The effect of lowering the RQ cutting point by one point for every three months of chronological age is that older children reading at the nine-year level will not be selected for remedial help. It may be desirable to make a few exceptions to this rule for children with very high IQs, but in general remedial teachers are concerned to develop fluent decoding skills rather than the more advanced comprehension and study skills. It is in fact at the lower levels and with the younger children that extra help is most needed. Younger children who have experienced failure need the security of a step-by-step programme, and are often unduly dependent on their teacher in the early stages. Remedial teaching should normally begin with a high rate of teacher–child interaction, but should involve a gradual weaning process, as the children develop the confidence to take bigger steps and to begin to work independently. Once a child has reached a reading age of eight years, six months, there are relatively few reading skills that he can learn better in a remedial group than in the classroom. If remedial teaching is offered to children reading at or above this level it may be good for their morale, but is unlikely to boost their reading ages more than good class teaching.

TABLE 10: *Suggested RQ cutting points for identifying backward readers in the junior school*

CA	RQ CUTTING POINT	RA EQUIVALENT
Less than 9y.	85	See Table 8
9y. 0m.	84	7·6
9y. 3m.	83	7·7
9y. 6m.	82	7·8
9y. 9m.	81	7·9
10y. 0m.	80	8·0
10y. 3m.	79	8·1
10y. 6m.	78	8·2
10y. 9m.	77	8·3
11y. 0m.	76	8·4
11y. 3m.	75	8·4
11y. 6m.	74	8·5
11y. 9m.	73	8·6

Summary
In the first year of junior school the average child makes a growth spurt in word-recognition and phonic skills, but the backward reader is still laboriously acquiring a basic sight vocabulary and has a very limited awareness of word structure. However, many of the slow starters do learn how to decode words with consonant clusters and vowel digraphs in the course of the first year, and reach the seven- to eight-year level of attainment.

In the second-year juniors the average child has sufficient mastery of word-recognition skills to be able to learn through reading, and can record his experiences and opinions in connected prose, whereas the backward reader is still at the stage of sight vocabulary and phonic skills, and may be unable to produce written work which can be read by anyone else. The kind of help that the backward reader requires may not be available in the ordinary class, unless the teacher is able to provide resources for learning which enable him to work independently for part of the time.

In the third and fourth years of junior school there are still some children who are uncertain about the function of letters in words, and are unable to blend sounds, but the majority of backward readers have passed this stage and are mastering the phonic skills which the average child learned two, three or four years before. Once they reach the seven- to eight-year level of attainment they can read simple books and follow written instructions, so it becomes much easier for the class teacher to organize special programmes of work for them. This work should be directed not only towards the acquisition of specific skills (such as phonic, comprehension or spelling skills) but should also aim to make reading and writing relevant to the children's own needs and purposes. It is only in this way that learning and thinking in the context of print becomes an absorbing activity; in other words, that the backward child becomes sufficiently motivated to want to read independently.

The selection of children for special reading provision should be based first and foremost on reading attainment, and it is suggested that up to the age of nine all children with a reading quotient of 85 or less should be given some form of extra help. Progressively lower cutting points are suggested for older children, since it is more important to make provision for maximum numbers at an early age (when backward readers are more dependent on their teachers) than for older children who can read reasonably well but who do not develop their own skills by taking opportunities to read and learn independently.

All backward readers with attainments below the suggested cutting points should be given extra help, including those of low intelligence in the ordinary school (i.e. IQs 70–85). Regression formulae which take IQ into account in predicting expected reading levels should not be used in order to exclude dull children from special reading provision, although they do have a use in giving some idea of the reading attainments to be expected of highly intelligent children. However, even when used for this purpose a regression formula may be misleading, for the relation between reading backwardness and IQ is less marked at high than at low IQ levels.

Backwardness in secondary schools

The best available estimate of the incidence of severe backwardness in reading in secondary schools comes from Sampson and Pumfrey's (1970) survey of 205 comprehensive schools and 65 secondary modern schools. Only 70 per cent of the schools initially approached provided complete data, and two large LEAs known to have a high incidence of backwardness refused to co-operate in the survey. The sample included only well-established comprehensive schools, and secondary schools which were nominated by the LEAs themselves. These sampling limitations all mean that the number of backward readers reported is likely to be an underestimate, particularly in view of the fact that the 1971 NFER survey showed that the proportion of backward readers in the average secondary modern school is double that in the average comprehensive school.

Teachers were asked to estimate the numbers of children in remedial departments who were 'non-starters, i.e. children with reading ages of seven or below'. The results obtained were that 26 per cent of the 'remedial' pupils in comprehensive schools were considered to be non-starters, compared with 23 per cent in the secondary modern schools. (NB the LEAs had been asked to select secondary modern schools which were 'comparable' with the comprehensive schools.) The remedial departments in these schools provided for seven per cent of all pupils on roll, but in two-thirds of the schools included no pupils above the third year, and in one-third of the schools none above the second year. One is therefore justified in stating that between two and three per cent of the children in the schools surveyed were reading below the seven-year level.

On the basis of the NFER national surveys, Start and Wells (1972) have suggested that reading standards in secondary schools declined slightly between 1961 and 1971. It is difficult to be sure of this, as only 56 per cent of the schools selected for the 1971 survey supplied information.

The NFER survey included children in grammar and direct grant schools, as well as in comprehensive and secondary modern schools, but the standards in comprehensive schools were found to be representative of the country as a whole (not including public schools). This means that we may take the results of Sampson and Pumfrey's survey as a fair index of the national incidence of severe backwardness (bearing in mind the fact that it may be an under-estimate).

It is therefore necessary to approach the results of the NFER survey itself with extreme caution. It seems most unlikely, for instance, that only 3·2 per cent of 15-year-olds have reading scores at or below the nine-year level.

The NFER survey was bedevilled by a multitude of mishaps, but one serious source of error was the high absentee rate (34 per cent) among those about to leave school (at Easter). Pumfrey (1969) mentions a survey of eight secondary modern schools in which it was found that the average reading age of Easter leavers was one year below that of summer leavers. It seems highly probable that a large proportion of poor readers and non-readers escaped the NFER net because they were truanting at the time. Another weakness of the survey was that the nine-year level of reading attainment was estimated, not by testing nine-year-olds, but by extrapolating from the scores of 11-year-olds.

Local surveys are much more valuable than national statistics when considering the need for special reading provision in secondary schools. There are very few published accounts of surveys of this kind, but Hill and Moorehead (1971) give some details of the Manchester survey mentioned by Pumfrey. In eight secondary modern schools in slum areas it was found that at the age of 15, 2·2 per cent obtained RAs of seven years or less, and 8·3 per cent scored at or below the nine-year level. Hill and Moorehead pointed out that statistics of this kind are notoriously hard to obtain. Very little of the information they collected from LEAs has been published elsewhere, and in one case it was stated that a researcher who had carried out a longitudinal study of 300 children was unable to publish the results, as he would thereby lose the co-operation of the LEA.

In 1961 reading standards in problem areas and in slum areas were investigated for the Newsom Report. Performance between schools was shown to vary considerably, with average scores at 15-plus in secondary modern schools ranging between ten-and-a-half and 15 years. Schools in problem areas obtained mean scores about seven months below the national average, and schools in the slums about 13 months below average. The best performance from a school in a slum area was an average score at the 14-year level. The over-all average for secondary modern schools was at the 13-year level.

The greatest problems are usually to be found in schools in inner city areas. In one London secondary school the author (1969b) found that 25 pupils in the second- and third-year classes obtained Schonell spelling ages of six years, six months or below. This represents a massive problem of illiteracy in a particular school. In this case a special effort was made to ensure that all pupils on roll were tested. If this is not done, or if results are based solely on teacher estimates, it is likely that the results will appear more acceptable. In 1970 the Centre for Learning Disabilities asked teachers in eight London secondary schools to put forward the names of severely backward readers. It is very doubtful whether all of the pupils in this category were identified, as numbers reported varied between two and 14. Out of 68 children who were subsequently interviewed and tested, 48 proved to have reading or spelling attainments below the seven-year level. One-third of these had reached their 14th birthday. None of them scored above the national average (SS 100) on the English Picture Vocabulary Test, but there can be no doubt that their illiteracy had restricted the development of vocabulary as well as other linguistic skills. In order to give a more realistic impression of the problems facing teachers in inner city secondary schools, a selection of comments made by head teachers is given below:

CA 13y. 10m.   EPVT 80

[1]BRA 7y. 1m.

Described as 'a real tough nut' by his primary school, he has a belligerent attitude to authority and is often a source of trouble. Progress in reading has been poor. He is at present reading book 4 in the *Wide Range Readers*.

CA 13y. 5m.   EPVT 76

BRA 7y. 1m.

'Arrived in England from St Lucia at the age of nine not speaking English. Following a recent medical examination, he has been recommended for admission to a Day Special School for the ESN. He has an IQ of 81 and is a very poor reader.'

CA 12y. 6m.

BRA 6y. 10m.

'Low attainment in junior school and here. Great difficulty in spelling. Good at games. Has attended remedial classes here. His attendance was good in the junior school, but erratic here.'

CA 14y. 8m.   EPVT 65

BRA 6y. 2m.

'Parents are of Cypriot origin and he speaks Greek at home. Poor academic record throughout school career. Has few interests but has always been anxious to learn. Some improvement slowly over the years from remedial teaching here. Attendance very good.'

CA 14y. 0m.   EPVT 89

BRA 6y. 5m.

'Has attended tutorial class from the junior school until this year. Started with a severe speech defect which he has practically overcome. Had made slow but steady progress in remedial classes here, but very reluctant to write. Good attendance.'

[1]Burt (Rearranged) Word Reading Test scores (corrected).

CA 12y. 1m.   EPVT 75
No score on Burt test.

'Very poor academic record from junior school onward. Appears to have no special interests or abilities. He was given special tuition in the junior school and has attended remedial classes here, but has made little progress. His attendance has been extremely bad.'

CA 13y. 5m.   EPVT 77
BRA 5y. 11m.

'Came here from the West Indies in time to spend only a few months in primary school. He appears to have had a very sketchy junior school education and has had some difficulty in communication. A date has been made for an ESN examination. He attends remedial classes here, but has made no progress in reading at all. His attendance is irregular, but has improved lately.'

CA 13y. 9m.   EPVT 75
BRA 6y. 3m.

'Admitted to the school as a non-reader. His parents have opposed attendance at a centre.'

CA 13y. 11m.   EPVT 93
BRA 6y. 6m.

'Comes from a broken home, and is a poor attender. He has attacked a teacher and is a constant source of trouble. School reports have recommended individual attention since 1968.'

CA 14y. 3m.   EPVT 86
BRA 6y. 11m.

'This boy is on probation and has a serious police record involving violence. He is very often absent from school.'

CA 14y. 3m.   EPVT 86
BRA 6y. 2m.

'His attendance has always been poor through ill-health. Is slightly deaf and probably spent some of his junior years deafer than he is now. Has been to remedial classes all his time here, and his reading has improved a little. Last year had individual reading lessons at Child Guidance Centre. Intelligent in conversation and good at crafts.'

Some of the children described above are rebelling against a system of education which has failed to meet their needs. Others are the victims of social injustice or of unhappy family relations. The older they get, the harder it becomes to teach them, but many can progress if they are given a genuine opportunity to learn. As Ablewhite (1967) has shown, it is possible to raise the average attainment of secondary 'remedial' children to a 12-year level by the age of 15. Almost all children, no matter how limited their receptive vocabulary or verbal intelligence, should be capable of reaching a nine-year level of word recognition by the time they leave school. The number of words that can be read (either in isolation or in context) by the average nine-year-old is between 2000 and 3000 (Gates and others, 1938), and this corresponds to the number of words understood by the average six-year-old (Smith, 1926).

Not all backward readers in secondary schools have difficulties as severe as those which have been described. In one inner-city comprehensive school known to the author, seven per cent of first-year children obtained RAs of seven years or less, but a further 15 per cent scored at the seven- to eight-year level and another ten per cent at the eight-to-nine year level. These figures are based on a total of 293 children, the 1971 and 1972 intakes. The non-verbal intelligence scores of the first-year children were close to the national average, with a mean of 98. About a third of the backward readers (35 per cent of the boys and 22 per cent of the girls with RAs of nine years or less) scored 100 or above on the non-verbal test. The proportion of backward readers with non-verbal IQs of 90 or above was 60 per cent.

In this sample there was, as one would expect, a relationship between the degree of backwardness and non-verbal IQ. However, the high incidence of backwardness could not be explained by lack of intellectual ability. As many as 12 per cent of the first-year children were unable to write their names and addresses in a manner which would ensure correct delivery. Even the 20 non-starters with reading scores below the seven-year level included children in the average range of non-verbal ability. Their average IQ on the NFER DH test was 88.

Of course, there were some dull children among the backward readers, but not all of the dull children were backward in reading. Of the 13 children with non-verbal IQs in the range 70–79, four were certainly not backward, and two had RAs of more than 11 years.

In this particular school a non-verbal test of intelligence was used, and it is probable that mean results on a verbal measure would have been somewhat lower. Bernstein (1960) found that working-class boys obtained much lower verbal scores than middle-class boys in a public school, but that there was a much smaller difference between the groups on a non-verbal test. Verbal ability also tends to be lower than non-verbal ability among backward readers (Belmont and Birch, 1966; Clark, 1970). It is important to remember that backward readers have not had the same opportunity as normal readers to extend their general knowledge and other verbal skills through reading, and that this differential factor becomes increasingly important as children grow older. This is not the only explanation for depressed verbal scores among backward readers, but it is certainly relevant at the secondary stage.

Hebron (1957) studied 1546 pupils in secondary modern schools in order to consider the curricular needs of children with special abilities and disabilities. The most common problem she found was that of superiority in spatial and arithmetic skills when compared with verbal skills (including reading). The pattern was about twice as common in boys as in girls. It was associated with character traits of independence, self-confidence and perseverance. The largest proportion of these pupils were in B streams, and many of them would have been suited to technical courses if their reading had been adequate. A much smaller group of pupils showed specific backwardness in reading, compared with relatively high performance on all other tests of intelligence and attainment. Some of these pupils were later offered grammar school places.

Measuring backwardness

It is generally accepted by remedial teachers that children are ready for discharge once they reach a nine-year level of attainment. At this stage a pupil should be able to extend and develop his reading competence without the support of a remedial teacher, and at the same time many teachers are doubtful of their ability to take children beyond this point.

In some cases the backward reader seems to have reached his limit at the nine-year level, because he cannot understand the vocabulary or the concepts used. Even if he does seem to be capable of making further progress, the range of language which is available at the nine-year level is so great that the remedial teacher hardly knows where to start.

The sliding scale of reading quotients suggested in table 10 for junior children was intended to establish minimal levels of attainment which could be achieved by all children, given adequate help. If we extend the same scale into the secondary age-range, we find that the cutting point for special provision never exceeds an RA of nine years (see table 11). Of course, in some cases it may be desirable to give special help to highly intelligent pupils who are reading above these levels, particularly if they are likely to be handicapped in examinations by inadequate reading and/or spelling.

It may at first sight appear to be unrealistic to expect all children to reach the minimal standards of attainment set out in table 11. However, even the dullest children should be capable of reaching these standards. Morgan (1971) has described his work in a residential special school,

TABLE 11: *Suggested RQ cutting points for identifying backward readers in the secondary school*

CA	RQ CUTTING POINT	RA EQUIVALENT
11y. 0m.	76	8·4
11y. 3m.	75	8·4
11y. 6m.	74	8·5
11y. 9m.	73	8·6
12y. 0m.	72	8·6
12y. 3m.	71	8·7
12y. 6m.	70	8·8
12y. 9m.	69	8·8
13y. 0m.	68	8·8
13y. 3m.	67	8·9
13y. 6m.	66	8·9
13y. 9m.	65	8·9
14y. 0m. and over	64	9·0

where the average IQ is in the middle 50s. Many of the children come from deprived homes and more than a third are maladjusted, according to a psychiatrist. Yet when a group of 20 children recently left the school at the age of 12-plus, an educational psychologist found that their average RA was eight years, one month. The special provision for backward readers in Morgan's school is of de luxe quality,[1] and a great deal of individualized work is provided. The children learn how to work independently using audio-visual aids and automated teaching aids, but at the same time they are involved in a full range of normal lessons and a considerable amount of project work. Unlike many backward readers in ordinary schools, they are really given a chance to learn.

Summary
The numbers of illiterate children in secondary schools are considerably higher than one is led to believe from national surveys commissioned by the Department of Education and Science. We have no reliable figures for the number of illiterate school leavers, but between two and three per cent of all children attending secondary schools have reading ages of seven years or less and are completely unable to write anything intelligible. In addition to these non-starters, there are many more children who fall in the 'semi-literate' band, with reading ages of between seven and nine years.
In inner-city working-class areas the average standards of reading are about one year below the national average, and the incidence of back-

[1]In January 1975 Morgan's work received international recognition in the form of a special award from the International Federation of Learning Disabilities.

wardness is between two and three times the national average. At least two per cent of 15-year-olds are likely to be illiterate in these areas.

Approximately one-third of backward readers entering secondary schools are of average or above intellectual ability, and there are more boys than girls in this category. Some boys with reading problems are considerably more gifted in the field of non-verbal and spatial ability than in verbal reasoning.

It is not plausible to explain severe backwardness in reading at secondary level in terms of limited intellectual ability. Almost every adolescent (except the severely subnormal) is capable of achieving literacy if placed in a positive educational environment.

Chapter Three

Literacy in a Social Context

The validity of all research results is limited by the measuring instruments used. When we look at research which examines reading and language skills in a broad social context, we see that some of the measuring instruments are very blunt, and that many of the things one would want to measure are difficult to isolate. Although a great deal of work has been done, we are not yet able to say how effective educational intervention can be in preventing and in putting right a situation in which large numbers of children learn very little at school. As stated in Chapter 1, most of these children are from the manual working classes,[1] and it is very tempting for teachers to attribute their poor response to schooling to 'environmental disadvantage' or to 'cultural deprivation' or to 'a bad home'.

The chances of a child being a poor reader at seven-plus are about three times as great in manual working-class families as in other families (Davie and others, 1972). This is illustrated in table 12 which shows a substantial difference in reading standards even within the Registrar-General's occupational class 3 (skilled workers), depending on whether or not the father was a manual worker.

Similarly, Morris (1966) found that: '80 per cent of the fathers of the poor readers were manual workers, and of these about half were unskilled. In contrast, 28 per cent of the fathers of the good readers were manual workers of whom the majority were skilled or semi-skilled.'

There is strong evidence that the academic performance of children in the poorer socioeconomic groups gets relatively worse as the children

[1]Nisbet and others (1972) compared the reading standards of 11-year-olds in Aberdeen in the years 1962 and 1972. They found that standards had declined in children with fathers in semi-skilled or unskilled occupations, but not in those with fathers in the professional and managerial classes. One is reminded of anecdotal evidence from teachers who tell of children who cannot see why they should study when their own parents have achieved a high material standard of living without consulting books. There may perhaps be more children who feel this way now than there were in the early 'sixties.

get older. Barker Lunn (1970) noted a progressive decline in the reading quotients of working-class children between the ages of seven and ten, and Halsey and others (1973) found that mean receptive vocabulary scores (English Picture Vocabulary Test) declined between the ages of five-plus and 11-plus in schools in designated Educational Priority Areas (EPAs). Additional evidence from the West Riding suggested that this relative decline continued throughout the secondary school period. In the USA the Coleman Report (1966) showed that the gap between median scores of minority and majority group pupils was wider in the 12th grade than in the first grade.

TABLE 12: *Reading performance at seven-plus according to occupational status of father (from Davie and others, 1972)*

	PROFES-SIONAL	INTER-MEDIATE	SKILLED NON-MANUAL	SKILLED MANUAL	PARTLY SKILLED	UN-SKILLED
% poor readers	8·3	14·7	13·9	30·4	37·2	48·3
% average readers	37·5	38·8	43·1	41·0	37·9	34·3
% good readers	54·3	46·6	43·0	28·7	25·0	17·3

Poor academic performance is frequently associated with feelings of failure, frustration and unhappiness. Davie and others showed that the seven-plus backward readers are approximately four times as likely to be rated as severely maladjusted by their teachers as are adequate readers. Teachers complain most of their restlessness, anti-social behaviour and rebellious attitude (Barnett, 1972; Chazan and Jackson, 1971; Peaker 1971; Rutter and Graham, 1970). This kind of behaviour is relatively more common in the lower socioeconomic groups anyway, according to Davie and others. Stott and others (1970) showed that these 'over-reacting' types of disturbed behaviour become increasingly common up to the age of nine, i.e. during the critical period for the acquisition of reading and writing skills. Of course, over-reaction is not the only possible response to failure and frustration. Another common pattern is worry about personal worth and about acceptance by other children (Crawford, 1968; Gregory, 1965; Morris 1966). Again, other children react to failure by becoming depressed, and Barnett noted that more backward readers than controls were so described.

Backward readers often have a poor self-image (Lawrence, 1971), although they may try to hide this fact from those around them. Children are certainly aware of their success or failure in school, and know very well whether they are liked or disliked. In an interesting study of absenteeism in a secondary remedial department, Ralphson (1973) found that while there was no significant association between reading ability and frequency of attendance, there were moderate correlations between sociometric status and attendance. It is perhaps not surprising that some children feel that there is no point in going to school. Nash (1973) found that children allocated to a remedial class in one secondary school had been perceived in extremely negative terms by their primary teachers. Observational records of teacher–pupil interaction in one of the primary classes showed that many of the teacher's comments to the unfavourably-perceived lower-ability children had been unhelpful. Nash emphasized that a child's academic self-concept is influenced by the way he is treated by teachers and by other children. Gillam (1974) found that 15 boys in a remedial class thought of themselves as less happy and less confident than did 23 boys in a middle-band class in the first year of secondary school. Moreover, for the remedial, but not for the middle-band boys, total self-concept scores (as measured by a semantic differential technique) were significantly correlated with reading scores ($r=0.49$). The boys in the remedial class placed 'confidence' relatively high in a list of desirable attributes, but placed 'success' and 'popularity' very low, perhaps because they were genuinely unable to think of themselves in these terms. Gross (1974) studied some personality characteristics of 28 poor readers in the first year of a comprehensive school, and confirmed Lawrence's finding that many backward readers are prone to feelings of self-reproach, guilt and inadequacy. It is when these feelings are so strong that a child is forced to deny them that quite unrealistic ideas of competence or lack of it develop. Gross found that good progress in reading over a six-month period was associated with an increase, and poor progress with a decrease, in the extent to which the children were able to admit that they were anxious and socially inadequate. A degree of realistic self-dissatisfaction is a healthy thing, but after years of failure and humiliation it is not surprising that many children are unable to face learning situations in which they become aware of their own limitations.

It seems likely that relatively little of the maladjustment seen in backward readers is primary. Barnett failed to find significant differences in family dynamics (as perceived by the child in the context of the Bene-Anthony Test of Family Relations) between backward readers and controls, except that the fathers of his backward boys apparently took little interest in their progress and rarely read to them or helped them with their reading. Moreover, Barnett carried out a follow-up study which goes against the theory that reading failure is often caused by an 'emotional blockage'. He found that the ten children who made the most progress (all of whom were reading at or above their age-level on follow-up) showed no similar improvement in social and emotional adjustment, and were in fact slightly less well adjusted at follow-up than the 22 children who had made the least progress. Malmquist's (1958) study suggests that much of the behavioural disturbance that accompanies reading failure arises from a negative reaction to the social and learning situation in school. He found that 40 per cent of the children in his sample who later became poor readers showed nervous symptoms before going to school, compared with 34 per cent in the sample as a whole—but that at the end of the first year at school (average age, seven years, nine months) the poor readers showed much poorer concentration, less persistence, more nervousness and submissiveness, and tended to lack confidence both in learning and in social situations.

If behaviour disturbance in a backward reader is often the result of the child's failure to adjust to the standards of work and behaviour expected by teachers and readily adopted by many of his peers, one would expect that in schools and areas with a high incidence of reading failure the backward readers will show fewer signs of maladjustment than elsewhere, because they will stand out less as failures. On the other hand, if reading problems are caused by emotional problems in a majority of cases, one would expect a higher incidence of maladjustment among backward readers in schools and areas where reading standards are low. A comparison of the data collected by Crawford and by Davie and others shows that in Liverpool, where mean reading scores at seven-plus were six months below the national average, significantly *fewer* poor readers (22 per cent) were rated as maladjusted than in the National Child Development Study (37 per cent). This comparison is a fair one in that the children were at the same stage of schooling, very similar reading cut-offs points were used, and the same criterion of maladjustment was employed (BSAG). We have to conclude that maladjustment among backward readers depends to a great extent on how other children, the parents and the teacher view the child's failure to learn. It is certainly possible that certain school attitudes, practices and types of organization simply exacerbate the situation for children from poor homes who may have little experience of books and 'educational' toys, and who may find it difficult to accommodate to new social conventions.

Given that so many learning and behavioural problems occur in children from the manual working classes, we need to examine the correlates of such problems in these children. We shall look at differences between regions, between schools, between homes, and between individuals before making an informed guess about the most important causal factors. We shall then consider whether educational intervention is likely to prove effective in overcoming some of these problems.

Regional and area variations in reading standards

Clark's Dunbarton survey (referred to in Chapter 2) showed that satisfactory reading standards can be maintained even in largely industrial areas. The National Child Development Study showed that reading standards are generally higher in Scotland than in England and Wales, even though there were more working-class families in Scotland. Whereas 36 per cent of families in London and the South-East are middle class, only 22 per cent are so classified in Scotland. Yet average reading scores in Scotland at seven-plus were shown to be nine months above those in England and Wales, and backwardness was less common (in the ratio of 2:3 for a cutting point one year below CA). Among the possible reasons for this Scottish superiority in early reading standards are the following differences reported by Davie and others:

1 Scottish parents read to their children more regularly than English parents.

2 Scottish parents have higher educational aspirations for their children than English parents of equivalent socioeconomic status.

3 Scottish children settle down more quickly after entering school, and fewer of them are said to be unhappy there (four per cent compared with seven per cent of English children, according to mothers' reports).

4 The speech of Scottish children is clearer than that of English children.

5 School attendance rates are higher in Scotland than in England and Wales.

6 Systematic phonic instruction begins earlier in Scotland (in 95 per cent of schools before CA six years) than in England (62 per cent before six years) and Wales (69 per cent).

Also, within England itself there is evidence that reading standards are not necessarily low in economically depressed areas with a predominantly working-class population. There is more poverty and unemployment in the north of England than elsewhere, school buildings and physical amenities are relatively inferior, and comparatively few students proceed to sixth-form and further education (Taylor and Ayres, 1969). Yet the National Child Development Study showed that reading standards at seven-plus were in fact slightly higher in the northern region than elsewhere in England and Wales.

Apart from the slight superiority of Scotland and the north of England, and the slight inferiority of Wales,[1] reading standards at seven-plus

[1] An inferiority which has since disappeared (Horton, 1973).

were almost the same in each region in 1965, and did not vary with average wage levels in different parts of the country. In rural areas, where earnings are especially low, average reading scores fall only a little below those obtained in urban areas (Morris, 1966; Chazan and others, 1975). It is evident, therefore, that if there is a direct relationship between socioeconomic status and reading in this country, it is to be found within cities, within local communities and within schools, rather than between larger areas such as counties and regions.

Crawford (1968) carried out a survey of 790 Liverpool children, drawn at random from the entire city. She compared reading standards and intelligence scores (Stanford-Binet) in seven different residential areas, and found considerable differences between the best and the worst areas (see table 13).

TABLE 13: *Reading and IQ in two contrasting areas of Liverpool at CA 7–8*

AREA	NO. OF CHILDREN	MEAN IQ	MEAN RA (BURT)	% BACKWARD > 20m. RA
Dockland	137	97	6y. 7m.	37
Outer residential (southern)	76	112	7y. 9m.	15

Similarly, Goodacre (1967) in her survey of 100 London infant schools found that average reading scores were lowest in schools serving lower working-class areas, and highest in middle-class suburban areas. Evans (1972) replicated this not unexpected result. Interestingly, his data for 'deprived' areas showed proportionally more boys among the complete non-starters and fewer girls among the advanced readers than in 'settled working-class' and 'suburban residential' areas. This leads one to consider the possibility that reading is often taught in such a way that it is rejected by boys from manual working-class families in which practical and sporting activities are valued more than 'book-learning'. It also makes one wonder why girls who come from a poverty-stricken background rarely shine academically. It could be that girls have to bear more of the burden of home chores in the poorer families, and it may also be relevant that the majority of jobs available to women in industrial areas are unskilled and badly paid.

Wilson (1971) examined home, school and neighbourhood correlates of reading and intelligence at seven-plus and at ten-plus in 4554 children in Northern Ireland. His results show quite clearly that home and neighbourhood deficiencies impinge less on boys than on girls, and that their main effect is to reduce the numbers of achieving girls.

e effort involved in controlling a pen. Part of a test designed to measure hand dominance.

is book is 'for real'. The children and their teacher have all had a part in making it.

A group of infants needing extra help start the day with a teacher and a classroom themselves.

A spacious and stimulating class environment with a reading corner and a listening centre.

At the same time, Wilson found that backwardness in boys was chiefly associated with a neighbourhood anti-school attitude as expressed in poor school attendance figures.

Both Wiseman and Wilson (1967) showed that, in general, home and neighbourhood variables had a bigger influence on the numbers of bright children than on the incidence of backwardness. This point was also made by Ferguson and others (1971) who attempted to predict school success in Swansea by using socioeconomic variables alone. They found that measures such as family size, population density, incidence of broken homes, distribution of supplementary benefits (and other criteria which have been used to identify educational priority areas) were more useful in picking out specially favoured schools than in identifying the disadvantaged ones. The relationship between home, school and neighbourhood variables and individual IQ and attainment test results can easily be exaggerated. Wilson found that less than a third of the inter-pupil reading test variance was associated with these environmental measures (55 variables in all). The Plowden National survey results (DES, 1967) might at first sight seem to conflict with Wilson's findings, but both the parental attitude measures and the school measures in this survey are contaminated by indirect measures of intelligence and attainment (such as expected and actual 11-plus success). Wilson pointed out that measures of this kind are likely to reflect attitudes and expectations that are based on actual as well as hoped-for performance.

The evidence from the Plowden National survey and from the NFER follow-up to it (Peaker, 1971) suggests that there is a slight tendency for the links between socioeconomic background and school performance to become stronger as children get older, and at the same time for the influence of school variables to decline. Wilson's study points in the same direction, and also focuses attention on certain clusters of economic and social disadvantage which are associated with deteriorating school performance. For example, there was evidence that in areas of high unemployment, poor school performance was more of a problem at ten-plus than at seven-plus. Moreover, particular problems associated with being a Catholic in Northern Ireland (such as large families, overcrowded and sub-standard living conditions, difficulty in getting a job) had apparently no bearing on school attainments at seven-plus, but were correlated with reading attainment at ten-plus. Unfortunately, one has no means of telling how far the environmental factors here operate directly upon morale and motivation. What is most interesting, however, is the fact that indices of 'deprivation' such as family size and overcrowding (which are generally agreed to be important correlates of educational performance) were not, within the Catholic community, associated with poor attainments at seven-plus. It may be that these things are considered to be normal and are not perceived as special handicaps by Catholics—indeed, it is likely that they apply to Catholics in all walks of life in Northern Ireland.

In the light of the evidence summarized above, it would be possible for an environmentalist to argue that a large part of the observed differences in IQ and reading scores could be produced purely by the action of the environment. Even if there is an underlying genetic difference in ability between the unskilled poor and the élites of suburbia, it can only be a matter of a few IQ points, and can by no stretch of the imagination be held to account for the observed difference in attainment. We have seen how part of this difference is due to the specially favourable conditions in middle-class areas, schools, and homes; how another part is produced by a wastage of talent among working-class girls; and how in exceptionally bad living conditions severe educational and social problems are to be expected. On the other hand, we have seen that the relationship between poverty and educational performance is not a simple one, especially when we come down to the individual case. There are some notable exceptions to the general pattern, and much seems to depend on how the families and the communities concerned view their position and their chances of betterment.

Variations in reading standards between schools

Several authors who have reviewed the evidence (e.g. Kelsall and Kelsall, 1971; Little and Smith, 1971; Halsey, 1972; Chazan and others, 1975) have concluded that the influence of the home on school performance is much greater than that of the school. Teachers who feel powerless to prevent some of their pupils from falling increasingly behind their peers in attainment and in standards of behaviour as they get older, may find this reassuring. The point may, however, be disputed. Goldstein (1972) has argued that previous research involving measures of environmental and home factors, parental attitude and school circumstances has simply failed to account for the observed differences between schools. He believes that inappropriate measures have been used, and he is certainly right as far as school factors are concerned, since objective methods of assessing teacher performance or classroom interaction have rarely been used as part of a larger survey. At the same time, pupil-consensus measures of the social environment of the classroom are still in the early stages of development and application (Marjoribanks, 1974).

There is general agreement that there *are* very marked differences in attainment between schools, even within a socially homogeneous area. For example, Evans (1972) pointed out that one school in a deprived area (which was committed to the formal teaching of reading) had less than eight per cent of its children more than two years behind in reading at the end of the infant stage, whereas another (which served an area of slightly higher socioeconomic status) had as many as 86 per cent who were backward by two years or more. Chazan and others found that significantly fewer teachers of infants in deprived urban areas set aside a daily time for 3R work (six out of 19 teachers), compared with rural areas (nine out of 11 teachers), settled working-class areas (eight out of 11 teachers) and middle-class areas (five out of seven teachers). This is certainly one way in which progress in reading can be affected. Unfortunately, what passes as a progressive approach (incidental help with reading in the course of an 'integrated' day) can in inexperienced hands amount to a state of near chaos. Cane and Smithers (1971) showed how much performance at seven-plus is influenced by systematic teaching, as well as by factors such as lack of discipline and extraneous noise. Their study concerned 12 schools in lower working-class areas and four in middle-class areas, over two years of infant schooling. Reading readiness tests were given to reception classes, and word-recognition was measured at seven-plus. The schools were ranked according to their success in teaching reading after initial readiness had been accounted for. It was found that none of the twelve schools in working-class areas achieved such good results as those of the least successful schools in a middle-class area. At the end of infant schooling, 15 per cent of the girls and 30 per cent of the boys in the working-class schools were still on Book 1 of a reading scheme. This is more than twice the national average, as determined by Pringle and others. The majority of backward readers were to be found in the four least successful schools. One school in particular had very poor results, with an average standardized score of just over 80. Here there was little reading instruction in the reception class, and no use of phonics. There was no timetable and no restriction was placed on the children's movements. The children seemed free to 'follow their own ways and interests and not pay too much attention to the teachers'. Observers felt that the headmistress and the reception class teacher were hostile in attitude towards the local population. All four teachers in the school frequently commented on parental lack of interest and on the 'extreme poverty of the childrens' cultural backgrounds', without producing specific evidence of this. On the other hand, neutral observers felt that the children were on the whole well clothed and cared for, and that their standard of speech was 'better than one would expect for the area'. All of the schools were studied in considerable detail, and it was found that the most successful working-class area schools differed from the least successful in the following ways:

1 Teachers did not wait for children to show an interest in reading but exerted direct control over the childrens' learning.

2 Fewer classes were considered to be out of the teacher's control.

3 Early instruction in the sounds of letters was common.

4 They were in relatively quiet surroundings, whereas all the unsuccessful schools were in noisy surroundings, three of them being near railways.

It should not, however, be supposed that these results justify a massive swing to formal authoritarian methods in infant schools. In two of the successful schools there was a friendly, permissive atmosphere but *reading* was not allowed to suffer because of this. There were set periods of reading instruction when the teacher assumed direct control of either a group or the whole class. Observers felt that relations between teachers and children were relaxed and informal, even in the schools ranked highest for teacher direction. However, the considerable variation between the 12 schools certainly could not be explained in terms of home or parental factors. The schools had very similar catchment areas, and the differences between them were clearly due to internal factors such as teaching methods, teachers' attitudes towards readiness, and the role and influence of the head.

We cannot be certain about the disturbing effects of noise in the unsuccessful schools. It may have been one of the reasons why phonic instruction was rarely given in these schools. It is much more difficult to hold the attention of children in noisy surroundings than in quiet ones, and virtually impossible to provide any training in listening skills which call for precise discrimination.

Also, Lasky and Tobin (1973) have shown that children thought to be at risk as cases of learning disability are adversely affected significantly more than controls on listening tests by hearing an irrelevant speech message. It is therefore probable that such children find it particularly difficult to concentrate when those around them are talking about something else – and we have already seen that this situation is particularly common in deprived areas. Extraneous noise makes it necessary to raise one's voice – so the distracting effect of conversation is presumably increased in a noisy environment. Interestingly, Elliott and Pumfrey (1972) found that children who were unable to tolerate high levels of noise made very little reading progress during a one-year period. The sample in their study consisted of 16 socially maladjusted boys of low average intelligence and poor reading attainment, from two junior schools in an educational priority area.

Wilson's Northern Ireland survey drew attention to another way in which schools might improve their reading standards. Test performance at seven-plus, but especially reading as assessed by the primer criterion, was better in those schools which regularly gave 'homework' (often in the form of reading). This finding was quite independent of any socioeconomic and neighbourhood influences, as was Wiseman's similar finding at the age of ten-plus in Manchester. Wilson also found that, although streaming had little effect on mean test scores, it was associated with a somewhat lower incidence of backwardness. Other school variables, such as size of classes, pupil/teacher ratio, school equipment and library provision, had virtually no effect on reading scores. Kemp (1955), Coleman and others (1966), Morris (1966), DES (1967), Wiseman (1967), Peaker (1971) and Little and others (1972) are among those who may be cited in support of similar negative results. The evidence about the age and experience of teachers, as well as about teacher turnover, is somewhat conflicting – but Wiseman found that younger children did seem to be adversely affected by inexperience and a high turnover rate, whereas older ones were not.

An attempt was made in the Plowden National Survey to rate the effectiveness of teachers, but the HMI gradings used proved to have only small correlations with attainments. Morris, in her Kent survey, spent a great deal of time in observing how teachers taught reading in particular, and her results suggest that it would be worthwhile trying to develop more reliable and objective measures in this area. She found that 'pupils attending schools with outstandingly good reading attainment had considerably better[1] teachers each year than those in other schools'. In addition, the most experienced teachers and those who showed special competence in teaching reading tended to be responsible for high-ability classes in streamed schools, whereas the poor readers were taken by the weaker teachers and were in the junior years subjected to significantly more changes of teacher. Peters (1970) noted similar trends in the teaching of spelling. She found that teachers rated low on technical skill in teaching spelling were not only in charge of classes with poor spelling attainments, but produced much smaller percentage gains with those classes than did teachers with a systematic approach ($r = 0.48$.)

Morris considered that differences in reading attainment between schools depended not only on the quality of the class-teachers, but also on the competence of the head. On the basis of a detailed study of ten schools, she pointed to differences in the organization of special help for backward children, in the preparation of clearly defined schemes of work, and in the amount of practical classroom assistance rendered by

[1]This refers to qualifications, experience, interest in teaching reading, and ratings of classroom practice. It is not a matter of a formal versus a permissive approach, nor of phonic versus whole-word methods.

heads in schools with good and poor reading standards. In two of the 'bad' schools there was a prevalent belief that greater effort would be wasted on pupils without an academic bias.

Although it has been shown that there is very little relationship between attainments and the provision of books and other equipment at school level, it is not clear how far the unequal distribution of these resources among the bright and backward affects the incidence of brightness and backwardness. Morris made the following statement on the basis of her study of the accommodation and basic equipment provided in 91 classrooms: 'there is evidence . . . that juniors who need the most encouragement to improve their reading standards were generally given the least in terms of the material conditions of learning and teaching provided for them at school and classroom level.' Of books, Morris noted that 'not only were the "poor" readers found to be at a distinct disadvantage with regard to class libraries, but the books generally available to a sizeable proportion were both insufficient in number and unsuitable in content'.

One way in which both teachers and resources can be unevenly distributed within a school is, of course, by the practice of streaming. The NFER survey for the Plowden Report showed that the teachers of C and D streams have had, on average, six years less teaching experience than teachers of A streams. Moreover, there was a significant tendency for the lower streams to be given badly-lit classrooms. On the other hand, class sizes were smaller in the lowest streams. What one wants to know is whether any particular kind of organization is associated with small numbers of failing children. The evidence adduced by Wilson and Wiseman suggested that there are fewer severely backward children in streamed schools – in other words, that the advantage of being in a relatively small homogeneous class can outweigh the disadvantage of having a less experienced teacher and rather poorer classroom facilities. Whether or not this happens depends a great deal on local circumstances, as became evident in a survey of spelling ability which the author carried out in a relatively homogeneous working-class area of north-east London in 1967.

All second-year juniors in 16 schools were given Schonell's Spelling Test B during the summer term. After excluding immigrant children who had arrived in this country after the age of five, and all those whose parents did not speak English at home, as many as 20 per cent of the remainder performed at below a seven-year level (which means that they were unable to spell three-letter words reliably). The 'best' school had only four (five per cent) of its 'indigenous' nine-year-old pupils scoring below SA 7y., while the 'worst' school had 29 (26 per cent). When the schools were ranked from best to worst according to the proportion of backward spellers they contained, the importance of class size became evident, as shown by a Spearman rank correlation of 0·49 between mean class size and school incidence of poor spelling. The data was then examined for possible effects of school organization (see table 14), and it was found that schools which had a relatively small special class contained significantly fewer poor spellers. Streaming as such had no significant effect either on mean spelling scores or on the incidence of backwardness – unless, that is, a special class be considered a form of streaming.

TABLE 14: *The effects of school organization on the incidence of backwardness in spelling in second-year juniors*

	Unstreamed	TYPE OF ORGANIZATION Grouping by birth date	Streamed	Unstreamed and special class
No. of schools	6	5	2	3
Average size of class	33	34	33	33*
Proportion of immigrants	9%	11%	14%	8%
Proportion of poor spellers (excluding imm. group)	20%	19%	17%	12%†

*In unstreamed classes x̄ 38, in special classes x̄ 23.
†This proportion is significantly lower than with the other types of organization, at 1%, 2% and 10% levels (1-tailed test).

It will be seen from table 14 that the beneficial effects of a small special class operate quite independently of the overall average size of classes within a school. Neither can the effects be explained in terms of different numbers of immigrants in the schools concerned.[1] In fact it turned out that the four 'best' schools actually contained more immigrant children (13 per cent) than the four 'worst' schools (nine per cent). What seemed to matter was the size of classes, especially the classes containing large numbers of backward children. None of the four 'worst' schools had any special arrangements for teaching reading, and the age-group was made up of three or four mixed-ability classes of equal size. On the other hand, two of the four 'best' schools had a smaller class for slower pupils, while the other two headed the list for small class size (27 and 30 pupils respectively). One of these schools was streamed, and was the only school in the sample to have a part-time teacher speci-

[1]This finding is consistent with results obtained in the ILEA Literacy Survey (1969).

ally appointed to take groups of backward readers. It also had the highest proportion of immigrant children (18 per cent, according to the definition given previously) of all the schools in the study.

There can be little doubt that the influence of the head was important in creating better learning conditions for the less able pupils in the 'better' schools. As Morris argued, if the head is seen to be actively interested in reading, and in different problems, pupils will be encouraged. There is no evidence from the author's survey that female heads are any better than male heads in this respect, as the incidence of backwardness was the same (17 per cent) in five schools with female heads as in eleven schools with male heads.

However, one unexpected finding emerged, namely that girls were less likely than boys to be poor spellers in schools with male heads. This is shown in table 15, but in view of the small number of schools involved, the result may prove to be spurious. Moreover, it is not known whether the same tendency applies at the level of the class teacher. Further research in this area is needed.

TABLE 15: *Incidence of poor spelling in boys and girls according to sex of head teacher*

	PROPORTION WITH SA $< 7Y$.		
	Boys	*Girls*	*Significance of sex difference*
5 schools with female heads	41/214 (19·2%)	31/199 (15·6%)	Diff. n.s. (0·87 s.e.)
11 schools with male heads	102/436 (23·4%)	42/405 (10·4%)	Diff. sig. (5·0 s.e.) $p < 0.0001$

Schools differ considerably, not only in their internal organization, policy and quality of teaching, but also in the extent to which they truly serve the communities in which they are located. The Plowden report (DES, 1967), gave considerable emphasis to the correlation between parental attitudes towards education and pupil attainment, but hardly considered the possibility that schools themselves may be partly responsible for the growth of unfavourable parental attitudes.

A longitudinal study of the parental attitudes of slow-learning children has not yet been made, but the clinical experience would support the view that many of these parents become increasingly disillusioned with the services available during the primary years. The high degree of involvement of working-class parents in the West Riding EPA home-visiting programme (Smith, 1975) suggests that if positive steps were taken to involve parents in special educational programmes at all levels of schooling, there would be a good response, even in 'deprived' areas. As things are, Plowden found that working-class parents have about two-thirds as many conversations with teachers as middle-class parents have. The Plowden data also showed that schools in predominantly working-class areas tended to invite parents to fewer functions than schools in middle-class areas, and that fewer of those functions were arranged at times when fathers were likely to be available. At the same time, it was the manual working-class parents, not the middle-class ones, who expressed the stronger desire to be told more about the progress of their children, and who thought that teachers should have sought more information from them about special problems and difficulties with the children. As Cullen (1969) found, communication between home and school is often at its worst when a child is failing to make progress at school. Poorly educated parents feel helpless in the situation: they do not know what facilities are available, and they do not feel competent to tackle the problem themselves. They may be afraid to approach the school, but are likely to respond if approached. Chazan and others found that almost all parents, however poor their home circumstances, would welcome a teacher who visited the home to discuss the progress of their children.

Fryer (1973) described a parental involvement scheme in an EPA primary school. It was found that most parents took the opportunity of meeting teachers and coming into classrooms when they brought their children to school in the morning, and that many of them borrowed the public library books which were kept in the school for the purpose. Social and fund-raising events were supported by almost all parents. Occasional home-visits were made, although not as a routine duty. Unfortunately, insufficient work on this kind has been done for one to judge what might be achieved if parents and other adults were involved more actively in the life of their schools. It is not unusual for teachers never to meet the parents of at least one-third of the children they teach (Goodacre, 1968; Cullen, 1969). Cane and Smithers noted the patronizing attitude and lack of detailed knowledge about families on the part of the head-teachers in three of the four 'unsuccessful' schools in their study. They also found that 'children with at least average ability, or better, may be stereotyped as less able because they conform to expected appearance and personality of a child from a poor home'. Unfortunately, teachers are apt to underestimate both parents and children in working-class areas. Goodacre suspected that the parents who cannot take time off work to visit the school are often thought to take little interest in their children's progress. Barker Lunn (1970) showed that with both average and high-achieving pupils (though not with backward ones), teachers seriously underestimate the English ability of children from poorer social backgrounds.

An interesting parallel to the above-mentioned underestimation of the more capable working-class children is a dramatic finding by Rubowits and Maehr (1973), who were concerned with the amount of attention and praise given by 66 American trainee teachers to black and white children who were described as (but were not in fact) gifted and non-gifted. Measures of teacher–child interaction showed not only that the black children were ignored much more and praised much less than white children, but that it was the gifted blacks who came off worst, and the gifted whites best. These differential effects were greatest with those of the children's teachers who scored high on personality tests of dogmatism and authoritarianism, and were not present with all teachers. It is, of course, possible that similar effects operate on a social class as well as on a racial basis in this country. The American Coleman report showed that the educational achievement of racial minority groups was associated with teachers' attitudes towards integration. How far the attitudes of teachers can be changed by training which fully involves them in the life of deprived and multi-racial areas is not yet known, but there are signs that the problem is beginning to be recognized (Hannam and others, 1971; Fairman, 1972; de Zutter, 1973).

Home influences on reading standards

On balance, the evidence of research studies shows that children with difficult home circumstances are more often directly affected in their performance at school by lack of parental example, encouragement and help than they are indirectly affected by emotional tension in the home, even by family disruption. In homes where time, money and space are limited, there is a strong possibility that parents will be unable to spend as much time as they would like with their children, and will read little themselves. In addition, many parents are not interested in literary pursuits, and many do not feel competent to help their children with school work, as they themselves were backward at school. There is bound to be a correlation between these home factors and socioeconomic status, and if a multiplicity of disadvantaging factors combine in an individual family, the children will almost invariably find learning difficult.

All the major British surveys have shown that broken homes do not, as such, produce backward readers. However, Davie and others found that, while the absence of natural parents was not associated with reading standards in social classes 4 and 5, there was a very slight association in classes 1–3. Morris found that the fathers of seven out of

101 poor readers but also nine out of 98 good readers were either absent, dead or unemployed.[1] She also considered the possible effects of illegitimacy, parental neglect and over-protection, but found no significant differences between the poor and good readers.

In a study involving 160 negro mothers from differing social backgrounds, Hess (1968) related measures of family and community circumstances to reading readiness scores and to reading achievement two years later. Mothers were also observed and recorded in various situations, including trying to teach their children three simple tasks. The highest correlation ($r=0.61$ with readiness and 0.36 with later achievement) was with a composite measure of the mother's use of resources in the home (e.g. use of toys and reading to the child) and in the neighbourhood (parks, etc.). Measures of maternal teaching style were also found to be related to reading readiness and subsequent progress, especially the use of feedback and affective support. Moderate correlations were also obtained with measures of maternal involvement in community organizations and activities, and with feelings of confidence in dealing with the school. Lower correlations were obtained with measures of the mother's use of standard English and with methods used to control behaviour.

The Plowden national survey showed that parental interest in school work and progress was the biggest factor associated with school performance at infant level, and could be held to account for ten per cent of the within-schools attainment variance at top junior level. This factor was assessed by means of questions about time spent talking and playing with the child, the child's reading at home and parental satisfaction with the part played by the school. The literacy of the home is another important factor at all ages. These interest and literacy factors affect the numbers of good readers as well as the numbers of poor readers (see Wiseman and Wilson), and Morris found a significant differential social-class effect as far as good readers were concerned. Table 16 gives the relevant data.

TABLE 16: *Help given to poor and good readers by fathers analysed by occupational status (based on Morris)*

| | POOR READERS (n=96) | | GOOD READERS (n=90) | |
	Non-manual	*Manual*	*Non-manual*	*Manual*
Much or some help	5	20	58	21
Little or no help	8	63	4	7
	$\chi^2=0.57$ (n.s.)		$\chi^2=4.6$ (p$<$0.05)	

[1]Unemployment was not high in Kent at the time.

Plowden found significant social class differences in the following measures of parental behaviour and attitude: responsibility and initiative taken by parents over their children's education; the interest shown and the support given by fathers over their education and upbringing; parental interest in school work and progress; and the literacy of the home.

It is very probable that the relationships between such things as family income, material circumstances, standard of housing, family size and reading are indirectly mediated through some of the behavioural variables detailed above. Several workers, for example, have obtained significant correlations between family size and reading standards. Thus, in Crawford's Liverpool sample there were 25 children who had seven or more siblings. The average RA of this group near the end of the infant stage (mean CA 7y. 3m.) was 5y. 0m. Their complete lack of progress in reading could not be explained in cognitive terms alone, since the average IQ of the group was 91. No one factor could fully account for this, but Morris' finding that in large families parents (especially mothers) gave much less direct assistance with reading than in small families is undoubtedly relevant. Other indices of environmental disadvantage are probably also related to reading in indirect ways. Many families living in sub-standard, overcrowded accommodation simply do not have the time or space in which to settle down quietly with books. Fathers with small incomes typically work long hours of overtime. Those whose work involves considerable physical effort may be too tired in the evenings to concentrate on a book or to play with and read to their children. When mothers are working during the day they may have less time and energy to devote to their children.[1] Low income families (Field, 1973) simply cannot afford to buy many books and toys.

There are other still more direct effects of poor living conditions on school performance and/or social acceptability. Malnutrition, illness, dirtiness and poor clothing are among these. Children who appear tired, lazy and dirty can easily get a bad reputation with teachers as well as with other children. If these children are often late for school or attend irregularly, it may well be as a result of genuine sickness or hardship. Of course, older children sometimes positively reject a school which they feel has rejected them. Lesson refusal and truancy, as well as aggressive acts and a deliberate effort to obtain low marks (Rosenberg, 1973), are among the symptoms of rejection. Of course, some children

[1]Evidence on this point is conflicting. Care must be taken in applying national statistics to a particular area. There is evidence that in industrial areas, children of working mothers are *better* adjusted to school (Finlayson, 1964) and do not suffer in attainment (Fraser, 1959), compared with those whose mothers do not go out to work.

and their parents have every right to feel that not only school but society in general is against them. According to Field, more than 6500 children a year are separated from their parents and put into care because of homelessness or bad housing. Cases have been reported of children afraid to go to school in case their parents are not there when they get back, and of children unable to play and even to talk for fear of offending landlords.

Is compensatory education possible?

If one believes that the limits to a child's educational performance are determined almost entirely by environmental factors, the extent to which teachers can intervene to help low-achieving children is a function of the control teachers have over the relevant environmental factors. If, on the other hand, one believes that the limits to a child's educational performance are determined almost entirely by his genes, one will presumably not rest until one has brought his attainments up to the standard implied by what is claimed to be an assessment of his genetic potential.

The arguments for a substantial genetic element in the determination of cognitive abilities are not merely based on an analogy between the colour of the eyes and the ability to impress examiners. It is a fact that there are very large variations in the skills and abilities of children exposed to very similar environments, and as yet no selection of environmental measures has been proved to account for more than half of the variance in intelligence and attainment scores. Moreover, the evidence of twin-studies (summarized by Jensen, 1973) is sufficient proof that there are significant genetically determined cognitive differences between individuals. On the other hand, we have no direct measure of genetic factors, and the problem of disentangling nature from nurture is virtually impossible in adverse environments. One thing is clear. The results of IQ tests give a very poor indication of a deprived child's ability to learn in a more favourable environment. Hamblin and others (1971) showed that with systematic reinforcement an inner-city class of six- to seven-year-olds could gain 17 IQ points (on average) in one year. This kind of result makes us realize that if a working class child scores badly on an intelligence test, he is not necessarily going to be slow in learning, nor is he necessarily innately dull.

There have been a number of studies in which substantial gains in attainments and in intelligence scores have been reported (e.g. Bereiter and Englemann, 1966; Gray and others, 1966; Hawkridge and others, 1968; Deutsch, 1969; Blank and Solomon, 1969; Jacobson and Greeson, 1972). In the majority of cases (including Hamblin's study) the gains were gradually eroded when the special intervention programmes ended. This should not be taken as a criticism of the projects concerned, as in most cases they did not intend to bring about permanent changes in the schools. Pre-school programmes such as those of Bereiter and Englemann, Blank, Deutsch, Karnes and Weikart are not really likely to modify the practice of teachers who come into the picture one or more years later. In Jacobson and Greeson's study the children were followed up when they were still of pre-school age. It was found that IQ gains had been maintained reasonably well over a 14-month period, and were still ten points above the initial scores.

Impressive results have been obtained with very different teaching methods, and Weikart (1970) suggests that this may be because the projects concerned have been carefully planned, have been implemented by enthusiastic and committed teams of workers, and have had sufficient resources to organize activities which support classroom work. Thus, Bereiter and Englemann reported a mean gain of 26 Stanford-Binet IQ points in the two years, while Blank, using daily individual tutorials, obtained a mean gain of 14·5 points in four months. There was a similar outcome in the West Riding EPA Project (Payne, 1974), in that good results were obtained by two very different methods (the Peabody Language Development Kit and individual tutoring with an emphasis on abstract thinking and problem-solving along Marion Blank lines). Gains made during the nursery year were increased still more during reception year in the infant school. Even though the special programmes were not continued during the reception years, close links were maintained between the specialist project workers and the infant school. This is likely to have played a part in changing the usual pattern of scores when the initial impetus of action research is over. Another type of approach also proved effective in a West Riding community, leading to a mean IQ gain (Merrill-Palmer) of 12 points and bringing about changes in mother–child interaction (less negative reinforcement of the child's behaviour than in a control group). This was the home-visiting programme, the aim of which was to realize the abilities of mothers (and fathers) to extend and to create situations on the basis of the model provided by an educational visitor. It is a major achievement for a programme of this kind to succeed in its main purpose, but for permanent gains to accrue, parents may need a continuing contact with the education system if they are to enrich their child's learning in an appropriate manner in later years. A multi-purpose educational guidance centre like the Red House in Conisborough is one means of providing such contact.

Some workers have realized that short-term compensatory intervention is of limited value, and have therefore tried to provide a long-term solution, based on parent and community involvement. Among these is one project reported by Gordon (1967) in which home-visiting began when a child was only three months old. Modarressi (1974) described the Baltimore Early School Admission Project, in which parents were involved not only in a teaching capacity in inner-city schools, but in decision-making at weekly case-conferences held in school. The project is succeeding in its aim to encourage schools to become self-reliant systems, capable through joint efforts of parents, teachers and mental health workers of finding solutions to special learning and behaviour problems. Bailey (1974) reported on a 'Parents as Partners' programme in Rockwood, California, which also involves parents as classroom aides, in remedial work and in decision-making. Other approaches include 'free', community and model schools of various kinds. Some American developments in this field have been described by Little and Smith (1971), Blackstone (1973) and Stanley (1973).

Since then, Stenner and Mueller (1974) have claimed success for a large-scale compensatory education project in Chicago. So far, this has involved 2100 children in 11 'Child Parent Education Centres'. The centres are staffed by teachers, aides, teachers of parents (home economics), adjustment teachers, nurses, health aides, social workers, speech therapists and others, and each centre has a parent advisory council, which together with staff members helps to make decisions concerning the services available, as well as the curriculum. Children attend between the ages of three and nine, and the size of group is 15 (pre-school) and 20 (kindergarten onwards). These centres appear to be very special neighbourhood schools, and represent an effort to upgrade the quality of educational provision in poverty areas to a really significant extent. The total cost of the primary programme per pupil-year ($2290) is more than twice the normal cost of primary education in Chicago, but the authors consider that the results justify this. An early start is made with reading, and by the time the children reach the third grade, they are, on average, eight months in advance of national norms in reading, and 12 months in arithmetic. If it is assumed that further remedial, social and psychiatric intervention is not going to be needed for these children after they transfer to ordinary schools, the programme will have proved itself in terms of cost-benefit analysis. The authors attribute the success of the project to date to the following factors which were present in all centres: an early start, continuity for the children, parent involvement, and the use of structured language and reading programmes backed up by ample rewards and praise. Statistical analysis showed that 20 per cent of the pupil achievement variance could be attributed to the parental involvement aspect. Interestingly, the parents who played an active part were not any better off financially than those who did not.

It must be admitted, however, that many large-scale compensatory education projects have come up with disappointing results. The All Day Neighbourhood School Program in New York provided after-school 'clubs' for children with home difficulties, but no attainment gains occurred (US Commission on Civil Rights, 1967). The Higher Horizons cultural enrichment programme in New York cost only $61 per pupil per year extra, and Ribich (1968) found an average gain in attainment of only three per cent of a year compared with pupils in control schools. The gains made in the American Headstart programme were minimal (Westinghouse Report, 1969). The enormously expensive More Effective School Programme (Fox, 1968) brought about no significant improvement in attainments, even though total expenditure was practically doubled[1] in schools for up to three years. Findings like these led Little and Smith (1971) and Jencks (1973) to draw rather gloomy conclusions from their surveys of compensatory educational intervention.

It is, of course, possible that large-scale projects often fail because they simply offer more and more unproductive school experience. If nothing is done to change the relationship between schools and their settings, they may simply serve to intensify a sense of failure and frustration among the less academic children. Holt's (1964) description of how some children fail is certainly convincing, as is the powerful and well-documented appeal to public conscience by the School of Barbiana (1970). Keddie (1973), Goodman (1962) and Reimer (1971) are among those who have made some genuinely constructive suggestions for broadening the context of education and for humanizing what may be little more than a process of selection, regimentation and depersonalization. MacBeath (1974) made a related point: 'No matter how flashy or comfortable or home-like schools may be, if they are perceived as alien and unfriendly places, it is too much to expect that much learning will occur. Within this context even the most sensitive teacher cannot be expected to do much. It is important . . . that learning occurs in an environment which is not hostile, threatening, disapproving, coercive; that there is time and opportunity for the child to communicate his experience in his own language; that there are teachers who are able to tune in on the same wavelength and relate what is to be learnt to what the child perceives as important.' Kozol's (1967) personal experience in a Boston school (see Appendix B) illustrates how disadvantaged children can be made to suffer in the name of education.

[1]Most of the money was spent on more teachers, including four or five assistant principals per school. There was no over-all organization or in-service training programme to enable schools to make good use of the additional personnel.

On the other hand, most teachers could describe heartening examples of local commitment and creative involvement.

The success of some of the smaller compensatory education projects may well derive from the fact that it is sometimes possible to alter the balance of resources in such a way that disadvantaged and handicapped children feel that they have a real, genuine chance to develop. This is sometimes achieved in special schools and units, and in a few schools where the head is especially interested. As we have seen, significant educational progress can also result from work done with and by parents. Remedial drama, as described by Jennings (1973) offers another set of opportunities, and even a weekly chat with an interested and outgoing adult volunteer can not only boost the morale of slow-learners, but can make it more likely that they will respond when given extra help with their reading (Lawrence, 1972).

With a few notable exceptions, the idea of compensatory education has not yet been put into practice in Great Britain. We know relatively little about how far it is possible to modify the patterns of parent–child interaction from an early age, how to increase the numbers of parents who read to their children, and how to develop an atmosphere of educational co-operation between home and school. We have only begun to explore the possibility of providing relevant vocational courses and recreational facilities for both parents and children in areas of high unemployment. Further education departments make little impact on the problem of adult illiteracy (NARE[1], 1972), and offer no courses in training non-professional personnel for work in the classroom.[2] School-based preventive and treatment programmes for children with special problems very rarely operate in conjunction with parents and other community representatives. Little is done to modify counter-productive interaction patterns between teachers and failing children, or to influence the attitudes and expectations which so many teachers bring to their work from the suburbs. Teachers who do wish to improve provision for 'children in distress' can find themselves blocked by head-teachers or administrators. They have no direct channel of communication either with parents or with the LEA. An inflexible school organization sometimes means that small groups cannot be formed for specific purposes, and many children who need the experience of a small 'family' group and consistent adult care in a school setting do not get it. There are too few adults and inadequate resources for learning in the vast majority of the schools which have more than their share of learning and behaviour problems. Schools in crowded and noisy city areas do not even compensate for these basic

[1]National Association for Remedial Education.
[2]See Appendix C.

restrictions on a child's personal development by providing adequate play and recreation facilities, and enough space and sound-absorption for efficient learning.

On the basis of the evidence reviewed in this chapter, it seems fair to conclude that educational intervention is more likely to succeed if it diverts more effort *within each school* towards disadvantaged children and their families, than if educational priority areas are defined by socioeconomic criteria and more money and teachers are simply poured in. As Ferguson argued, the Plowden idea of positive discrimination should be applied to individuals as well as to entire schools and districts. At the same time, when new schools are built in poverty areas, they could be designed to be like Chicago's Child Parent Education Centres.

Chapter 6 of this book includes a number of practical suggestions for improving provision for backward readers. Formal recommendations in the context of teacher-training were also made by Booth and others (1974) to the DES Committee of Inquiry into Reading and the Use of English. These recommendations covered the areas of teacher expectations (of the needs and capacities of children and their parents), teaching methods, record-keeping and educational guidance, curriculum content, authority structure and ethos within schools, and special educational services. There is reason to believe that much can still be done to enable failing and unhappy children to realize their 'right to learn'.

Summary

The correlations between educational performance, behaviour in school and socioeconomic status are real, but correlations do not explain causality. Genetic and environmental factors which have both direct and indirect effects on school adjustment and progress are mediated through interpersonal interactions in school as well as out of it. These interactions are of major importance to children, and have been relatively neglected by researchers. Norms and expectations vary considerably between different regions, areas, schools and teachers, and so does performance in school. It is naïve to assume that the reasons for the relative failure of working-class children in the educational system must lie in the children or in their 'background'. In fact, home and neighbourhood variables have a greater effect on the number of high-achieving children than on the number of children who fail academically. If children develop a crippling sense of failure, schools must bear at least part of the responsibility. The distribution of resources within a school almost invariably favours the more able middle-class child, and makes a nonsense of the term 'compensatory education' as we at present understand it.

There is a growing body of evidence that schools and colleges are able to take positive steps to reduce the incidence of reading backwardness, to influence community attitudes and to overcome internal prejudices. Moves to give parents greater responsibility for and involvement in their children's learning are promising developments. Lack of example, encouragement and help handicap children more than adverse material circumstances. Children who are subject to physical and emotional stress out of school are not helped by teachers who devalue their friends and families, and who criticize their language, their appearance, their work and their manners.

If remedial and compensatory education are to work, it is not simply a matter of spending more money, but of redistributing resources on the basis of a new sense of social justice.

Chapter Four

Present Facilities

Pringle and others (1966) and Goodacre (1967) have reported on the organization of special help for children in infant departments and schools. After considering this evidence, we shall look at special provision in junior schools. We shall begin by examining the facilities for helping backward readers in a large urban area where it is normally left to the individual heads to allocate staff and resources as they see fit. Here we shall draw on some of the findings of the Inner London Education Authority (ILEA) Literacy Survey of 1968. Interim results were summarized in a document produced in 1969, and some further developments were reported in a paper circulated to schools in 1971. Further information about ILEA facilities and plans of action is contained in a discussion document called *Children with Special Difficulties* (1971b). The ILEA situation is of great interest, as the problems to be found in the inner-city areas of the metropolis are those which hit New York ten years ago, and which may well reach provincial towns in five years time.

We shall then consider the large-scale surveys of remedial education services carried out by Sampson (1969) and Sampson and Pumfrey (1970). Sampson asked LEAs in the North of England to report on their remedial services in and for primary schools. These were defined in terms of individual or small-group tuition. As the pattern of provision is different in many respects at secondary level, Sampson and Pumfrey carried out a second inquiry, obtaining responses from 61 LEAs throughout the country. Goodacre's (1971b) report on developments in reading provision between 1960 and 1970 is also referred to.

A small-scale survey of LEA provision was carried out by the author in 1971, to provide additional data for this book. Information was received from 11 boroughs and from 12 county LEAs. The reasons for including certain LEAs in the survey and for excluding others were subjective, but an attempt was made to include a number of areas in which provision was expanding, albeit on different lines.

References are also made in this chapter to two DES Education Surveys (1971 and 1972) concerned with slow learners in secondary schools and with immigrant pupils. Finally, the question of residential provision for children with specific reading difficulties is briefly considered.

Relevant findings from the national survey carried out by the Bullock Committee of Inquiry are summarized in Appendix G.

Provision at infant level

In most parts of the country children are admitted to normal schools at the age of four or five, even though they have quite obvious mental and physical handicaps. Only those with gross disabilities are placed in special schools at this age. However, it soon becomes evident that some children are not coping in the ordinary school, and they are referred to an educational psychologist or to a schools' medical officer with a view to special schooling or to treatment of some kind. Referral rarely leads to immediate action, so steps have to be taken to contain children for whom a permanent solution has not been found. This often takes the form of individual attention from the head-teacher.

Many of the children needing attention of this kind are dull and immature. The hurly-burly of a large class is too much for them. They are not used to taking turns, to waiting quietly, to the language of time, sequence, reasons and conditions. Other children may be quite bright in some ways, but are restless and hyperactive, or perhaps just boisterous and selfish. Some are frightened of other children; some are over-dependent; some act dumb or play helpless – in fact, the range of behavioural reactions is endless. Stott (1971b, 1974) has described some of the most common behavioural strategies that young children develop in their attempts to cope in a learning situation. What is not always realized is that children who are put forward by teachers in infant schools as being in need of special educational provision are almost invariably behaving badly or in an unusual way. It is their behaviour rather than their slowness in picking up the rudiments of reading and arithmetic that makes them stand out. In many cases, these children have a limited understanding and use of language, and some of them are unable to regulate their own behaviour in terms of linguistically formulated intentions and rules.

Pre-reading and reading activities are provided in small groups or on a one-to-one basis in many infant schools, and in some schools the emphasis is placed on language rather than on reading. It is, however, comparatively rare for structured language or perceptual-training programmes to be used. Some reasons for this are considered in Chapter 6, which is concerned with new developments rather than current practice.

Pringle and others (1966) in their study of 11,000 seven-year-olds found that seven per cent of the boys and four per cent of the girls were said to be receiving help within the schools because of educational or mental backwardness 'apart from anything which the class teacher may be able to do in the normal way'. This additional help is not, however, available in all infant schools, as it depends so much on the interest and support of the head teacher. Goodacre (1967) found that in only 17 out of 100 London schools was there a part-time teacher to give extra help with reading. In 48 schools in this sample no extra help was given, not even by the head teacher. Only two schools used parent volunteers as classroom aides. Some years later, steps were taken to improve matters in 50 schools in deprived areas in Inner London, by the appointment of one 'helper' between two classes. At the same time money was allocated to more than 300 schools and a refurnishing programme was started (ILEA, 1971b).

In the published report of the ILEA Literacy Survey (1971a) it was said that the primary inspectorate advocated 'a 5–8 "first stage" in combined primary schools instead of 5–7 with a special allowance for a suitable teacher charged with this extended responsibility'. This policy would of course eliminate the lack of continuity which sometimes occurs at seven-plus, but it might also result in a general lowering of standards. After the survey work of Morris, Goodacre, and Cane and Smithers (see Chapter 2), we cannot have a great deal of confidence in current practice in many infant schools.

The number of children referred to outside agencies during the infant stage 'because of difficulties which have affected . . . progress or behaviour in schools' exceeds the number who receive some form of extra help in school. Pringle and others reported referral figures of 11 per cent and eight per cent for boys and girls respectively. It is clear that referral does not always ensure effective intervention. Very few infant schools are served by peripatetic remedial teachers (e.g. six teachers to help with 'disruptive infants' in the whole of the ILEA in 1971), and Child Guidance Clinics are able to take on only a very small proportion of the children referred to them. Between two and four per cent of an age-group may be recommended for special schooling towards the end of the infant stage, and a similar proportion are given speech therapy (three per cent of the boys and 1·3 per cent of the girls, according to Pringle and others).

Provision at junior level

The quality of remedial education varies considerably between LEAs. It depends not only on the number of teachers with diplomas in remedial or special education, but on the standard of in-service training, the organization of special educational services, the support given by other local authority departments, the availability of suitable accommodation and the provision of a wide range of resources for learning. At its best, remedial education is tailored to the individual child, giving him genuine opportunities to communicate, to make discoveries, to express himself, and to develop habits of independent learning. On the other hand, what passes for remedial reading all too often amounts to a hastily-snatched half-hour with six children and a dreary reading primer. Where there is no effective LEA backing for remedial teachers, and in schools where taking the backward readers is thought of as a low-status soft option for the inexperienced teacher, standards are likely to be low.

This used to be the situation in the majority of Inner London schools. The ILEA Literacy Survey showed that, although a small proportion of children with severe reading difficulties attended groups organized by the Schools Psychological Service, the main responsibility for making special provision lay with head teachers. It is worth taking a closer look at the ILEA survey, which is the largest of its kind, covering 587 schools. It should be noted that since the survey was carried out in 1968 there has been a marked impetus within the ILEA towards improving the scope and standard of special provision. More teachers have been appointed, more money has been made available, in-service training has expanded, and a number of special units have been set up. However, there is still no over-all organization of the teachers and the services involved in helping backward readers. The impact of the various special units is almost negligible in an authority of such enormous size (approximately 330,000 children in junior and secondary schools).

In 88 per cent of the schools surveyed in 1968, help with reading was given in a withdrawal group or groups, and in 37 per cent of the schools some children received individual attention outside the ordinary classroom. It was comparatively rare for an additional teacher to go into a normal class to help with groups or with individuals (five per cent of schools). Special classes for slow-learners had been set up in 14 per cent of the schools. Estimates as to the proportion of children needing extra help with reading varied considerably, but were over 25 per cent in more than half the schools.[1] Actual provision fell short of estimated need only by some 20 per cent, but it was widely held that existing help was spread too thinly. For example, only one child in a hundred was getting daily individual help lasting more than 12 minutes and this attention was often given in normal class conditions.

The majority of teachers doing remedial work were ordinary members of staff. The survey showed that in most cases the teachers concerned had received little specific training in the teaching of reading. In 58 per

[1]See Appendix G.

cent of the schools none of the teachers had ever received more than a few general lectures on the subject.[1] The different forms of provision in ILEA junior schools in 1968 are summarized in table 17. This table does not take into account the very small proportion of children attending area remedial classes organized by the Schools Psychological Service.

TABLE 17: *Special provision for backward readers in 561 ILEA junior schools*

	% OF SCHOOLS
No help other than by class teacher	13
Special classes only	2
Class teacher and head teacher	9
Class teacher and one other	49
Class teacher and two others	24
Class teacher and three others	3

One rather controversial form of provision which is used in the ILEA and elsewhere is the special class.[1] These classes normally number 15 to 25 pupils, most of whom are of low intelligence. Criteria for placement in a special class vary enormously, and are usually determined by the head teacher. Children may be placed in special classes because of language problems, poor attainments or difficult behaviour, and this may mean that a few intelligent children are included among the dull majority.

It has already been pointed out that three of the four most successful schools in the writer's 1967 survey had special classes. In fact, they were the only schools in the sample of 16 to have smaller classes for backward pupils, although one of the streamed schools had two large equivalent 'C' streams! The special classes in these schools included only three pupils who were above average in verbal ability (EPVT scores of 100 or more).

Special classes were advocated in DES Education Pamphlet No. 46 (1964) which suggests that two such classes are needed to provide for slow-learning children in a typical junior school. In the ILEA survey only three per cent of the 587 schools surveyed had more than one special class. When there was only one special class it usually contained children from two or three year-groups, and the majority of special class pupils remained in the same class for more than a year.

The ILEA survey is valuable because it provides us with a baseline from which to work. When provision is left to individual head teachers in an authority with an extremely generous teacher–pupil ratio, we see that some extra help is provided for large numbers of backward readers

[1]See Appendix G.

from the time they enter the junior school, and sometimes even before this. In some schools the dullest children are taught in full-time classes, whereas the brighter backward readers may receive tuition in small groups or even on a one-to-one basis. However, in the majority of schools all backward readers receive the same kind of help, whatever their intelligence scores.

Most of the ILEA heads were aware of deficiencies in the kind of help they were able to provide. Four out of ten heads wished to devote more time to remedial work, and three out of ten wished that their remedial teachers were more qualified or experienced. One in ten argued for a general reduction in teacher–pupil ratio. It is, of course, impossible to tell whether this kind of action would significantly reduce the numbers of backward readers. No figures are kept regarding the efficiency of present types of provision. All that can be said without fear of contradiction is that large numbers of children reach secondary schools in Inner London still unable to read, and in some schools as many as 25 per cent of the 11-plus intake have RAs of less than eight years.

In different parts of the country attempts have been made to co-ordinate remedial reading services at LEA level, and this usually means reducing the autonomy of head-teachers in this respect. What normally happens is that a small clinic-based service gradually expands in scope until it can offer practical help to all schools. Remedial teachers and advisers become increasingly dominant within the service, and eventually the point is reached at which parallel school-based help is superfluous. There are, of course, other possible lines of development. For example, the LEA can take responsibility for allocation of personnel and resources according to objectively established need, leaving head teachers in charge of the day-to-day organization of remedial help. Another possibility is for remedial teachers to be responsible both to head teachers and to LEA advisers and to spend part of their time working in a centre in curriculum development, research and evaluation, or in-service training.

Sampson's survey of remedial education services at junior level was primarily concerned with centrally organized teams of remedial teachers. Of 59 LEAs, 39 maintained special services of this kind staffed by 'teachers additional to basic staff, who work either in special centres or on a visiting or peripatetic basis'. A typical service would consist of four full-time and 13 part-time teachers, with a senior educational psychologist in charge. Remedial advisers and organizers would often share responsibility for the service and in a few cases were in sole charge. In addition to the teaching duties, the remedial teachers were commonly involved in the testing of ability and attainment, and in advisory work.

The average remedial group consisted of six pupils. Approximately ten per cent of such groups had daily sessions, but the majority met two or three times a week.[1] A small proportion (eight per cent) met only once a week. Backward readers of all ability levels were included in these groups. Only about ten per cent of all pupils were considered to be of above average intelligence.[2] Many children who would at one time have been placed in special classes were receiving 'remedial' help, often from the beginning of junior school.

Children were normally selected for remedial groups on the basis of teacher referral. Screening procedures involving the testing of ability and/or attainment were in operation in only 20 per cent of LEAS. Provision varied in extent, but nine of the 29 LEAS who supplied detailed figures had places for between four and eight per cent of the junior school population and ten made provision for more than eight per cent.[1]

Sampson found that the majority of remedial teachers saw their task in terms of giving failing pupils the experience of success as they developed techniques of reading skill. A wide variety of books and games was normally available, and many teachers stressed the importance of interesting their pupils. The growing use of programmed instruction and of various kinds of teaching machine was welcomed by a number of teachers. Regarding method, two-thirds mentioned a phonic approach but not to the exclusion of everything else. However, it was also found that most remedial teachers worked in staff rooms, vacant classrooms, libraries or medical rooms, as they did not have rooms of their own. Much of the work was carried out quite independently of the class teacher. Little attempt was made to ensure that success was maintained during the rest of the school day, or after discharge from the remedial group.

If this is the position in those parts of the country which are fortunate enough to have a centrally organized team of remedial teachers, the standard of provision elsewhere must surely cause concern. Of course, there are bound to be individual exceptions, where interested heads and competent staff members have taken their responsibilities seriously. Yet the over-all picture is depressing: in areas without a centrally organized service we can expect to find untrained and inexperienced 'remedial' teachers working in almost impossible conditions. All too often these teachers are insensitive to individual differences and are either unable or unwilling to plan individual programmes of work.

Goodacre (1971b) summarized results obtained from a survey of 127

[1]See Appendix G.
[2]See Chapter 2, p. 43, for relevant survey data. It is likely that remedial teachers underestimate the intelligence of the children they teach.

LEAS in 1970, and made comparisons with data from a similar survey carried out by the NFER in 1960. Although there had been significant improvements during the decade, it was found that half the LEAs thought of remedial provision solely in terms of the provision made by individual schools. Despite a considerable expansion of schools psychological services, their remedial expertise was not reaching the many teachers trying to cope with backward readers in the schools. More was being done in the field of in-service training, particularly in conjunction with teachers' centres, and more teachers were available for work with small groups than in 1960. However, Goodacre concluded that only a minority of LEAs were tackling the problem of poor readers on a broad front by backing up school provision with sustained in-service education programmes, advice on reading materials, form of assessment, diagnosis, and remedial techniques. It was still a special occasion when extra funds were made available for materials, premises or additional services such as those found in reading, remedial or child guidance centres.

In order to obtain a more detailed picture of centrally organized remedial services at different stages of development, in 1971 the author decided to send a questionnaire to a number of LEAs throughout the country. Full co-operation was obtained in almost every case, but the ILEA (which had previously withheld co-operation when approached by Sampson and Pumfrey) failed to respond. The statistics obtained from this small survey are not intended to be representative of the country as a whole, but they do show how a number of LEAs (including some of the largest as well as some of the most progressive in the country) deploy their teams of remedial teachers. It should, of course, be realized that since local government reorganization in 1973, the picture may have changed considerably in some areas.

By relating the number of teachers (full-time equivalents) to the number of children helped, it was found the average 'case-load' of a remedial teacher was approximately 50. All LEAs gave details of their staffing, but some were unable to say how many children were receiving remedial teaching. For purposes of comparison it was therefore necessary to make estimates in these cases, based on an average case-load of 50. Details of LEA provision are given in table 18. It should be remembered that the figures given do not (except in the case of West Sussex) include children receiving reading help in small groups from teachers who are responsible only to head-teachers. The statistics for special education are taken from the *Education Committees Year Book* (1971/2) and include all types of special school. It was possible to include an estimate for the ILEA in table 18 as the author was able to ascertain the number of teachers employed in the remedial service organized by the Principal Psychologist.

TABLE 18: *Proportions of children receiving special and remedial education within the framework of organized l.e.a. services.*

	APPROX. JUNIOR AND SECONDARY SCHOOL POPULATION	% IN SPECIAL SCHOOLS	% RECEIVING REMEDIAL HELP
(a) Boroughs:			
ILEA	330,000	2·9	0·7 (est.)
Manchester	76,000	3·0	2·6
Kingston-upon-Hull	54,000	1·4	2·4
Edinburgh	52,000	2·3	6·4
Brent	33,000	2·7*	0·6
Hillingdon	32,000	1·7	0·7
Haringey	29,000	1·7	0·8
Waltham Forest	27,000	2·0	0·3 (est.)
Merton	25,000	1·2	0·3
Richmond	18,000	0·9	2·9 (est.)
Brighton	18,000	1·1	1·5 (est.)
York	15,000	1·8	0·4
(b) Counties:			
Lancashire	330,000	4·0	0·9
Cheshire	148,000	0·0	0·6 (est.)
Surrey	118,000	2·3	0·4
Staffordshire	103,000	1·4	7·5 (est.)
Glamorgan	97,000	1·1	7·5
Gloucestershire	76,000	1·5	1·0
Leicestershire	60,000	0·6	0·2 (est.)
W. Sussex	59,000	1·3	4·7 (est.)
E. Sussex	46,000	1·3	3·7
Shropshire	45,000	0·8	0·7 (est.)
W. Suffolk	21,000	0·0	4·0
Isle of Wight	16,000	1·2	1·2

*Personal communication.

The percentages given in the previous table are for children in both junior and secondary schools. However, provision is much greater during the junior years, and some LEAs do not provide external remedial support to secondary schools. Only four authorities were able to give a year by year breakdown of the numbers provided for. These figures showed that maximum provision was for second-year juniors. There would seem to be a tendency to rely on school resources for all but the most difficult children in the first year, and to use the external remedial service as a safety net. However, this practice is not uniform, and provision in some areas (e.g. Gloucestershire) is greatest in the first year of junior school.

As can be seen from table 18, there is considerable variation in the scope of LEA services. The most limited type of service normally consists of a class held at the Child Guidance Clinic. The next stage of development may be the establishment of area centres or special classes Alternatively, a peripatetic service may be started. Finally, a reading specialist is attached to each school, as in more than 80 per cent of the junior schools in Edinburgh.

In order to illustrate the range of different types and stages of provision, a number of LEAs have been selected for more detailed analysis.

Edinburgh

Provision for children with special educational needs is organized within the Department of Special Educational Services (Priestley, 1971). The department includes the Child Guidance Service with its associated teaching units, the special schools, and the adjustment services to primary and secondary schools. Most junior schools have a resident adjustment remedial teacher (often part-time) who takes groups of six to eight children for, in most cases, a daily session of 45 minutes. More than seven per cent of all juniors are given help in this way and the service has continually expanded since it was set up in 1948.

Children with more serious problems can be referred to units for severely disabled readers (60 places available) or to units for maladjusted children. In the reading units, individual attention is available if necessary and each teacher has a case-load of only 20 children (compared with 66 for a full-time adjustment teacher). In addition to some small units for children with acute problems such as 'school refusal', there are two day schools for children with emotional and behaviour disorders. Special school provision is comprehensive in nature and includes a nursery school observation group, an advisory and teaching service for autistic children, and a pre-work experience course for handicapped school leavers.

Assessment teams have been set up on which teachers, educational psychologists, social workers and doctors are represented. A centre for in-service training has also been established. This is available to all teachers who are in any way involved with the education of children with special needs.

Glamorgan (excluding Rhondda)

The Schools Psychological Service plays an important part in the field of special education. Each area psychologist works with a team of remedial teachers, headed by an advisory remedial teacher. Peripatetic members of these teams normally cover two or three primary schools, taking groups of six to eight children daily for one-hour periods. The dullest children are not helped in this way, but are placed in special classes for slow-learners after selection on the basis of standardized tests and interviews. The special classes are attached to ordinary schools and are limited to a maximum of 15 pupils. Approximately two per cent of the junior age-group is provided for in this way. Teachers of special classes are responsible to the local educational psychologist as well as to head teachers. Children with exceptional or persistent learning difficulties are taught individually at the area Schools Psychological Service Centre, and sometimes in their homes. Units for maladjusted children (eight to ten children) are attached to the area centres. Residential education is also available within the county, as are observation classes and special schools of various kinds. A recent development is the appointment of two Organizing Teachers of Remedial Education. These teachers give advice on the curriculum and teaching methods in all branches of special education, including remedial departments in comprehensive schools.

Classes for slow learners in secondary modern schools are supervised by the Schools Psychological Service and, although remedial departments in comprehensive schools are autonomous, a very close liaison does exist with the Schools Psychological Service.

Most children with learning problems are discovered as a result of the screening procedure carried out at the age of seven-plus, but apart from the teachers, parents and others can make direct referrals to the Schools Psychological Service. As a matter of routine, class teachers, head-teachers and school medical officers are asked to supply information when children are referred for special provision. Reports on children receiving help from remedial teachers are sent twice yearly to head-teachers and to educational psychologists.

Gloucestershire

In Gloucestershire, after routine group testing at 7 +, further screening tests are given to low-scoring children by county remedial staff. All children who are then selected for help by peripatetic teachers are discussed with the local remedial adviser, the head of the school and the class teacher. The teachers are said to welcome the remedial specialist to teach children in the classroom and they are increasingly willing to accept aids such as tape recorders, overhead projectors, etc. One of the benefits of the co-operation between specialist and class teachers is that teachers become more aware of the need to structure a reading programme, particularly in terms of language development. This means more oral work and a tendency to swing away from the use of a basic reading scheme.

This service is focussed on the first year in junior school, and five per cent of this age group benefit from it. If children do not respond, individual tuition is available, as well as programmed learning methods.

Hillingdon

The Schools Psychological Service includes a small team of remedial teachers working in centres and in 'unattached' classes. Teachers taking groups of children for remedial work in ordinary schools are not yet (1973) part of a co-ordinated service.

Some children needing remedial provision are identified by group tests, as part of a Borough Record Card System, and by individual reading tests towards the end of the first year in junior school. Others are referred at different times, and in special cases a report form is completed by the class teacher. Medical advice is sought as necessary. Remedial teachers report to educational psychologists once a term about the progress of children in their groups.

The Authority has recently (1973) appointed an Adviser for Special and Remedial Education and a Working Party on Special and Remedial Education will shortly be considering new developments in this area. Other developments are likely to include a screening procedure in all infant and junior schools: (a) at school entry (age five) to link with 'nurture groups'; (b) at age seven in the junior school to ascertain the need for special remedial measures.

Kingston-upon-Hull

The Senior Educational Psychologist is responsible for a team consisting largely of part-time remedial teachers. Most of these are peripatetic, but a small proportion work in one school only. The average case-load of a half-time teacher is 33 pupils in the age-range seven-plus to 13-plus. Provision in comprehensive schools is the responsibility of the head-teachers concerned.

A screening procedure is in operation at six-plus, seven-plus and eight-plus, which is designed to identify candidates for special schools as well as those needing remedial teaching. Head-teachers are always asked to supply relevant information on referral. Children with special problems may be taught by a teacher working at the Child Guidance Clinic or by an educational psychologist.

Lancashire

This authority has many more teachers working in remedial centres than in the schools. These teachers are normally responsible to divisional education officers, and work closely with educational psychologists. The teachers have little opportunity for advisory work, as none of them have as much as two days per week for non-teaching duties. Selection is in the control of the educational psychologists, who organize screening procedures in most divisions during the first year of junior school. Contact between ordinary schools and remedial teachers varies but there is generally not very much time for this. Discussions with the school often take place before a child is discharged and discharge reports are sent to head-teachers.

Difficult cases are sometimes given individual help by psychologists and sometimes by speech therapists. It is hoped to extend this kind of specialized help, particularly for children with a history of speech and language disorder.

Manchester

The remedial and advisory branch of the Schools Psychological and Child Guidance Service is staffed by area teams of teachers, based at their own centres. The remedial teachers select their own pupils in consultation with the staff of a school, usually after the administration of standard tests in the first junior year. In addition to the advisory work in connection with children receiving remedial teaching, each teacher is expected to offer the schools a more general educational advisory service (e.g. with reference to methods of diagnosis and remediation in the schools, classroom organization, etc.). One senior remedial teacher is concentrating on intensive advisory work in the infant schools in her area.

In-service training is given at the reading centres for all junior-school and a few secondary-school teachers, most of the work being undertaken by the four senior remedial teachers. Selected schools are allowed to recruit an additional half-time teacher, to release one teacher at a time for course attendance in school time. At the reading centres, teachers are also able to inspect, discuss and sometimes borrow or make equipment and materials, schemes and tests. An advisory service is offered not only to teachers (including head teachers), but also to inspectors, to special education advisers and to colleges of education.

Staffordshire

The service is organized by a Remedial Advisory Officer, assisted by area remedial advisory teachers. These teachers carry out screening and assessment procedures at the beginning of both junior and secondary stages.[1] Working closely with class teachers, they arrange for special groups to be set up within the schools, provide programmed material, and give training to part-time teachers who have been found and appointed to give remedial assistance. The advisory teachers have close contact with teachers of special classes and special schools. One of their duties is to work as part of a multidisciplinary team to advise on the

[1] The Remedial Advisory Officer reported to the author that the incidence of reading failure at 11+ and 15+ was now remarkably low. Those wishing to obtain up-to-date details of reading standards should contact the County Education Office.

s reading practice group uses the staff room. The children prepare passages silently before reading aloud.

ermanently established remedial reading corner in a room which is also used for other purposes.

Everyone in this Headmaster's office is involved in the

A phonic card game in the medical room

need for special schooling, and this calls for discussion with parents and head teachers. The remedial service is also responsible for organizing home tuition. The teachers act as a liaison between Child Guidance Clinics and the schools, and help to translate the recommendations of psychiatrists and educational psychologists into classroom terms.

In-service training courses for teachers involved with special education are held, a travelling mobile exhibition is available, and the support given to four local branches of the National Association for Remedial Education reflects the considerable interest and the increasingly high levels of professional competence expected in this field.

West Suffolk

This is a sparsely populated area, with no special schools. The remedial service is therefore really a special education service. Special classes (maximum 15 children) have been set up in the majority of primary schools, and regular screening tests are given in the first three years of junior school. A limited number of children with severe learning difficulties can be helped at a remedial centre or at an education guidance centre. Other children for whom special class provision is inappropriate are taught by peripatetic remedial advisory teachers.

West Sussex

Small-group remedial teaching in primary schools, and in selected infant schools, is conducted in the main by part-time teachers allocated on the basis of an annual survey of slow-learning children in the seven to eight-plus age-group. These teachers are responsible to head-teachers in the normal way, but are helped through programmes of in-service training conducted by remedial advisory teachers attached to the County's Psychological Service. Accompanying the training programmes is a useful series of booklets (Labon, 1971) concerned with various aspects of assessment and teaching.[1]

Provision at secondary level

Surveys

Remedial education in secondary and comprehensive schools was the subject of Sampson and Pumfrey's (1970) inquiry. Information was obtained from 65 secondary modern and 205 comprehensive schools, of which 90 per cent claimed to have remedial departments and/or classes. The range of numbers catered for was considerable, with an average of between seven and eight per cent of pupils on roll.[2] Full-time and part-time arrangements were equally common. Remedial classes

[1]Available from the Schools Psychological Service, County Hall, Chichester.
[2]See Appendix G.

existed in 40 per cent of the schools surveyed and the average size of these classes was 19 in comprehensive schools and 17 in secondary modern schools.[1] In those schools in which a group withdrawal system was used (40 per cent) the average size of groups was seven. Individual sessions were mentioned by 20 per cent of the schools, although this often meant that teachers gave up free periods or time during the lunch hour. One-third of the schools had remedial attention available for one to two years, one-third for three years, and one-third for at least four years.

Specialized accommodation was rare, the majority of teachers working in ordinary classrooms without sink units, work-benches, study carrels, or quiet areas. A substantial proportion of teachers (12 per cent) mentioned using accommodation such as store rooms, dressing rooms, landings and medical rooms.[1]

Only one in four teachers had received any special training.[1] This situation was much worse among part-timers than among full-timers. It was normal for a watered-down version of an ordinary curriculum to be offered in classes. Straightforward class teaching was used frequently by almost all teachers who taught whole classes. Project work was also popular, being used frequently by 48 per cent of the teachers and sometimes by 46 per cent. Outside activities and visits were rather less popular, with as many as 19 per cent of teachers having no experience of this kind of work.

Programmed instruction and audio-visual aids were used very little, with as many as 72 per cent reporting that they never used machines. This was said to be due to unavailability and cost in most cases. Those teachers who made frequent use of programmes (21 per cent) and machines (seven per cent) were well satisfied with these. They stressed that children could work independently with carefully graded materials, freeing the teacher to attend to others.

Sampson and Pumfrey found that secondary remedial pupils 'are not a group consistently defined in terms of IQ, academic deficit, or as a certain proportion of scholars. Rather, they would seem to be as many of the weaker brethren as staffing additions make it possible to attend to'. In many cases, ESN children were included in remedial departments.

The Department of Education and Science (1971) has also surveyed provision for slow learners in secondary schools. Head teachers considered that 14 per cent of their pupils were in need of special education.[1] About one-third (51) of the 158 schools surveyed had special departments for slow learners, and these made provision for 14 per cent of all pupils. A further 68 schools had special classes, while 'remedial sessions' were mentioned by most of the remainder. Only 16 schools sent pupils

[1]See Appendix G.

to outside centres, an arrangement which proved to interfere with the rest of the timetable.

None of the schools was found to have accommodation expressly designed for slow-learning pupils, and complaints about inadequate accommodation and equipment were common.[1] Suitable books and equipment were often in short supply. Only 16 per cent of the teachers had taken courses of specialist study lasting for at least one term,[1] and it was not unusual for young or even probationary teachers to be placed in charge of the slow learners.

The primary school record card was the most common source of information about pupils, although these often contained little more than the results of attainment tests at 11-plus. Details of relevant medical conditions were available in only 52 schools (33 per cent), owing to the policy of many medical officers to keep such information from teachers unless asked to report on particular cases.[2] Psychological and other advisory services had given guidance on the need for special educational treatment in 33 schools (21 per cent). The authors of the report expressed the opinion that in 73 per cent of the schools surveyed 'the information available was insufficient to give the teachers a clear diagnosis and assessment on which to base any specialized teaching'.

The majority of the schools surveyed grouped pupils by ability and in many cases the 'remedial department' was simply another name for the lowest streams. Class and subject teaching were normal, and it was rare for a special curriculum to be available for the slow learners. In many schools, help with reading consisted of 'little more than the reading of graded textbooks with prompting from the teacher'. Declining school attendance in the third and fourth years bore witness to the general inadequacy of the courses available.[3]

In areas which contain a substantial population of children from non-English-speaking backgrounds, there is an additional need for help with both spoken and written language. The DES Education Survey 14 (1972) pointed to a general neglect of the 'needs of these pupils when they are called upon to participate in normal classroom life and work, particularly at the secondary school phase'. The practice

---

[1] See Appendix G.

[2] The Bullock Committee of Inquiry (DES 1975) specifically recommends that medical records be made available to teachers.

[3] Reynolds (1974) drew attention to the variation in absence rates between nine secondary modern schools in a working-class area. The school figures varied between a minimum of 13 per cent and a maximum of 23 per cent for boys in 1972–3. Reynolds found that the pattern of attendance between schools was remarkably consistent over a six-year period, and suggested that some schools, but not others, are run 'in certain ways by staff with certain attitudes to prevent truancy and other behavioural problems'.

of assigning children with second-phase language problems to remedial departments was criticized because it usually results in over-large classes. Lack of special equipment and materials was a common finding, as was the lack of a permanent base or even a suitable teaching area. It was, however, possible to point to individual cases of good practice in which there was a high degree of inter-departmental co-operation, good staff and student morale, and relative success in examinations.

The inside story

One knows that young teachers sometimes break down under the strain of working in large inner-city schools. They are often ill-prepared for coping with the never-ending series of problems and crises they encounter. Some newly-fledged teachers are asked to carry heavy responsibilities. Others begin with idealistic schemes, but soon come to realize that their freedom of action is limited by constraints within the school itself. The timetable, the changes of room and teacher, the low status of the remedial department in the departmental pecking order, the lack of time, people and technical resources, all combine to demoralize teachers and pupils alike. In the context of the surveys summarized above, one becomes desensitized to 'horror stories', such as a probationary teacher in charge of a remedial department in one of the toughest schools in London, the growing practice of lesson refusal, truancy and the occasional eruption of violence. One has read Croft's *Spare the Rod* and Blishen's *Roaring Boys*. One has also read LEA press releases designed to convince parents that blackboard jungles do not exist. Teachers in inner-city areas know otherwise. What they do not know is just how many schools are as chaotic, noisy and depressing as the one they have heard of or happen to work in.

This question cannot be answered on the basis of research evidence, although the surveys that have been carried out suggest that there are fundamental deficiencies in accommodation, in school organization and in the curriculum for slow learners in the vast majority of secondary schools. Personal experience suggests that both pastoral and remedial staff in inner-city secondary schools live in a perpetual state of crisis. Many have undoubted skills and enthusiasm, but the odds are against them. The author believes that a major revaluation of provision for secondary children with special problems is needed, and that nothing is to be gained in the long run by attempts to avoid the issue. The following accounts by teachers of conditions in the remedial departments of inner-city secondary schools have been selected to illustrate some of the problems and some of the positive attempts to solve these problems that are being discussed in a great many staff rooms today. More far-reaching plans and some interesting new developments will be considered in Chapter 6.

We begin with an anonymous description, by an experienced teacher of slow-learning children, of her initiation into remedial work in a comprehensive school.

'On the first day of term, I went to my classroom which was situated on what had once been the stage. There was a general feeling of claustrophobia and chaos. The girls were sitting quite subdued and the boys were fighting and arguing. There were no reading books in evidence, so I looked in the cupboards for basic materials to occupy the 18 children. I found three series of readers and a Stott Programmed Reading Kit, but there was no practical equipment or suitable mathematics material. Pencils and paper were available but the main concern was to get hold of more books. One person asked at the first department meeting if the remedial department could have throw-out books from other departments.

'I was told that my children were not supposed to know that they were in a remedial class (one of four in the first year). During the first few days, however, when other teachers came into my class they looked annoyed. One child was pointed out as "a terror" and another as "a really bad one, that one". The obvious assumption was that these children were nuisances who must learn to behave. The children seemed almost to be sorry for me when they noticed that I did not often yell, threaten and give detentions. When they went to other teachers for lessons such as RI PE, and Art, they were expected to be hushed and quiet.

'A belief firmly held by the children was that work came from the board. The slow ones who needed remedial help became restless and did not even start, so the others became agitated as well and yelled angrily at them. All this brought about an acceptance of the situation in which they mucked about until fiercely reprimanded.

'Many of the children were in need of basic remedial work, and I would have loved to take them two or three at a time. This was in theory possible on Thursdays when another teacher came to take my class, but then I usually got a note telling me to stand in for a teacher who was away sick.'

Perhaps this teacher should have known what to expect, and should have prepared herself more fully before the beginning of term. She did at least have a room of her own and a fairly small class. But she had previously worked in a special school, where there were no serious shortages of material and where the chances of building up good relationships with the pupils were not undermined by other members of staff who had low expectations of the pupils and gave them inappropriate work to do.

When no home base is available, and when the teaching load is split among too many teachers, the situation is even worse. Scott described some of the problems in an ILEA comprehensive school where the teacher turnover is high and where part-time schooling has been adopted for some pupils because of the shortage of teachers (*Times Educational Supplement*, 26.10.73). One-third of the children were said to have had reading ages of eight years or less when they entered the school. One teacher said: 'Because many of them are poor readers, they are not sure where the handouts and constantly revised timetables tell them to be. . . . When they finally get in to the right classroom it takes time to settle down. All too often it is a relief teacher who appears to say simply, "Get on with your work".' Another teacher summarized the needs and problems of the children in one class in the following terms: 'Four kids could work by themselves. Twelve needed close supervision. Ten others needed remedial teaching. Three had extreme behaviour problems. And when I'd grasped that little lot, two Turkish-speaking kids arrived. So we just had to let them sit there.'

The greater part of Ablewhite's (1967) book is an attack on un-imaginative remedial teaching for backward readers in secondary schools, and is documented with evidence from one particular school collected during the years 1945-53. There was no overall increase in the initial reading attainment of successive intakes to the remedial groups or classes during this period, but there was a remarkable increase in the amount of progress made when subject teaching together with the remedial withdrawal groups were abandoned. To begin with, when no special provision was made for the lowest stream, the average reading age of the stream increased from eight years, seven months at 11-plus to only nine years, two months at 15-plus, an almost negligible gain of seven months in four years. When subject teaching was abandoned, and the backward children stayed with one teacher in a special class, average reading gains went up dramatically to 18 months RA per year. Ablewhite described a considerable amount of expressive and project work, and relatively little formal teaching in these classes. One year the backward readers spent their first three years in a special class. Their mean RA increased from eight years, five months at 11-plus to twelve years at 15-plus – a remarkable achievement. The telling thing about the statistics given by Ablewhite is that every year the progress of the remedial children virtually stopped if no special help was given or when help was discontinued. Ablewhite drew the following conclusions: 'The failures must be together and they must have the same teacher all the time. The teacher must be free to work as he pleases in an all-purpose room and he must have reasonable freedom to order unusual material as well as material which will duplicate that ordered by the specialists, for he will want paint as well as the art specialist and he will want wood and a small quantity of good tools. . . . There will be no stigma: theirs will be the most interesting room in the whole school. Perhaps they will leave school without the benefits of a formal course of history, geography, English literature, mathematics or general science, but they . . . never did benefit much from such courses anyway. On the other hand they will be able to read. They will be first-class people from an employer's point of view because they will be used to working as a team and will be thinking of their work-mates rather than, selfishly, only of themselves.' If Ablewhite is right, then schools which produce gains of only two to three months RA per year in the slowest groups are neglecting their responsibilities.

It is interesting to see how fashions swing. Special classes for slow learners have been tried out for some years. Sometimes they work, as in Ablewhite's study, but sometimes they do not. If the teaching is uninspired and proper facilities are lacking (i.e. a permanent base equipped as a multi-purpose resources room suitable for individual and group work), a special class is likely to fail and to become a disturbing and divisive influence within the school. It is to avoid the undesirable effects of segregation that mixed-ability classes in conjunction with a withdrawal system for remedial work are now being introduced into an increasing number of comprehensive schools.

Williams (1969) described this process of transition in a Bristol comprehensive school. He was worried about the self-image of the children 'in the dimmers' class', and by the fact that the 'remedial classes, for the older children particularly, were becoming pools of maladjustment'. In a class of 20, with a majority showing a disturbed pattern of behaviour, the stable children were being adversely affected. 'If they wanted the attention of the teacher, they too had to indulge in attention-seeking behaviour, or, if they were not prepared to do this, do what they could on their own and then withdraw into fantasy or play until the teacher was free to attend to them.' Williams claimed that the most severely backward pupils benefited from the new withdrawal system in that they received individual attention or intensive help in very small groups. The teacher concerned also visited the homes of most of these children and 'established a good relationship with the parents'. Williams felt that the lower ability children were taking part in more evening activities, and were less isolated within the school. However, he was aware that the new scheme provided for very few children, and he was in no position to judge the success of the counselling scheme which was introduced to help pupils showing poor adjustment.

Dean (1973) also described the changeover from remedial classes to small withdrawal groups, this time in an ILEA secondary school. 'We have an intake which usually includes about 40 per cent who need remedial help, but we have only one remedial trained teacher.

'In the past, we have tried picking out a remedial class by various means in each year, leaving the rest in the main stream of the school. Necessarily, much of the remedial class timetable has to be taken by ordinary subject teachers, who usually regard the remedials as "different", and consequently they become so. By the end of their first year, each remedial class has become a problem group, whereas the equally backward children left in the ordinary classes have not, on the whole.

'I decided to regroup them into three classes, and . . . 39 children were invited to join the withdrawal groups. Seven of them were virtual non-readers, 22 had a reading age below 8 years. . . . The average chronological age was 11 years, 11 months.

Games, technical studies, housecraft and needlework lessons were not affected. . . . Twelve teachers became involved in taking the groups, of which there were seven of various sizes, the largest of eight children. . . . Help offered included some maths and writing, although reading was the main target.

Twelve weeks later, we finished assessing the results. Two children had left, and five were absent, so could not be retested. The average improvement was 0·8 years in three months, the range of improvement from nil to 3·7 years. The most spectacular success was one boy who changed from a depressed non-reader in April to a cheerful, chatty book-worm with a reading age of 9·7 years in July.

Several of the apathetic, sad children started smiling and talking freely, asking questions and volunteering information. . . . Some of the behaviour problems have improved, too . . . . The staff who have helped . . . have found working with small groups interesting and rewarding. They have come to know some of the dreaded remedials quite well, and have found that they are not so difficult and different after all.'

Residential provision

LEAS are sometimes faced with the problem of trying to place a child with a specific reading difficulty in a residential school. This may be desirable for a number of reasons: (a) separation or loss of parent(s); (b) mental or physical disability of parent(s); (c) unresolvable family conflicts which hinder progress; (d) lack of adequate local non-residential provision; (e) the child's inability to respond except in an environment specially geared to his needs. If the child is unsuitable for placement in a special school for educationally subnormal or maladjusted pupils, he needs special teaching in a school where the academic pressures are present, but not overwhelming.

In recent years, a number of residential schools have begun to specialize in remedial work, notably Millfield School, which has a remedial department with perhaps the best pupil–teacher ratio and the most lavish collection of special resources in the country. LEAs do, on occasion, use independent schools for residential provision, since, so far, no LEA has set up its own residential unit or school solely for children with specific learning difficulties. However, a few independent schools of this kind do now exist. One of these is Brickwall House, Northiam, Sussex, which has places for about 80 'dyslexic' boys aged ten and above.

Not all the boys at Brickwall House are severely retarded in reading and spelling, and only about ten per cent have reading ages of less than eight years. The teaching groups are small (four to eight boys) and more than half the pupils receive individual remedial help. There is a considerable emphasis on oral work in most subjects, and on the accuracy of reading and spelling in the remedial sessions. In 1972-3, boys receiving remedial teaching improved by an average of one year in both reading and spelling (personal communication). A breakdown of progress scores by attainment levels showed that those starting the year at the ten- to 12-year levels made just as much progress as those starting at the eight- to ten-year levels. This suggests that the school succeeds in providing an atmosphere that is conducive to the development of literacy, for at the more advanced levels of reading, one would expect relatively little progress if the pupils did not continue to learn in ordinary lessons and in their own free time. Of course, there are some poor results, especially among those with multiple disadvantages and handicaps. However, a failure to achieve a high standard or written English does not always mean that the battle is lost. Pupils are sometimes provided with an amanuensis when they take public examinations, just as if they were physically unable to write. This gives them a better chance to express on paper what they are well able to express orally, and so achieve a pass. They will not, of course, pass if facts are lacking of if their grammatical and linguistic weakness extends to oral as well as to written English.

A large proportion of the pupils at Brickwall House are sponsored by LEAs. As there is no official category of handicap called 'dyslexia', most of the boys have been officially classified as maladjusted. In many cases, this is a matter of administrative convenience, but it is an unsatisfactory state of affairs, both for the individuals concerned and for the school. Technically, retarded readers should be classified as educationally subnormal, but this term has come to be equated with low intelligence, and is offensive to many parents. Perhaps a new category of 'severe learning difficulty' would be more appropriate in this context, and should be written into future legislation.

Summary

Provision for children with reading difficulties varies greatly between schools and between LEAs. It is relatively good in areas where there is a strong LEA remedial service. Where the main responsibility for the allocation of staff and resources lies with individual heads, the needs of the backward reader tend to be low on the list of priorities. Although most schools have some arrangement for 'hearing children read', this has apparently little effect in reducing the numbers of backward readers.

The most common method of giving extra tuition is by withdrawing groups of about six children from their classrooms. The groups are normally taken by 'floating', part-time, or peripatetic teachers rather than by their class teachers. Most of the teachers doing this work are inadequately trained, poorly equipped, and do not have access to a resources room designed for small groups.

Full-time special and remedial classes are more common in secondary than in junior schools. We do not know whether this form of provision is better or worse than the withdrawal group system, but it is often criticized because it tends to isolate both children and teachers from the normal life of a school. There is, however, some evidence that special classes are better than no special provision at all.

Surveys of remedial education facilities and services have repeatedly shown that improvements are needed in the selection of children for extra help, in the organization of individualized programmes of work, and in the relationships between specialists and class teachers. Reports from selected LEAs show that considerable progress has been made in some areas, both in the scope and in the quality of special provision. However, much remains to be done, especially in secondary schools in inner-city areas.

Chapter Five

Attempts to Evaluate Special Provision

The effectiveness of remedial reading

There have been no large-scale studies comparing taught and control groups. However, we do have information about the rates of progress that can be expected from backward readers who do not receive specialized remedial help. Barnett (1972) followed the progress of 60 retarded readers selected from a school population of 459 boys. These children were the most retarded as defined by a regression formula which took into account the correlation between reading scores and IQ. The mean Schonell Reading Age at the end of infant school was five years, four months. When these children were re-tested two years later, the average score on the Vernon Test was just eight years and at the end of the third year of junior school their mean score was nine years, two months. Only two of the children had been given remedial lessons other than whatever help was available in the schools, yet they had progressed at the average rate of 1·4 months of reading age per month.

Similar results were obtained by Clift (1970), who measured the progress of 112 Shropshire children who scored below 85 on the NFER Sentence Reading Test. Clift found that although no specialized remedial help was available, scores on the Daniels and Diack Test improved by one year during the second year of junior school. Collins (1961) also found that his control group who had not received remedial teaching (n=20) made 40 months progress in reading during a 40-month period.

If we assume that backward readers are likely to progress at a rate of one month of reading age per month without special help, it is reasonable to expect better results than this as a result of remedial teaching. Gains of between one and a half and two months of reading age per month may be taken as a norm for remedial work, but more striking gains than these have been reported. Chazan (1967) and Carroll (1972) contributed useful reviews of relevant studies. Cashdan, Pumfrey and Lunzer (1971) reported a mean gain in reading age of 21 months in 11 months of remedial teaching for a sample of approximately 1200 junior children. They also found that backward readers taught individually or in pairs made no more progress than those taught in groups of three to six children, but that in remedial groups of seven or more children the gains were substantially less. In an unpublished study of 28 children who attended remedial classes in Brent for periods of a year or more, the author found that rates of progress were highest in the first term of tuition but progressively declined until at the end of the first year they were down to one month of reading age in one month of tuition.

As several authors have pointed out, the variance in reading progress scores is often large. The average figure can be misleading as a few children will have made massive gains and some will show little or no change. For example, in one comparative study of conventional and automated instruction, it was found that four out of 16 pupils gained less than one unit of RA per unit of time, five gained between one and two units, five between two and three units, and two more than four units (Moseley, 1969b).

Attempts to predict which backward children are most likely to make rapid progress have not met with much success (Clift, 1970; Barnett, 1972). Authors tend to agree that neither IQ nor personality factors have much predictive value (see Chapters 2 and 3). Lytton (1966) approached this question on a *post hoc* basis, by comparing eight boys who had responded well to remedial teaching with eight who had not.

It was found that the groups did not differ significantly on father's occupation, family size, living space, conditions of the home or amount of parental encouragement. However, adverse family relationships were less common in the 'good' than in the 'poor' group. Delayed speech development and reading problems in other members of the family were significantly more common among those who made little progress. This finding suggests that there is a 'hard core' of children who are (perhaps in common with other members of the family) ill-equipped to master communication skills. It is possible that special teaching techniques are required for these children, but no firm evidence on this point has yet been produced.

Comparisons of remedial teaching methods have generally proved inconclusive (Georgiades, 1967; Bateman, 1969; Silberberg and others, 1973), but Burt and Lewis (1946) showed that with 10- to 11-year-olds a change of method as such is more often than not a good thing. This suggests that at this age what is needed above all else is a boost to morale. Method may be more important with younger children and for those with severe learning difficulties. However, the majority of backward readers have certainly developed all the basic skills required for reading by the age of ten. Some of them make good progress even without remedial help at this age.

The research of Collins (1961) is cited less often than it used to be. Now that remedial services are an established part of the educational scene, it is uncomfortable to be reminded that perhaps they would not stand up well to the rigours of cost-benefit analysis.

Collins set up three matched groups of 20 retarded readers randomly selected from ten schools. The average age of the groups was nine years, ten months and mean RA was six years, eight months. One group attended a remedial centre for twice-weekly lessons during a six-month period. The school group were taught by peripatetic teachers, and the third group consisted of untreated controls. All three groups were given follow-up tests seven months, 19 months and 27 months after the tuition period ended. As shown in table 19, the control group ended up at virtually the same level as the taught groups. The control group made a big advance (14·3 months) during the last year in the junior school, which cancelled out the initial advantage of both tuition groups.

TABLE 19: *Gains in reading age made by three matched groups in Collins' study*

	CENTRE	SCHOOL	CONTROL
Average gain during 6-month tuition period	15·2m.	16·5m.	8·3m.
Overall gain in 40 months (selection – follow up)	40·5m.	41·5m.	39·7m.

This study includes a longer period of follow-up testing than is normally practicable. It proves that spontaneous improvement can take place in backward readers, but it does not prove which of the following conditions were critical: (a) the pupils were in the last year of the junior school when they put on a spurt; (b) the pupils who improved most rapidly had reached a reading age of eight to eight and a half years; (c) three or four reading tests had previously been given to the pupils in little more than a year. It should be remembered that the improvement took place in classes in which great emphasis was put on reading standards not only because some pupils had extra lessons, but because repeated testing was carried out. We cannot generalize from Collins' results to schools in which regular testing is not carried out, and in which special help is not provided for at least a few individuals. Neither can we be sure that the argument applies to the completely illiterate 'hard-core', with attainment ages of seven years or less.

Lovell and others (1963) reported results which confirmed those of Collins. In this study the children were less backward, with an average reading quotient of 85. Two groups were compared, 50 children who attended a remedial centre full-time, and 50 controls. The children were selected from the same schools, so, as in Collins' study, we have a situation where those backward children who did not receive special help were probably aware of the fact. The centre group received remedial teaching for an average of 11 months but when tested 41 months after the initial selection tests had been given, were no better off than the untreated controls. While the centre group had gained 49 months reading age, the mean gain made by the controls was 50 months. Again, we see that spontaneous improvement can occur if no remedial teaching is offered. As Lovell did not report interim test results, we do not know whether the controls made their biggest spurt in the last year of junior school, but this is certainly possible, as the mean age at follow-up was eleven years, two months. A comparison of the gains made in the studies of Collins and Lovell shows that the rates of progress were comparable. Lovell's controls did make somewhat greater progress, but they were both younger and brighter than Collins' controls.

In Collins' study, remedial help was first offered to nine-year-olds approaching the end of their fourth year in school. It is much more usual today to provide remedial lessons for first-year juniors, and this undeniably boosts both performance and morale. Few teachers would argue that backward readers should have to sit still and put up with their frustrations because they may 'catch up' three or four years later. In Lovell's study the average age at which remedial teaching was begun was seven years, nine months. Immediate gains were made and within an average of 11 months the children in remedial centres had reached an average RQ of 99.

Shearer (1967) produced evidence of gains both during remedial teaching and follow-up, which suggests that some form of continuous remedial support is worthwhile. The average age of his tuition group was nine years, six months, and the average RA when tuition began was six years, six months. The non-tuition group were rather younger (eight years, ten months) and more backward ($\bar{x}$ RA=five years, six months). Details of progress are given in table 20.

TABLE 20: *Mean progress of tuition and non-tuition groups (from Shearer)*

	TUITION (n=46)	NON-TUITION (n=22)
Mean progress during 12m. RT	30m.	—
Over-all gain in 58m. (selection – follow up)	50m.	32m.

On this occasion the remedial group showed a clear advantage at follow-up. They had been discharged at the average age of ten years, six months, with an average RA of just nine years. After discharge, 24 of the tuition group received no further remedial help, as was the case (personal communication) with the controls. The average rate of progress of this sub-group after discharge was only 0·3 months RA per month, compared with 0·7 months RA per month for those who continued to receive help in the remedial departments of their secondary schools.

Pinnington (1971) reported on a follow-up study of 35 children who had attended a remedial teaching centre twice a week. Their average RA when admitted to the scheme was just six years and the mean IQ was 91. Mean progress during tuition was 1.64 months RA per month, and this fell to 1·05 months RA per month during the first 17 months after discharge. These children were discharged from the remedial centre at a relatively low level of attainment ($\bar{x}$ RA 7y. 11m.), which suggests that the most important function of remedial provision is to give the children an initial boost. The six 'best' cases attended for short periods and had no physical disabilities. Those who made least progress included three with articulatory defects and one with sinus trouble. It was felt that they needed more specific auditory-vocal training than the teacher was able to provide.

Pinnington's results differ from those of Shearer, Lovell and others (1962, 1963) and Moseley (1969b) in that a higher rate of progress was maintained after discharge. In none of these other studies (involving more than 400 children altogether) was mean progress after discharge from remedial teaching more than six months RA per year. The only important difference seems to be that most of Pinnington's subjects were followed up while they were still in the junior school, whereas the follow-up periods in the other studies were mainly at secondary level. It is possible that a slower rate of progress is normal for secondary remedial children than for top juniors. The fastest rate of reading growth by the control group in Collins' study was during the last year of junior school, and Ablewhite's evidence (summarized in Chapter 4) suggests that unless a real effort is made, progress during the secondary stage may be almost negligible. Rigley (1968) found that even with two one-hour remedial lessons a week, 119 backward secondary pupils on the Isle of Wight made an average gain of only ten and a half months RA in the first four terms after the appointment of a remedial advisory teacher. Lytton (1967) found that children who were in secondary schools when followed up 16–18 months after remedial teaching were, on the whole, making little or no progress, whereas younger children who were followed up while still in the junior school were doing considerably better. A significant finding from the ILEA (1974) evaluation of support services for remedial work in four areas of special difficulty was that while there was relatively little improvement in work and behaviour as a result of increased expenditure, there was an actual *decline* in a control group of children needing remedial help in schools where no extra money was available. This decline was more marked at secondary than at junior level.

Some teachers have drawn the inference from well-known studies such as those of Collins and Lovell that six months of remedial teaching is too little for a permanent impression to be made, and that discharge is premature at an eight-year level of attainment. It is now common practice to discontinue remedial teaching after a nine-year or ten-year level has been obtained on more than a single occasion. This opportunity for 'consolidation' may mean continuing small-group tuition for a period of years. Pinnington's results tend to show that this may be wasteful of resources. Even with 'consolidation', reading progress may decelerate after special teaching in small groups is ended. It looks as if some pupils flourish only in small groups with a considerable amount of attention from a friendly teacher. Or it may be that some children learn best when they are given the opportunity to play games or to respond to a machine. When they return to a large class where they receive less attention and where the resources for learning are more limited, they again lose heart. It is also possible that many children are more keenly motivated to reach a *Daily Mirror* level of reading (RA nine to ten years) than to progress beyond that level.

In none of the studies summarized above are details given about the liaison between psychologists, remedial teachers and schools, but it is reasonable to suppose that this was minimal. If children who have received remedial help remain in the same classes after discharge, their teachers may fail to adjust their expectations to the point of requiring higher standards of work. For this reason it is important that in streamed schools a bright backward reader should be promoted from the 'C' stream as soon as he has the slightest chance of coping with more advanced work. In practice, however, this rarely happens without a specific recommendation from an educational psychologist or remedial adviser.[1] In unstreamed schools, it is particularly important that class and subject teachers should have good working relationships with remedial specialists so that they may perhaps change their attitudes towards their 'thickies' as they begin to improve. Without new goals and expectations, it is only to be expected that the remedial successes

[1]Lovell and others followed up 84 children who entered streamed schools after discharge from remedial centres. Almost three years after discharge, 59 (70 per cent) were in the bottom stream, 20 (24 per cent) were in intermediate streams, and five (six per cent) were in top streams. None were in grammar schools.

will in time perform only at an average level for all their class. Collins argued that this would not happen if all of the advantages of a good remedial service were available in the school on a continuing basis. The fact remains that they are not.[1]

Evidence that children with learning difficulties are sometimes treated differently from those without such difficulties in the ordinary classroom comes from an interesting observational study by Bryan (1974). It was found that the children with learning difficulties were ignored by their class teacher three times as often as controls when they tried to speak to him. While they received just as much praise and encouragement as controls, they received significantly more criticism. Teachers spent neither more nor less time interacting with the slower learners, but spent relatively more time in pointing out their errors. The children showed poor concentration and sought diversions when the teacher was not with them. They sought attention from other children, but were ignored by their peers significantly more than controls. Bryan showed that this pattern of interaction could be broken in remedial lessons, where teachers were more positive, spent more time with the pupils, and were rewarded by increased attention to instructions and to tasks. It has yet to be established whether remedial teachers who deliberately intervene in order to modify unproductive patterns of interaction in the ordinary classroom are able to achieve their aims. Although failing to prove this point, the findings of Bruininks and others (1974) are relevant. In a study involving 1299 children, it was shown that in inner-city schools where resource-room teachers were working on a daily withdrawal and consultative basis, dull and backward children tended to be given above-average sociometric ratings by same-sex peers.[2] Apart from this, very little work has been done in this most important field.

In some secondary schools (Goodwin, 1974; Rushworth, 1974), a highly flexible type of organization has developed in which teachers of mixed-ability groups are actively involved in helping the backward readers. Rushworth describes how a training programme for English teachers, parents and sixth-formers was set up, and how 70 first-year pupils reading at or below the eight-year level were given four periods a week of 'extra English' in groups of five or six, taught by their own English teacher. Each of these groups had 'a parent and sixth-former who hear pupils read, thus freeing the teacher to work with individuals or pairs'. This scheme was a success in that the average increase in reading age was 1·5 years, and in that only four pupils 'have continued to show serious behaviour problems manifested in the primary schools'.

[1]See Appendix G.
[2]Interestingly, the reverse was true in suburban settings.

The effectiveness of special class and special school provision for backward readers

The evidence presented in Chapter 3 suggests that special class provision is better than no provision at all for slow-learning children. In circumstances in which even a special class of 25 children is thought of as an exciting innovation, this may be so. However, special schools and special classes can become institutionalized. If this happens, there may be certain disadvantages attached to this kind of provision.

There is always a danger that the special class can become a place of no return. This is particularly likely to happen if special class provision is available throughout a school. If it is left to the special class teacher to put forward children to return to ordinary classes, he may prefer to keep some of his improved pupils knowing that he will be asked to exchange them for others with more serious behaviour problems. Similar problems occur in connection with special schooling.

Another danger is that the special class or school can become a 'dumping ground'. If it is thought of as being full of 'baddies' or 'thickies', the children in it may deteriorate in social adjustment. The stigma of being in a special class or school is likely to be increased if the provision is physically isolated, poorly equipped, or in some way institutionalized. However, a special class can be a place full of opportunities if it has a good teacher, ample space and special resources for learning.

Lewis (1972) studied the self-concepts of 100 adolescent boys in day ESN schools, and found that they had a level of self-regard comparable to the general population. As they did not think of themselves as more stupid, or as greater nuisances than boys in the middle streams of comprehensive schools, it was thought that their main frame of reference was that provided by the school itself. Children who had spent more than five years in day ESN schools thought significantly more of themselves than those who had been there less than five years. This suggests not only that special schooling can provide an unrealistic yardstick of human behaviour, but that the stigma value of special provision is likely to be at its highest in settings which are not insulated from the wider educational context. In a study of streaming in 50 New York schools, Passow and others (1966) obtained results which are consistent with this interpretation. The slower pupils perceived their present status as higher and had higher aspirations in streamed classes than in broad-range ability groups.

The American equivalent to a school for ESN pupils is a special class (which is normally attached to an ordinary school) for EMH (educable mentally handicapped) pupils. In the USA, children in special classes are exempted from the normal requirements for 'passing grades'. This of course adds to the stigma attached to special classes. Dunn (1968) concluded that research supports the view that, in the context of the grade promotion system, special class placement is usually unnecessary, if not a mistake. Four relevant studies are summarized below.

Goldstein and others (1965) compared the progress of 57 children in special classes with that of 69 in ordinary classes. The children were six- to seven-years-old, and the two groups had mean IQ scores of 77 and 79 respectively. Although the overall differences in intelligence and attainment scores after four years were not significant, there was some evidence that the more able children had benefited from normal school placement, whereas the least able had done better in special classes. There was no difference in anxiety about learning to read, even though the pupils in ordinary schools tended to be using books which were too difficult for them. Children in special classes were found to be more willing to attempt difficult questions, perhaps because standards were lower and they were less likely to be ridiculed. On the other hand, other children reported playing with special-class children less often than with the equally backward children in normal classes. Meyerowitz (1962) reported that first-grade special-class children (n=60) were significantly more self-derogatory than a matched group of children (n=60) in normal classes. In another study (1967a) he found that special class placement makes it more difficult for a child to adjust to his neighbourhood peers. The same author (1967b) found that parents of EMH children in special classes tended to devalue their children more than parents of similar children placed in normal classes.

British research suggests that separate schools for moderately dull and backward children may also be a mistake. Ascher (1970) compared two groups of secondary pupils, 31 in remedial departments, and 31 in ESN schools. The average IQ scores of the groups were 75 and 74 respectively. The reading and arithmetic attainments of those in special schools were lower, which may have been partly due to the nature of the selection process. Gains over a one-year period were also less in the special schools, despite the advantage of smaller classes. We should remember, however, that Ascher's ESN school sample must have been among the brightest in their schools. Remembering the findings of Goldstein and others (quoted above), we should not jump to the conclusion that duller children would also learn more quickly in ordinary schools.

Hodge and Bain (1971), in a study of eight secondary ESN schools in Glasgow, found that the average IQ was 68 (n=1101). Similar results were reported by Williams and Gruber (1967). Hodge and Bain reported that the average reading age in six schools at the average chronological age of 13 years, three months was seven years, eight months, whereas pupils who were about to leave (average age 15 years, nine months) were only 11 months more advanced. The special school children had the advantage of slightly smaller classes than in ordinary schools, with an average class size of 25. The burden of devising special reading programmes fell on the class teachers, as very little guidance was given by outside experts. In one school with 138 pupils, as many as 118 (86 per cent) had not been seen by an educational psychologist in the previous five years. Modified secondary courses were offered, and in no case were these based on diagnosis of specific learning difficulties and allocation of pupils to different groups for special remedial treatment. Virtually no attempt was being made to use programmed learning techniques. No audio-visual methods were being used to develop reading skills. If this is all that a special school has to offer, one must certainly question the wisdom of providing so-called special education in separate school buildings.

For an evaluation of special class provision for children with emotional difficulties and behaviour problems, we again have to draw on American experience. Morse and others (1964) carried out a large-scale comparative study of classroom-based treatment methods for disturbed children. Backwardness in reading was a common problem in the classes concerned. Among the types of programme considered in this survey were:

(a) Psychiatric-dynamic (ten classes). Here the emphasis was on relationships rather than on academic attainment. Teachers tended to be passive and undemanding, allowing children to group themselves and encouraging them to evaluate their own work. Both teachers and parents spent a considerable amount of time in consultation with clinic staff.

(b) Psycho-educational (20 classes). Here an attempt was made to measure both intellectual and personality variables by psychological tests and to devise appropriate educational programmes. Periodic discussions were held with the psychologists concerned.

(c) Psychological-behavioural (three classes). The approach here was to emphasize structured remedial exercises, and to keep meticulous records.

(d) Educational (22 classes). These classes were set up by special education personnel, and contact with psychological services was peripheral.

(e) Chaotic (one class). The teacher was described as permissive.

It was found that the pupils preferred the psycho-educational classes. They said that they had established better relationships both with teachers and peers, were less anxious, and thought that they would soon return to a normal class. Pupils in psychiatric-dynamic classes were less optimistic on all counts, including teacher–pupil relationships. Teachers in these classes were unable to report the same improvement in control of pupil behaviour as claimed by those in psycho-educational settings. Children in the psychological-behavioural classes claimed to be on good terms with their teachers.

These results favour the retention of a structured 3RS programme in units and schools for maladjusted children. The idea of allowing disturbed children freedom from a normal curriculum in order to 'work through' their difficulties is not supported. Pringle and Sutcliffe (1960) showed that even disturbed children in residential care can respond well to a programme of systematic teaching. Here, opportunities for play and creative expression were provided by the teacher, but were closely linked with reading and writing activities. In this study the teaching was on a one-to-one basis, but this is not an essential requirement. In an unpublished study linked with an Open University (1973) film about a resource-room approach to learning difficulties, the author found that good results could be obtained with deprived and maladjusted children if special resources were brought into the classroom. The setting was an 'opportunity class' of 11 children who had been removed from junior schools in the area because of their disturbed behaviour. For a period of ten weeks the first part of each morning was devoted to the special programme. The children would be split into three or four groups according to the nature and severity of their difficulties. A welfare assistant helped to operate tape-recorders and other audio-visual equipment (which included a group-paced tape-slide unit for up to six pupils). The teacher used a variety of skill-building materials, as well as her own experientially-based programmes written at two different levels of difficulty. It was found that the average rate of progress during the 20 weeks which ended with this special intervention was 1·6 months RA per month. A comparison of pre- and post-diagnostic test results suggested that children who had used appropriate materials in order to overcome problems of auditory discrimination and visualization had benefited from these, and the teacher herself recorded an improvement in work habits when she completed Stott's (1971b) schedule 'Guide to Poor Learning Habits' on the second occasion.

The possibility of applying behaviour-modification strategies in curriculum design and in classroom management is yet another issue. Hewett and others (1969) described a rigidly programmed system whereby checkmarks were given for starting and working on tasks and for behaviour related to levels on a developmental sequence. It was found that this system was effective in improving concentration and in producing arithmetic gains in the five classes for emotionally disturbed children in which it was used. However, the experimental classes did not make greater gains in reading than the control class over a one-year period. This may have been because the rewards were not made contingent upon successful performance of reading and writing assignments. Hamblin and others (1971) described a number of projects in which behaviour-modification techniques proved highly effective in accelerating various aspects of learning, including reading.

We do not really know whether special class provision for maladjusted children is effective, or whether other measures would be just as good or even better. Special classes and special schools can be criticized because of the stigma attached to them and because of the undesirable effects of segregation. Expectations may be low, and children may be adversely affected by being in contact with a higher proportion of disturbed peers. An ILEA report (1971b) claimed that some of their day maladjusted schools 'have been disheartened by the unrelieved succession of disruptive children and have felt unable to admit more, so that children remain on the waiting list although there are vacancies in the schools'. There can be little hope of improvement for children admitted to such schools. It may, in the long term, be better to invest in preventive programmes such as those described by Cowen and others (1966), Bailey (1974) and Modarressi (1974). This will mean that schools will become more capable of containing and helping their problem children.

Special classes and resource rooms for children with learning disabilities are a relatively new feature of the educational scene in America, Holland and other parts of Europe. The author does not know of any well-controlled evaluation studies of the relatively small number of special schools for such children, but some work has been done in special class and resource room settings. Cruickshank and others (1961) carried out a well-planned study designed to test out the Strauss-Lehtinen concept of education for brain-injured children (involving the elimination of distracting background stimuli). Differences between experimental (n=20) and control groups (n=20) were minimal after one year and again at follow-up. We have already seen that there is little evidence in favour of special classes for slow-learning children. There are bound to be exceptions to this rule, as in the school described by Ablewhite (see Chapter 4, p. 102). However, large teaching groups are not advantageous. Large groups made up of children from different classes, meeting perhaps four times a week in different rooms as timetabled, and taught by different teachers, must surely be a recipe for disaster: yet this type of organization still exists in secondary schools. Even in much more favourable circumstances (Ebbutt and others, 1974), relatively disappointing results were obtained with a teaching group of 25 girls in a London secondary school. Here there was a stable, well-equipped environment, with two teachers available plus occasional help from visiting students. Although some individual and group work was possible, the major part of the 12 hours per week spent in the remedial setting was devoted to taking the class as a group through a phonic-based programme. The test results at the end of the year showed a mean gain of 11 months RA in a period of 10 months, and indicated that many of the girls had simply failed to learn and apply the content of the programme. It is, of course, virtually impossible to prevent this from happening in such a large group, although, with two teachers it should be possible for pupils to learn how to take some responsibility for assessing their own progress with individualized programmes.

Weiner (1969) argued that resource rooms are preferable to special classes for children with learning disabilities. A resource room is 'a specially staffed and equipped room designed to lend supportive assistance to students and teachers'. Weiner's teachers never worked with more than three children at once, and were allowed time 'to conduct in-the-class observation and teacher-to-teacher conferences', yet they were able to provide for more children in this way than if special classes had been set up. Timetabling was flexible, varying from one to five periods per week. Results were presented for four teachers, each working in a resource room attached to an elementary school, and each responsible for planning individualized programmes of work. All of the children concerned had IQs of 90 or above, yet had failed the previous year's grade. They were selected after a complex diagnostic procedure on grounds of their hyperactivity, dissociation, figure-ground reversals, distractibility, perseveration and behaviour disorders. In a 10-month period 61 such children made mean gains of 14 months in reading, seven months in spelling, and 11 months in arithmetic.

There is, of course, no reason why the resource room should not be used by a considerable number of teachers. It can also serve several different functions: e.g. a working area for children, a training area for helpers, a meeting-place for parents and others, a preparation area for teachers, and a resources area for borrowers. As yet, there has been no evaluation of this kind of resource room (or rooms) in this country, as the idea is relatively new. It does, however, have the advantage of great flexibility, and will be explored again in the next chapter.

The effectiveness of psychotherapy and counselling in helping backward readers

The theory that backward readers have an emotional 'blockage' which is the primary cause of their reading difficulty has not received much empirical support. The evidence summarized in chapter 3 suggests that it is more likely that emotional and behavioural problems stem from reading difficulties than the other way round. Whether or not this is so, remedial treatment often involves the learning or re-learning of positive emotional and behavioural responses.

Psychotherapy and counselling are both directed at helping a child to resolve emotional problems, but the efficacy of these procedures has not yet been objectively established. Intuitively, one feels that children cannot but benefit from regular contact with adults who try to provide a context in which new insights can be gained and new patterns of behaviour explored, but the research literature is much more negative than one might expect (see reviews by Levitt, 1963 and Kellner, 1967). It is possible that both psychotherapy and counselling are experienced by many children as peripheral to or different from their daily lives, and that they are relatively ineffective procedures unless they are directly linked with attempts to modify the environment or patterns of interaction with peers and with significant adults. The author knows of no evidence that interpretative psychotherapy is of any benefit to backward readers. Most published studies are concerned with play therapy and non-interpretative forms of 'talking treatment'. Pumfrey and Elliott (1970) pointed to serious deficiencies in many of these studies. Sample sizes were invariably small, periods of treatment usually short, and in several studies variables were not properly controlled. They concluded that the case for the value of play therapy for backward and disturbed junior children is unproven.

One study by Bills (1950) is sometimes taken as firm evidence that emotionally disturbed backward readers can benefit from as few as six individual and three group non-directive play therapy sessions. However, the seven children who did make substantial gains in reading, both during and in the 30 days following the therapy period, were hardly typical of backward readers. Five of them were girls. The average RA of the group was actually above their average chronological age, and four of them had IQs of over 145. Yet these children had been placed in a special class for slow learners (n=22). This alone may have damaged them psychologically. Pringle (1970) found that 'able misfits' like these are typically lacking in confidence and tend to be anxious and withdrawn. Their teachers frequently underestimate their ability. The experience of play therapy may well help these children. Attention, acceptance and an opportunity to take the initiative may be among the key factors. The most one can conclude from Bills' study is that some able children who have already mastered the basics of reading can make further gains if something is done to encourage self-expression and to make them feel more confident.

Rather different results were obtained by Elliott and Pumfrey (1972) with boys from educational priority areas. These authors were unable to demonstrate any significant improvement either in reading ability or in adjustment in a group of eight socially maladjusted boys of average intelligence and poor reading attainment, as a result of nine weekly sessions of non-directive play therapy. A control group made equal gains during the same period and during a subsequent 12-month follow-up period. Children with higher IQs and the more emotional children made the greatest short-term improvement in adjustment in the therapy group. Those who were the most hostile to adults in the therapy group made the smallest reading gains. It has been convincingly argued by Hamblin and others (1971) that non-directive techniques present an opportunity for aggressive children to learn how to be even more aggressive. The evidence reviewed by Hamblin fails to support the cathartic hypothesis that the 'therapeutic' acting out of aggressive impulses (whether in fantasy or in reality) serves to reduce the need to be aggressive. Elliott and Pumfrey found that the mean post-therapy gains in word-recognition were actually greater in the control group (20 months RA in one year) than in the treated group (six months RA in one year). Although the samples were small in this study, the groups were well matched in terms of ability and social adjustment, and had been randomly allocated to treatment and control groups. One has to consider the possibility that play therapy may be positively harmful for some children, in that they are placed in a relationship with an adult which bears little relationship to the rest of their experience, and which may be mutually unrewarding. Middle-class, conforming girls of high intelligence probably respond best to the play-therapy experience, but working class, restless, aggressive boys of limited ability almost certainly need a different kind of approach.

Lawrence (1971) claimed that individual counselling sessions are of considerable benefit to backward readers at junior level, and (1972) that non-professional counsellors are just as effective as a professional like himself. He reported mean gains of the order of three months RA per month for 24 children over a four- to five-month period, compared with normal one-month gains for a control group. Good results were obtained with dull children as well as with the brighter ones. However, Lawrence felt that 'counselling alone is not likely to help those children with specific perceptual difficulties'. He suggests that many children do have perceptual problems at the infant stage, but that these disappear with maturation, leaving a backward reader 'with a poor self image and lack of confidence in his ability to make progress in reading'.

In a subsequent study carried out with four matched groups of backward readers in one junior school, Lawrence and Blagg (1974) found that the best results were obtained by a group who received both individual counselling and unsupervised group work with a graded series of reading games. While good progress was also made by a group who received counselling only, the two groups which functioned without any close contact with an adult gained at the slower (normal) rate of only one month of RA per month. One of these groups used reading games, and the other non-reading games. Lawrence concluded that 'attention to the child's emotional life in an attempt to improve his self-esteem is of paramount importance in the reading situation'. He also felt that self-initiated learning for backward readers is preferable to the 'inculcation of certain skills by repetitious exercises', a practice which may be too close to previous failure situations.

Lawrence's counsellors presented themselves as people who wanted children to be happy in school. Those who achieved significant rises in reading attainment were themselves socially uninhibited, and spontaneous in manner. They were alert for opportunities to praise the children, and discussed with them such topics as family and peer relationships, hobbies and interests, aspirations, worries, and attitude towards school. This role is, of course, one which teachers might normally hope to perform, remedial teachers above all. In fact, the remedial teacher in Lawrence's first study was able to combine the roles of teacher and counsellor with some success. Yet if teachers had already been meeting the need, Lawrence's volunteer counsellors might not have achieved such good results. It may be that teachers and volunteers in this country will eventually develop a genuine working partnership, as in the Baltimore service described by Modaressi (1974). One would like to see closer links between counsellors and teachers than in Lawrence's project. LEAs would do well to support further action-research along these lines, especially in an inner city context where those who counsel are faced with problems of communication which may challenge some of their basic assumptions.

It is fascinating to read that positive results have been reported with non-professionals as counsellors when the majority of studies involving professionals have been relatively unsuccessful. Could it be that a confident, common-sense, avuncular approach may provide the child with a better model than the tentative, theoretically-inspired, detached approach of some professionals? Again, it may be a better strategy to dwell on a child's strong points and to encourage him in his real-life projects, than to make him even more aware of his problems and to provide him only with opportunities for the expression of fantasy.

Whatever the reason, the non-directive Rogerian approach to counselling which was used in a major experimental project reported by Winkler and others (1965) did not seem to help retarded nine-year-olds. This study involved 108 retarded readers, selected by a regression formula. As well as the usual 'reflected' comments made by the counsellors, the activities included role-playing, drawing, story-telling and model-making. However, those receiving either individual or group counselling did not improve in grade points more than others who listened to records and stories, and others who received no help at all. While this is a clearly negative result, it should be noted that the interval between pre-tests and post-tests was only 11 weeks. This is a long enough period for gains to show up on reading tests, but it may be too short for overall performance in class to be affected.

At secondary level, counselling is usually carried out on a purely verbal basis, rather than through the medium of play or art expression. Positive results have been reported by Shouksmith and Taylor (1964) for 12 high ability children, and by Harris and Trotta (1962) for four out of a group of eight relatively non-disturbed under-achievers.[1] However, Fisher (1953) found that 11 delinquent boys who were given non-directive group therapy as well as remedial teaching made no more progress than those who received remedial teaching alone. Similarly, Cheatham (1968) found no difference in reading progress or in self-concept scores between a group of six children who received remedial help plus 16 group counselling sessions and six others who received remedial teaching only. What did happen, however, was that the counselled group became apparently less interested in getting on well with other children. Cheatham thought that this was because the counselled group became more aware of in-group feelings and developed its own sense of identity.

Broedel and others (1960) found that the academic performance of 29 bright under-achievers actually fell during the period of counselling. Self-ratings of adjustment remained unchanged, although the counsellors themselves and other observers felt that there had been an improvement. Baymur and Patterson (1960) gave a favourable interpretation to their data on improvement in adjustment and attainment in two counselled and two non-counselled groups. In this study, however, counselling had no effect on study habits. The statistical analysis of the rest of the data was in fact inconclusive, because of the small size of the groups (eight per group) and (possibly) the short duration of the treatment.

The studies summarized above strongly suggest that non-directive counselling methods are unhelpful or irrelevant for backward readers, except perhaps for a few highly intelligent pupils. This does not, of course, mean that more effective kinds of 'talking treatment' will not in

[1]No objective data were reported in support of the assertion that these students obtained better grades. The authors found that not all of the students took the sessions seriously, and concluded that they had made a mistake in including one girl who was a bad influence!

due course emerge. It may be that approaches which include modelling, role-playing and simulations which deal with the times when a poor reader feels inadequate, may help to develop the ability to cope and to learn with a reduced level of anxiety. McCollum and Anderson (1974) reported than an Adlerian approach to counselling (which seeks to develop a sense of mastery and responsibility in making decisions) was effective in helping to raise the word recognition scores of 24 learning-disabled pupils. Again, however, this was a short-term study, and does not in itself provide a firm research base.

Unfortunately, very little work has been done which is relevant to the needs of slow learners in inner-city secondary schools in this country. The published research deals almost exclusively with children thought to have hidden potential. Moreover, in most cases the pupils were given counselling whether or not they sought help, and usually for the sake of experimental design rather than as a means of dealing with a crisis situation. It would, therefore, be premature to expand counselling services, or 'sanctuaries' for pupils with behavioural, emotional and learning problems, before first attempting to provide more favourable and humane learning environments for them.

The need for action research at LEA level

The greater part of the research summarized in this chapter was initiated by individual academic researchers rather than undertaken as part of a developing remedial service. When research and evaluation are built in to a new or existing LEA service, it seems that the results are seldom published. We therefore have little means of telling whether LEAs take this aspect of their work seriously.

Goodacre (1971b) found that about two-thirds of all LEAs surveyed were unaware of any research activities in their area. Perhaps the most common form of evaluation used at LEA level is a survey of reading attainment. About one-third of all LEAs in England and Wales claimed to carry out reading surveys from time to time. More sophisticated projects are rare, and there is little attempt to evaluate different forms of special provision. Of the 22 LEAs surveyed by the author in 1971, 11 were able to point to evidence that was being or had been collected in order to evaluate their existing remedial services. In one case the evidence was in the form of a report by an HMI. Five LEAs carried out annual surveys of attainment. These were also used for screening purposes,[1] and in one area were used to allocate extra teachers to schools in greatest need. Only two LEAs referred to records of progress of children receiving remedial teaching, and only one (Lancashire) had done follow-up testing of children who had been

[1]See Appendix G.

discharged from remedial centres up to three years previously. Five LEAs referred to other types of research projects. A comparison of ITA and TO had been made in remedial centres and in special schools in Lancashire. ITA and diacritical marking had been evaluated in Shropshire, as well as the use of a diagnostic spelling test at eight-plus. The Frostig (1964) teaching materials had been evaluated in Waltham Forest. In Sussex, the Talking Typewriter had been in use, and careful records of progress had been kept. In Richmond, a most ambitious project was being carried out, which involved intelligence, attainment, personality and attitude testing of some 2000 children.

The ability to carry out research and continuous evaluation of this kind is a valuable form of expertise. Educational psychologists are at present more active in this field than advisers and teachers. They are trained in experimental and survey methods, and there can be little doubt that these skills are under-used in many LEAs. No account has been published in this country of an attempt to initiate and to monitor a comprehensive service for children with learning difficulties. More is being done along these lines in one American public school system alone (Levine and others, 1972) than in any national project in the United Kingdom.

Summary

It is an established fact that worthwhile gains in tested reading achievement occur in response to remedial teaching, not only in isolated instances, but throughout entire LEA services. Without this help the immediate gains are very much less, although the long-term results may be the same.

The best results are obtained in groups of up to six children, but little is known about optimal prescriptions for individuals. Some children make extremely rapid gains, but others make little or no progress over long periods of teaching. In general, the law of diminishing returns seems to apply, so it does not make sense to prolong remedial help for those who do not respond without making a major adaptation to the programme.

In order to prevent the usual decrease in rate of learning once remedial help is terminated, it is suggested that some form of continuous support to teachers and pupils should be one of the responsibilities of a remedial specialist. This support need not be intensive if the remedial programme has succeeded in helping the pupil to learn independently, and if his teachers try to ensure that his classroom experiences becomes more positive. The need for support of this kind appears to be greater in secondary than in primary schools.

When children with reading problems are also dull and/or badly behaved, they are frequently segregated in special units, classes and schools. There is little justification for this practice in terms of attainment criteria, except in the case of children of extremely low ability (towards the bottom end of a typical school for ESN pupils), or where there is multiple or very severe handicap. Children who are partially segregated may be more aware of their own deficiencies than those who are completely segregated, but provided they have a favourable learning environment, this is not necessarily a bad thing. Even maladjusted children benefit more from a regime in which there is an emphasis on individual learning programmes, than from a *laissez-faire* approach with an emphasis on vaguely defined aspects of emotional growth. The resource-room approach to special provision makes it possible for children with learning difficulties and with behaviour problems to be helped in the ordinary school. This form of provision can easily be linked with preventive programmes and with classroom-based intervention.

Children with reading problems are unlikely to learn unless they find the activity both useful and enjoyable. Counselling support from an adult who wants them to succeed at school can have a beneficial effect, if it is perceived by the child as relevant to his learning and as an enjoyable boost to his morale. Play therapy and non-directive counselling frequently lack these qualities, and their value is correspondingly doubtful.

Chapter Six

Learning Difficulties: The View from Here

A recurrent theme in this book has been the poorly co-ordinated and relatively unsuccessful efforts of clinicians, teachers, social workers and others who are paid to help handicapped and deprived individuals. Inadequate resources, both human and material, has been another cry. Established services such as special schools for slow learners, child guidance facilities, and remedial classes have been examined and found wanting. A number of experimental and innovative approaches have been described and examples of what seems to the author to be good practice at LEA level have been examined. The problem is, how to bring present provision for children with special educational needs up to the standard of the best that is currently available.

The big discrepancies that exist between schools and between LEAS are to a large extent produced by the influence (or lack of influence) of individuals in key positions of power. Headteachers, advisers, senior psychologists, chief education officers, committee members and MPS are the most influential of these. It would be an interesting exercise to attempt to relate local standards of special educational provision to the personal involvement of such people with the problems of handicap. Correlations would probably be high, and the conclusion would probably be drawn that too many important decisions are left to too few individuals.

If the educational needs of the handicapped and disadvantaged are to be properly met, the whole issue must be opened up to public debate and to community involvement. At the same time, the professionals in the field must seek to improve their services and to overcome many of the difficulties inherent in specialization. This in turn means taking a fresh look at training, which needs to have a common core of theory and practice for all those involved in the educational enterprise.

There is no doubt that special skills and personal qualities are needed for working with children who do not easily fit in to the normal school regime. The problems that arise are sometimes difficult to understand,

and often cannot be resolved without examining the total situation of the child and family concerned. Any one specialist (such as a speech therapist or a school counsellor) needs to be familiar with almost the whole gamut of common physical, psychological, social and environmental problems. The overlap between different branches of special and compensatory education is in fact so great that it does not make sense for them to operate in isolation. Edinburgh has taken the bold step of bringing together all special educational provision within a unified service, and this must surely now happen elsewhere. Redlands College, Bristol, has set up an Education Special Services Unit to serve the county of Avon, with the aims of providing an organizational link between specialist agencies playing a part in the initial and in-service training of all the relevant professions, promoting interdisciplinary research, and establishing a resources unit. Again, this is an example which LEAs would do well to follow.

In this chapter we shall consider some of the educational problems which need special assessment, and shall look at various methods of assessment. It will be found that assessment cannot be considered in isolation from treatment, and that parents and class teachers have an important part to play in both. Decision-making about special provision is seen as an ongoing process involving all parties concerned. Decisions need to be based not only on the child's present level of functioning and the need to acquire new skills, but on expectation levels and on the possibility of creating a total context for learning in which the child's personal and social development will not be thwarted. While the emphasis is here placed on reading, it should be remembered that similar strategies could be developed for assessing and for coping with all kinds of personal and learning problems which occur in schools.

The assessment of reading and allied difficulties

Reading readiness and prediction

At nursery and infant levels it is possible to carry out valuable preventive work which will not only have a directly beneficial effect in helping certain children to adjust to school, but will reduce the later incidence of reading failure.

Some children come to school with very obvious limitations, such as very little speech, an inability to play co-operatively, difficulty in handling a crayon or a pencil, or failure to understand what is happening in pictures. All of these skills, and many others, are important in themselves, whether or not they are involved in the process of learning to read and write. Some are best assessed by systematic observation

f a unique resources room in a residential special school. The children with typewriters are following an audiovisual programme.

Learning how to learn by using a computerized training machine. Correction of errors and practice routines are automatically provided.

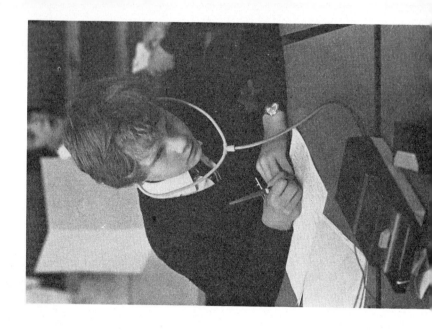

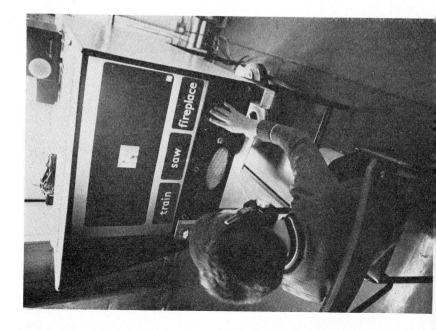

(preferably using developmentally graded check lists) and others by formal tests.[1]

Attempts to predict later reading levels on the basis of a child's performance in the first four months of schooling have not met with much success. This is perhaps not surprising since the early months are a time in which many adjustments have to be made, and performance is often very variable. The evidence reviewed by Downing and Thackray (1971) suggests that teachers' judgements are marginally better predictors of future reading level than are readiness tests of various kinds. Both are better than IQ tests.

The ability to name letters (which usually reflects a degree of directed experience with books) is one of the best single predictors (de Hirsch and others, 1966, Muehl and Kremenak, 1966). Most studies show that accuracy of prediction is not greatly improved simply by adding tests to a battery. For example, de Hirsch and others used 37 kindergarten tests, but achieved no better prediction of the performance of 53 children at the end of second grade from the battery than from the following measures:

letter naming;
word recognition;
name writing.

In this study, subjective judgements of distractibility and work attitude were better predictors than the majority of diagnostic tests used. Moreover, some of the tests which did show significant correlations (e.g. the Bender Visual-Motor Gestalt test, and measures derived from story-telling) may have done so only because they themselves are correlated with general intelligence. When Keogh (1965) held IQ constant, she found that kindergarten Bender scores did not predict third-grade performance in reading (n=127). There were many children with poor Benders who subsequently learned to read normally.

Thackray (1971) carried out an extensive study of 238 children, using an anglicized version of the Harrison-Stroud tests which were given in the first term of infant school. He reported only moderate correlations with later reading achievement. Thackray and Thackray (1974) have since published a revised version of these readiness tests. The visual discrimination test is a word-matching task, the auditory discrimination test demands awareness of initial sounds in spoken words, and the vocabulary test involves drawing a line under one of four pictures. None of these tests makes significant demands on sequencing skills, on powers of visualization, or on successive integration of information. Muehl and Kremenak found that all but one of the Harrison-Stroud tests were poor predictors of reading progress. It must be said that Thackray

[1]See Appendix G.

E*

and Thackray have failed to take into account the findings of recent research concerning information-processing in children with learning difficulties, and have presented tests of unknown test-retest reliability and poor predictive validity (see table 21).

TABLE 21: *The predictive validity of three reading readiness tests (from Thackray and Thackray (1974))*

	CORRELATIONS WITH READING ACHIEVEMENT ONE YEAR LATER
Visual discrimination	·48 – ·58
Auditory discrimination	·46 – ·54
Vocabulary	·48 – ·58

A somewhat different approach identifying children 'at risk' in learning to read has been developed by McLeod (1969), who has published a School Entrance Check List. This consists of 20 items which discriminated at the ten per cent level of significance between 43 backward readers and 43 other children randomly selected from the same classes. Most of these 'controls' were in fact advanced in reading for their age. The items included in the Check List are:

vision;
hearing;
early separation from parents;
nervousness and depression;
over-activity;
speech and language development;
knowledge of left and right;
family incidence of reading/spelling problems.

There is ample research evidence for the association of all these problems with reading failure. However, certain relevant areas are not covered, in particular visual-motor skills and anti-social behaviour. Moreover, McLeod's sample consisted largely of middle-class parents who had referred their children to a University Reading Clinic. More than half the children were seven-year-olds, but the sample did include all ages from six to 12. It is difficult to generalize from a study of this kind, but further validation would probably be worthwhile. It is important for teachers to know whether behaviour and learning difficulties have already been noted by parents, or whether they appear only after the child comes to school. If the infant teacher has a good picture of a child's pre-school development she can start off where the child is, and will fill in the gaps as she gets to know him.

A considerable amount of research effort was put into the Swansea Evaluation Profiles (Evans, 1972). In all, 144 potential predictor variables were employed in a sample of 627 children entering infant departments and followed up at seven-plus. Developmental tests, behavioural questionnaires, and data from home-background, medical, and school schedules were used to predict future reading test results and teacher ratings. For various reasons, measures of letter-recognition, letter sequence matching, immediate memory-span, phoneme-blending, and expressive language were not included in the analysis. Other highly specific but undoubtedly relevant variables such as the teacher's relationship with the child, parental relationship with the school, parental interest in school work, educational aspirations for the child, the child's reading at home and certain medical information with possible neurological implications were also discarded without good reason. The omission of these measures may have reduced the predictive validity of the battery to the level of 0·65 (by regression formulae) and 0·60 (by simplified risk score). Teachers' estimates of future performance and a simulated 'reading' test involving paired-associate learning were the best single predictor variables left ($r = 0.51$).

The level of prediction achieved by the simplified version of the Swansea Evaluation Profiles is too low to be of practical value, and has been achieved on other occasions by using teacher estimates alone, or even the results of a single test. A correlation of 0·6 accounts for only 36 per cent of the criterion variance. More than half of the most backward children at seven-plus will have been missed by the screening procedure carried out rather more than two years before. Moreover, some of those correctly identified by the screening procedure may well be victims of a 'self-fulfilling prophecy'. Reception class teachers were asked to estimate whether at eight years the child would be:

likely to need the help of a full-time special class or class for slow-learners;
in need of extra help in a normal class through a remedial teacher;
an average pupil;
a good pupil;
an exceptionally good pupil.

This kind of estimate opens the door to all kinds of biased judgement and to the Pygmalion effect.

The 'at risk' grouping criteria suggested by Evans draws attention to a child's social background, to his non-verbal intelligence and to his behaviour. For example, a deprived-area child of average non-verbal ability whose father left school at 14 is more likely to deteriorate in school performance during the infant years than a child whose father left school after the age of 14. Similarly, a bright child in a settled working-class or advantaged school is likely to deteriorate during the infant stage if he has behaviour problems, and to improve his position if he has none. The whole approach is very simplistic. It omits many relevant combinations of circumstances, and has little relevance to the planning of individual programmes. Indeed, by focusing attention on deficiencies in the child and in his home background, one may fail to observe the here-and-now interaction, and may avoid the challenge of adapting the curriculum to the child.

If continuous assessment and diagnostic teaching were to become established in schools, it would no longer be necessary to attempt to predict progress over long periods of time. The notion of 'intellectual capacity' will have to be revised once it becomes commonplace for large IQ gains to be made by disadvantaged children when placed in a more favourable learning environment (see Chapter 3, p. 77). The paradox is that the more effective our intervention programmes become, the more difficult it will be to predict future levels of attainment. It is time that teachers and psychologists abandoned attempts at prediction and got on with the job of making special provision for *all* children with learning difficulties. If children are apparently unable to learn, we should assume that we have not as yet found the right way to teach them. The value of test-batteries and teacher assessments should lie first and foremost in their direct diagnostic implications.

As we saw in Chapter 2, Hirshoren found that a single kindergarten measure of sequencing skills (the visual-motor sequential test on the experimental version of the ITPA) is as good a predictor of reading ($r=0.61$) and of a composite measure of achievement ($r=0.71$) as any complex battery of readiness and IQ tests. Measures of sequencing skills are, however, much more important as diagnostic pointers than as predictors. Sequential processing is essential to the development not only of reading but also of language and other pre-reading skills. A substantial proportion of children who later have difficulties in reading show various developmental delays in the pre-school years. Phonemes, syllables and words may be misplaced, and sentences may be abbreviated in their speech. On the receptive side, some children are unable to act on a series of instructions. This may or may not be accompanied by difficulties in sequential processing of non-verbal information, which may be revealed by an inability to solve puzzles which require a specific series of operations. This whole area of sequencing skills, memory-span, temporal order perception, cross-modal coding, attention switching, information-processing, and awareness of redundancy merits more intensive and exhaustive research. Some promising lines of inquiry are described in Appendix D, but we do not yet have the answers to several fundamental questions. We do not know yet how far the growth of these skills is limited by developmental factors as well as by varying degrees of neurological dysfunction, and emotional tension. Moreover, it is sometimes difficult to distinguish between a specific sequencing difficulty and a more general intellectual deficit. Sequential processing is essential to the development of coherent argument and to the planning and execution of learning strategies. If these areas of cognitive functioning are impaired, our first impression may be that the child concerned is dull. Only later may we discover that his vocabulary and concepts are well above average.

Existing reading readiness tests may be failing to measure some of the most important perceptual and cognitive variables. Many such tests involve simple matching procedures and often a multiple-choice format which makes no significant demand on sequencing skills. A search for variables which really do affect a child's chances of learning to read would probably lead into areas such as sequencing skills, associative learning, language development, noise-tolerance, learning styles and strategies. The author (1975) has developed a battery of tests along these lines, giving a profile of strengths and weaknesses which is directly translatable into a teaching programme. The process of test development is not yet complete, and the diagnostic value of the tests will not be established until it can be shown that teachers who implement remedial programmes suggested by the test profiles achieve better results than others who do not use the tests. A controlled experiment in the London Borough of Barnet has been set up to evaluate this approach. The Activity Sheets, which are the basis for designing remedial programmes are reproduced in Appendix F. This kind of approach to screening, diagnostic testing, school-based in-service training and evaluation is fully in accord with the Bullock recommendations (see Appendix G).

Diagnostic teaching
Hammill (1971) has listed several advantages of informal 'diagnostic teaching'. These include the lack of specific information regarding educational strategy from many formal tests, the problem of day-to-day variability in performance, and low subtest reliability. One clear advantage of informal assessment by a teacher who is working with an individual child over a period lies in the elimination of mistakes due to day-to-day variability. Furthermore, children can benefit from the experience. They can see the relevance of procedures which lead

quickly (perhaps the same day) to specially planned exercises and activities.

An experienced teacher often feels that he can do without tests and schedules of any kind. Particularly in a small group situation, the strengths and weaknesses of individuals become apparent and can be picked up by sensitive and unflurried observers. However, not all teachers have these skills and even for those who have, there are definite advantages to be gained from a systematic approach to record-keeping. This is particularly true if a child is referred to a specialist for assessment or when he changes class or school.

If diagnostic teaching in small groups were a normal feature of nursery and infant education, and if record-keeping were systematized, it would be unnecessary to carry out large-scale screening surveys in the last term of infant school, or at the beginning of junior school. The main purpose of such surveys (recommended in the DES green paper *Children with Specific Reading Disabilities*) is to estimate the need for special provision, rather than to select individuals for such provision. This purpose could just as well be achieved through the use of check lists, developmental schedules, diagnostic and criterion-referenced tests. Schools and LEAs sometimes draw up their own check lists and scales, as in Croydon (Wolfendale and Bryans, 1972). Others use existing published schedules. Some of the reading readiness check lists described by Downing and Thackray appear to be useful, particularly their own inventory. Ilg and Ames (1950) produced a developmental schedule showing the order in which reading skills are normally acquired, and a rather more detailed list covering phonic skills has been compiled by Carver (1970). Carver's list is based on extensive research, but not all these check lists have been scientifically constructed. In theory, one should start with a list of all the factors which are conceivably relevant, and progressively refine this after field trials and item analysis. Goodacre (1967 and 1968) described the early stages in the development of a reading readiness estimate, and substantial progress has since been made by Banks (1970). A similar approach was involved in the construction of Stott's Bristol Social Adjustment Guides (1971a) and Rutter's Behaviour Questionnaire (Graham and Rutter, 1970), and is being extended by Stott (1971b) to the observation of individual learning styles.

An important development in the field of diagnostic teaching is the informal reading inventory.[1] This can be used, not only at the onset of tuition, but as a regular form of assessment. The informal reading inventory, as defined by Johnson and Kress (1964) consists of a series

[1] The use of such inventories is recommended by the Bullock Committee of Inquiry.

of prose passages of increasing difficulty, rather like the Neale *Analysis of Reading Ability* (1958). Each passage may or may not be followed by comprehension questions devised by the user. These inventories may or may not be an improvement on standardized tests. So much depends on the selection of passages, and the nature of the questions. They are of unknown reliability and validity, but in the hands of an experienced teacher are certainly valuable. One of their built-in advantages lies in the scoring system used. Three levels of reading accuracy are normally used: the *independent level* (99-100 per cent words correct), the *instructional* level (91-98 per cent words correct) and the *frustration* level (word recognition 90 per cent or less). When the pupil discusses his performance with the teacher, he can be helped to formulate short-term as well as long-term goals.

If a readability formula is applied to the passages in the inventory as well as to other reading matter available, it is possible to guide a child to select books which he will be able to read with no help from the teacher (independent level) or with fairly close prompting and help from the teacher (instructional level). Some measures of readability are rather cumbersome, and others are crude and unreliable. After experimenting with a number of formulae, the author has come to favour the Mugford Readability Chart (1970).

One of the advantages of informal reading inventories and tests of paragraph reading like the Neale *Analysis of Reading Ability* is that one can observe many aspects of reading behaviour which may not show up with word-recognition tests. Variables such as reading speed, clarity of speech, expression and intonation, use of context, keeping the place, impulsivity and perseverance can be evaluated, and a more detailed analysis of hesitations and pauses, and types of error can also be undertaken. If the teacher is serious about this, he will not make snap judgements about all these variables after a single test session, but will tape-record the child reading passages at independent and instructional levels and will analyse the recording in a number of different ways. For speed, the norms given in table 22 may be found useful. These are based on Taylor's (1957) study for silent reading and on the Neale test (extrapolated) for reading aloud at independent level.

Reading rate depends to a considerable extent on whether a child reads word by word or whether he can perceive words and phrases as larger meaningful units. This becomes evident if one analyses a passage read at the independent level in terms of hesitations made at inappropriate places, and pauses not made at appropriate places.

An examination of the types of error made in reading and in spelling is often suggested by the authors of tests and by those who advocate

TABLE 22: *Approximate age norms for rate of reading at independent level*

| | RATE (WORDS PER SECOND) | |
AGE	*Silent*	*Aloud*
7	1·2	0·4
8	1·7	0·7
9	2·3	1·1
10	3·0	1·3
11	3·6	1·5
12–14	4·3	1·7
15–17	4·9	1·8

diagnostic teaching. Considerable attention has been paid to the symptom of reversing the order of letters and sounds. Here a note of caution must be sounded. There is very little normative evidence regarding the frequency of different types of error, although Tordrup's (1966) study does answer a few of the basic questions. Tordrup found that with 231 normal five-to ten-year-olds asked to read 100 words, the ratio of order reversals to other types of error actually increased with reading accuracy. The absolute number of order reversals was least in the top third of the groups, but was equal in the bottom two-thirds. In a second experiment involving 130 backward readers aged nine to 13 years and 92 normal readers aged seven to eight, Tordrup again found that the ratio of order reversals to other types of word-recognition error increased with reading ability, and showed that this ratio was identical in normal readers and in older backward readers of equivalent reading levels. It seems, therefore, that at the age of nine and above no great diagnostic significance should be attached to order reversals in reading. However, a different pattern emerged when spelling errors[1] were considered. Here it was found that the ratio of order reversals to other types of error decreased as spelling ability increased, and that backward pupils made proportionately more order reversal errors than average pupils of equivalent spelling ability.[2] Finally, when the spelling mistakes made by 214 normal readers and 103 backward readers in the ten to 12 age-groups were compared,

[1] Lyle (1969) found that writing sequence reversals were factorially independent of letter-orientation errors and letter-order errors in reading.

[2] Nelson and Warrington (1974) found that order reversals in spelling were also characteristic of children who could read well, but had a specific spelling difficulty. Analysis of WISC profiles suggested that these children had certain other difficulties in the sequential processing of information but no over-all language deficit.

Tordrup found that the following types of error were relatively more frequent among the backward readers (p $<$ 0·05):

confusion of consonants;
omission of sound;
omission of syllable;
phonic rendering;
order reversal.

It is interesting to note that there were no differences between normal and backward readers in the proportions of mute letter, addition of sound, addition of syllable, confusion of vowel sound, and doubling errors. In other words, the spelling errors which are found more often in backward readers are associated with auditory discrimination and sequencing problems. The higher proportion of omission errors (18·7 per cent) in the backward readers is consistent with the idea that for some of these children there is a limit on the number of letters or sounds which they can process efficiently. Lovell and others (1964) found that in a test of copying sentences, there was a sharp increase in the number of errors made by 30 nine- to ten-year-old backward readers when the length of a word exceeded three letters. A similar increase in errors was found among a group of 50 normal readers of equal non-verbal intelligence when the word-length exceeded six letters. This three-symbol limit is of great importance, as it is also a critical cut-off point on tests of phoneme-blending and digit span (Moseley, 1972b).

Without normative data it is virtually impossible for the teacher to evaluate the significance of the word substitutions, additions, and omissions that may occur during informal assessment or testing. Much depends on whether meaning is realized or lost, and on whether substitutions bear a close resemblance to the appropriate words. It is equally difficult to judge whether a child has predominantly auditory or visual problems if all one has is a sample of his reading or writing. In order to provide a starting-point for diagnosis at the level of auditory and visual confusions between single letters, the author (1974) has grouped pairs of letters on the basis of auditory-vocal and visual similarities as reported by Whetnall and Fry (1964), Dunn-Rankin (1968) and Morley (1972). The following confusions are auditory-vocal and cannot be visual in origin: d/t e/i f/s f/v g/k l/r l/y r/w s/t. Of these, the following are also common in the speech of children with poor articulation: d/t e/i f/v g/k. The following confusions, on the other hand, are visually based, and cannot be explained in terms of poor auditory discrimination or indistinct speech: a/o b/g b/h c/e d/h d/p f/k g/p h/n h/y i/l j/y l/t m/w n/r n/u p/q v/x v/y x/z. However, other letter confusions can be either visual or auditory-vocal in origin, and these are: a/e a/u b/d b/p d/g f/t k/t m/n s/z. It is evident than no reliable judgement regarding the nature of a disability can be made on the basis of letter substitution errors in the above 'mixed' category.

The roles of class teachers and specialists

The value of diagnostic tests of various kinds is discussed in more detail in Appendix D. While class teachers can learn how to administer and interpret tests which measure various kinds of reading and writing sub-skills, those tests which are only indirectly related to reading and writing are best left to the specialist. On the other hand, class teachers are perfectly capable of learning how to administer group screening tests, but testing should not be carried out in groups of more than 20. It is desirable to have two teachers present. The children should be separated so that it is not possible for copying to occur. Advisers and psychologists can train class teachers in the details of test administration, stressing close adherence to the instructions. However, as screening tests are not intended to be the sole basis for placement in a remedial group, it does not matter whether they are 100 per cent accurate. Jackson (1971b) and Pumfrey (1974) have produced useful guides to published tests.

The assessment of interests, attitudes, self-concepts, social relationships and behaviour patterns cannot be dealt with in detail here. Class teachers usually rely on an intuitive approach, but there is something to be said for more thoughtful and detailed analysis. Systematic observation of selected children can lead to fresh insights, and the class teacher is in the best position to carry out such observation. Hopefully, fruitful discussion will ensue, and for this specialist support may be needed. In Dade County, California (Levine and others, 1972), class teachers are requested to keep notes of classroom crises and the individuals concerned for three weeks, before discussing their problems with a specialist teacher. This procedure could easily be adopted for British use. Another possibility would be for teachers to tape-record their own lessons and discuss the classroom interaction with colleagues. Others may prefer to invite an observer into their lessons, so that detailed records can be kept and discussed shortly afterwards.

While it is important for educational psychologists, counsellors, remedial teachers and other consultants to obtain an accurate picture of what happens in the classroom, it is just as important for class teachers to find out how their children respond to individual attention or in a small group. Diagnostic testing and the assessment of a child's personal qualities should not be shrouded with mystery. There are, of course, occasions when confidentiality must be respected, but there are many aspects of the specialist's work which are not properly understood by class teachers. There are other aspects which are as irrelevant as many teachers suspect. Better communication between specialist and class teacher will, hopefully, lead to more reliable and efficient means of assessment, both formal and informal.

In her surveys of remedial education, Sampson found that individual testing of IQ or testing for special disabilities is not general when children are put forward for remedial teaching. Perhaps this is less alarming than it sounds. There is in fact no evidence that children who have been through a conventional psychometric assessment respond any better to the teaching that is subsequently offered than do those who have been through a less sophisticated set of procedures. It has been claimed that subtest information from individually-administered tests of intelligence is useful in planning special teaching procedures (Burkholder, 1968, Levine and others, 1972), but firm evidence is lacking. The author has developed a method of grouping WISC subtests according to their three main factor loadings (Moseley, 1972b), but has found that this analysis does not enable one to predict progress made in response to remedial teaching. Even the basic question of whether training should be specialized with regard to the kind of dysfunction cannot yet be clearly answered (Bruininks, 1970; Sabatino and Streissguth, 1972). Levine's project in Dade County and the author's work in the London Borough of Barnet should, however, answer some of these questions.

It would certainly be premature to throw all intelligence and diagnostic testing out of the window. In the past, the large number of WISCs and Binets carried out by educational psychologists on backward readers have at least proved one point: that many children, thought to be dull by their teachers, are in fact well equipped intellectually. Crawford's research is definitive on this point. Reading ability more than any other single variable colours teachers' estimates of intelligence. Intelligence tests provide a corrective here, but group tests can serve the purpose just as well as individual tests. If class-teachers used group tests such as Young's (1964) Non-Readers' Intelligence Test or Brimer and Dunn's (1962) English Picture Vocabulary Test (neither of which depend on reading ability), they would become aware of the verbally bright children with specific reading difficulties.

At the same time, it must be acknowledged that the one-to-one assessment situation has great potential as part of a total diagnostic-remedial strategy. It provides optimal conditions for learning and feedback. Certain diagnostic tests (especially those requiring motor responses) have to be given individually. Feelings can be expressed and explored in a relatively private and supportive atmosphere. One has therefore to discover the best way of using what are bound to be limited opportunities for individual specialist work as an integral part of the intervention process.

One way of combining informal and formal methods of assessment is for an educational psychologist or advisory teacher to work with an individual child for four to six sessions. This approach is justifiable only if some form of special provision is available when the sessions come to an end. A diagnostician will only cause resentment if he raises a child's hopes of learning to read, only to let him down by putting him on a long waiting list. Extended assessment enables the diagnostician to discover a great deal about the pupil – his strengths and weaknesses, his interests, his behaviour in a learning situation, and the kinds of teaching that he needs. It will also become apparent whether a child has any severe emotional difficulties, and then an attempt can be made to direct the parents' interest and concern into appropriate channels. Most important of all, findings and practical suggestions can be passed on to the teachers who will be chiefly responsible for implementing a special educational programme.

Extended assessment has several advantages for all parties concerned. The child is given the security of knowing that a real effort is being made to understand his difficulties and to offer him a genuine opportunity to learn. It is important for him to realize that there is no need for him to try to hide his problem from his parents and from his teachers. The psychologist or remedial teacher can invite both parents and teachers to attend one or more of his assessment sessions, and can afterwards discuss future plans with them. This would not be done if for some reason the child resisted the idea very strongly or if the diagnostician had reason to believe that it would only increase the pressure put on the child. However, as Stott (1974) argues, there are very few parents who are unable to play an active role in helping a child with reading or spelling difficulties. If the problem and the future learning load is explained to them, they are usually quick to realize their own limitations and to come to give praise when praise is due. Parents should not be asked to learn the technicalities of remedial teaching, but they can play a valuable part in listening to a child's own account of a book he has been reading, in telling and reading stories, in helping their child to select books at an appropriate level for independent reading, and in checking through assignments. They should be discouraged from taking an authoritarian or busybody role, and it should be left to the child to ask for help in the course of his reading or with his assignments if he needs it. He should also be given the choice as to which parent he goes to for help or for checking.

It is most important that during the period of extended assessment the child should experience a high degree of success on a number of limited tasks, that he should have the opportunity of showing his parents and possibly his class teacher what he can do, and that he should be introduced to new ways of independent learning. He should also be told that he will be expected to become increasingly independent and responsible in his approach to learning, and should be praised and rewarded for each step he takes in that direction.

If at all possible, the child himself should be involved in planning a special educational programme. The child's preferences may be irrationally based, but little will be accomplished if he is compelled to join a group or class against his will. While a backward and demoralized child is not always the best person to judge his own needs, it is rare for a pupil to refuse extra help with his reading once the nature of the problem has been explained to him by someone he trusts. Even if an apparently wrong decision is made, it can be changed on another occasion.

The teacher who takes over from the diagnostician after the assessment period will usually find that the pupil is already on the right path. The changeover should not represent a complete break, since it will often be desirable for the diagnostician to make a periodic review of the progress of all his cases. There should not of course be a complete change of remedial method at the changeover. If it is found that the child needs special resources which are not available in the school, these should either be borrowed from a resource centre or purchased.

Remedial and language advisory teachers have an important part to play in LEA screening procedures and in the educational assessment of individual children. They should not be expected to deal with the more extreme cases of physical disability or psychological disturbance, but should none the less be treated as responsible professionals in the fields of special education and educational guidance. They can, and sometimes do, carry out a large part of the work that is normally attempted by educational psychologists. As argued above, their assessment should be based not only on test results, but on classroom observation and on the child's response in a more structured learning situation. They should be able to help other teachers plan detailed programmes of work and should make periodic checks to see whether all is going well or whether some rethinking has to be done. Continuous assessment rather than once-off psychometry has been recommended for immigrant children by the Department of Education and Science (1973), and by a British Psychological Society working party (1973) for children with learning disorders. These recommendations cannot be put into practice unless large numbers of teachers are equipped for the task through full-time and in-service courses.

The organization of programmes for children with special problems

Infants first

Special programmes at infant level have attracted much more attention in the United States than in Great Britain. Published language development, auditory training and perceptual-motor programmes have been available in the United States for many years, and now some have appeared over here. Details of such materials are given in Appendix F.

Teachers of infants normally have very large classes and their opportunities for giving individual work are severely limited by this constraint. Yet individual and small-group work are more important at this age than at any subsequent period. Some children find it difficult to adjust to the demands of a larger group and need the experience of a small 'family' group and consistent adult care in the school setting. The need for special provision at infant level has led in the ILEA to the formation of experimental 'nurture groups' (Boxall, 1973; ILEA, 1974). The concentration span of many infants is extremely limited, and some kind of feedback is needed for almost every response they make. If the hierarchy of skills involved in learning to read (Merritt, 1969) is to be covered at all systematically, major changes in standard infant practice are necessary. Even when a structured programme is set up by advisory staff (Jones, 1969), it is unlikely to achieve a great deal unless sufficient staff are available to permit flexibility of group size.

There are several ways in which small groups or one-to-one teaching can be arranged, e.g.:

(a) training children to work in pairs, giving each other knowledge of results, or the one helping the other;

(b) making greater use of auto-instructional devices and programmes;

(c) using a permanent specialist member of staff either in the classroom or in a specially equipped group or resources room;

(d) arranging for peripatetic specialists to attend schools (i.e. a part-time version of (c);

(e) using supply or 'floating' teachers to release the class teacher;

(f) using non-qualified help in the classroom – this need not be restricted to paid classroom auxilliary help, but can involve college students, volunteer sixth-form help and interested parents;[1]

[1] See Appendix G.

(g) reducing the size of classes;

(h) part-time attendance for all or some pupils to achieve a part-time reduction in size of classes;

(i) extending the school day, with half a class coming an hour early and the other half staying an hour late;

(j) extending the school year, with staggered holidays, so fewer children are in school at any one time than at present.

Few of these approaches have been tried out on a large enough scale for any firm conclusions to be drawn. However, Hamblin (1970) found that six- to seven-year-olds learned to read more quickly when working in pairs than when paired with adult volunteers. McNeil (1964) and Hamblin and others (1971) described how five- to seven-year-olds enjoy and profit from daily periods of interaction with 'responsive' machines. Some of the compensatory education programmes described in Chapter 3 certainly show promise. Some LEAs (e.g. Croydon and Haringey) have set up multi-purpose Language Resource Centres. The concept of a resource centre was advocated by Halsey and others (1973), but on a more strictly local basis. The resource centre would act in support of local schools, to store and disseminate information on learning and reading problems and on the various programmes and materials available, to provide specialist help for the schools and opportunities for in-service and initial training. Some kind of focus for encouraging and co-ordinating local initiative is clearly needed if organizational and curricular changes are to have a chance of success. Resource centres could in certain areas be attached to colleges of education. The initial training work reported by Fairman (1972) would not be difficult to organize in the context of a local resource centre. Teachers in training could then be given the experience of getting to know individual children, of preparing schemes of work based on their interests, and of sharing in the learning process both inside and outside the classroom.

It is a widely held belief that early intervention can prevent many learning difficulties from arising. A reduction in class-size in the early years of schooling is perhaps the most obvious preventive measure that could be taken. The present policy of smaller classes for older children is at variance with the developmental progression from dependence to independence in learning and in social functioning. The present system is bound to produce a high rate of failure, while providing optimal tutorial conditions only for the Oxbridge elite.

According to Malmquist (197?) a different kind of thinking prevails in Sweden. There the size of classes has been reduced to a maximum of 25 at the ages seven to nine, and 30 at the ages ten to 16. Every teacher of the first three grades has a weekly two-hour period for tutoring children in need of help. In addition, classes are divided in half for part of their 3R work. In the first grade (six to seven years), one half of the class has 3R work for the first two hours of the day, while the other half comes to school for the next two-hour period, during which the first half can play.

In the same paper, Malmquist refers to the large number of remedial reading classes (163) and reading clinics (71) in Stockholm alone (1971 figures), and says that 'in any rural or urban community throughout the country, a specialist working two hours a week with a child can be hired and paid for by the national school authorities'. Malmquist's (1969) study showed that remedial instruction during the first years of school was indeed an effective preventive measure. Ellson and others (1968) reported on a field study in which paid non-professional individual tutoring was tried out in 20 Indianapolis schools with six- to seven-year-olds. This, too, proved effective, but only if a tightly structured programme were followed and only if each child had *two* daily 15-minute sessions. Ellson thought that the unstructured tutoring approach failed with this sample of disadvantaged children because the 'progressive' ideas of permissiveness, accent on self, stress on play, and under-estimation of the need for rules and standards are contradictory to the traditional attitudes and expectations of lower socio-economic groups.

While there is much that can be done within our infant and first schools to improve provision for children with learning difficulties, the role of parents is also extremely important.[1] One reason for this is that mothers and fathers who read provide the best possible model for children to imitate. Halsey and others (1973) recommended that ways should be explored of raising the educational level of the home and the community, by helping parents to reinforce the child at home with suitable materials and encouragement, and by involving parents in the work of the school. Valuable work can be done here by individual teachers, especially if they carry out home visits. Malmquist tells us that the Swedish Royal Board of Education has actually stipulated that class teachers are responsible for making regular contact with the home.[2]

There are a great many difficulties experienced by children in school which relate to such basic needs as eating and going to the toilet

[1] See Appendix G.

[2] The us Education of All Handicapped Children Bill (1973) takes parents' involvement to the point where they have the right of access to their child's records as well as the right to request an independent evaluation of learning difficulties.

(Moore, 1966). Some of the problems could be resolved by better communication between, and by action taken by, parents and teachers. Moore drew attention to the need for better facilities: 'Classes small enough to allow for attention to individual needs, adequate space and equipment, classrooms designed for sound absorption, improved dining facilities and pleasant indoor lavatories with simple bolts'. It should not be forgotten that schools as well as parents stand to gain from an open discussion of issues such as these. For, unless the community at large becomes aware of the difficult conditions under which many children and their teachers work, little will be done to improve matters.

Literacy for all
This is not an impossible goal. We all know of infant teachers who can justly claim to send no non-readers to the junior school. If present provision for backward readers were improved in a number of important respects, it would be a rare event indeed for a child to reach secondary school reading or spelling at or below the seven-year level.

For this to happen, the proportion of time and resources devoted to complete non-starters has to be increased. While this does not imply that all non-readers should be given one-to-one teaching, it does mean that a very carefully graded programme should be organized for them. Non-starters respond best if given regular but short periods of activities for which suitable rewards are available. The length of each activity and the nature of the rewards should be matched to the individual, taking into account his ability to work independently and in a group. Some of the activities can be carried out in the classroom, whereas others are better done in a resources room or at a reading centre of some kind. If a child can function only in a one-to-one situation, the teacher or other specialist working with him must see it as part of his task to integrate him first into a small group and then into a larger group. If one-to-one teaching is continued too long, the child may become overly dependent on the teacher and may even manipulate the teacher into continuing to see him individually for year after year.

Once a minimal seven-year level of literacy has been reached, a child's ability to function well in a normal class depends less on his attainment level than on the organization of work in the class, on the child's ability to work independently, and on whether the child feels that his efforts are likely to be rewarded. If the remedial teacher relies too much on formal teacher-directed methods in his work, it is unlikely that his pupils will learn how to take increasing responsibility for their own learning. But if he prepares his pupils to work independently with structured reading programmes, and then helps the class teacher to use and extend these programmes in class-time, the chances that initial gains will be increased are much greater.[1]

Much depends, of course, on the skill and interest of the class teacher and on the physical constraints of the classroom. Perhaps justifiably, some remedial teachers feel that they must hang on to their pupils because they could never undertake the task of trying to modify a class environment which offers no hope to the backward reader. When the class is very large and in the hands of a supply teacher who is experiencing discipline problems, this point of view needs no defending. It was seen in Chapter 3 that smaller classes help to reduce the incidence of severe backwardness. There is no doubt that it is much easier to organize small-group and individual work in small classes. Olson (1971) reported on an observational study of 18,528 classrooms, in which it was found that an individualized approach was most commonly applied in groups of up to five pupils. With group sizes of between six and 15 pupils, rather less individualization was possible, and less again with between 16 and 25 pupils. With more than 26 pupils, lessons consisted largely of standard exercises, question and answer, lecture and testing, and with 36 or more pupils there was virtually no group work, individual work, discussion or pupil reporting.

While a strong case can be made out for improving specialist provision for children with learning difficulties outside the classroom, it is probably even more important to create favourable conditions within ordinary classrooms for the individualization of work for slow learners. If this is not done, a significant proportion of children will continue to be denied an education appropriate to their abilities and aptitudes.

It was argued in Chapter 3 that the principle of positive discrimination should not be applied at the level of areas, nor even of schools, but should operate in favour of disadvantaged and handicapped individuals within a school. This can be done if funds are available for such a purpose, as in the case of the ILEA Special Difficulties Budget. Schools that wish to improve their facilities can apply for grants, and in this way new reading resource rooms, quiet rooms, special equipment, etc. can be obtained.

This approach could be developed in several important ways and could become the standard procedure whereby schools improved their provision for children in need of special education of all kinds. First, ways could be found of involving class teachers and community representatives in the formulation of proposals to be put forward to the ILEA. Second, proposals could be submitted by school panels

[1] See Appendix G.

(Booth and others, 1974) as well as by headteachers. Third, some kind of evaluation and accountability could be built in to all projects approved.

When one considers the diverse and changing problems that require special intervention of some kind, it becomes obvious that a flexible approach is needed. Flexibility is needed in planning size of groups, in timetabling, in bringing in appropriate specialists as needed, and in moving from a segregated to an integrated regime. This can best be achieved if, as in Edinburgh, there is a unified department of Special Educational Services, which provides special facilities in ordinary schools as well as in segregated settings. A department of this kind would be able to allocate resources on the basis of proposals put forward by schools, as suggested above. With a unified department, it would also be relatively straightforward to transfer children from one setting to another, if necessary. At present there are often serious delays in providing special educational treatment, which result from poor inter-departmental communication and from inter-professional rivalry, as well as from a shortage of places. In some cases, as with speech therapy, there is often poor communication between the professionals concerned with a particular child. This situation would be greatly improved if all professionals concerned with special educational treatment had defined roles within a unified department.

We shall now consider the full range of settings and the kinds of special educational programmes which LEAs may wish to provide in order to reduce the incidence of illiteracy and semi-literacy in schools. Although for convenience these are described separately, they should really be viewed as parts of a flexible, dynamic service, through which children move towards the point at which they become able to learn independently in an appropriate type of group. After all the possibilities have been outlined, we shall examine the resource room and resource centre approach to learning difficulties. In the author's opinion, this model is applicable not only to the entire range of reading problems, but also to the greater part of special educational provision.

With one-to-one attention, a wide range of programmes can be carried out. Many of these can be implemented in group situations just as effectively, but some cannot. There are three main reasons why individual attention should sometimes be provided:

(a) the child has a unique problem which can be dealt with effectively only if there is an ongoing process of diagnostic appraisal;

(b) the child's behaviour cannot be adequately controlled if he is in a group;

(c) privacy is required.

It is not necessary to add a fourth reason, such as (d) child and teacher or child and therapist need to establish a mutually-rewarding relationship, because good relationships automatically result if an empathic and suitably-skilled adult takes into account the child's needs under headings (a) to (c).

It is clear that certain kinds of speech and language programme require individual attention. Speech therapy, and all forms of dialogue (whether intended to develop concepts, to explore feelings or simply to exchange experiences) are cases in point. Unless confidentiality is at issue, it is desirable for the teacher or therapist to work very closely with others who know how the child behaves in a group or in his normal class. In some cases, the same person might work on an individual basis with a particular child, and also see him in a group. One of the most valuable aspects of individual work with a backward reader is helping the child to understand his own problems more clearly and to formulate his own goals, both short-term and long-term. Another very important part of the work is to find out what best motivates the child, and if necessary, to make radical changes in the systems of feedback, rewards and punishments. Specialists are unlikely to achieve much here if they see the child infrequently and work in isolation.

Children who cannot function in a group can sometimes be prepared for social integration by working on a one-to-one basis. In many cases, the teacher or therapist needs to interact with the child indirectly, through shared or complementary activities, or by assigning certain functions to mechanical or electronic devices. Those whose attentional difficulties appear to derive from cognitive and perceptual deficits may respond well to structured programmes into which a high degree of immediate feedback has been built (Moseley, 1969b). Behaviour-modification techniques as well as non-directive methods have a part to play in the therapeutic process, but it is extremely doubtful whether a completely unstructured approach is of any value. The evidence reviewed by Hamblin and others (1971) shows that one does not learn to control aggression simply by 'acting-out' one's aggressive impulses.

Teachers, as well as professional counsellors, psychotherapists and other workers, often find themselves in possession of confidential information with which children have trusted them. It is certainly important that children who want to talk about personal or family problems should be able to do so in privacy. Very often the first person they want to approach is their class teacher, so some arrangements should be made in every school for this. As we saw in Chapter 5, there is a gap in junior-school provision for personal contact between child and adult, a gap which can be filled by non-professional counsellors, according to Lawrence. At secondary level the need for pastoral care is undoubtedly great, and privacy is an essential requirement at times. The school counsellor, as seen by Hamblin (1973), would be in a good position to make constructive use of confidential information. Hamblin believes that counsellors should be involved in the curriculum, helping to resolve problems concerned not only with interpersonal relationships but also with intermediate goal-setting, the analysis of learning tasks, and the elements of decision-making.

Hamblin summarized his argument in the following way:

'(1) That the counsellor has to intervene actively in the pupils' lives within the school. In conjunction with his fellow teachers he must arrange supports, reinforcements and modify the environment to give a pupil the maximal chances of success. He is therefore incorporated into a team of teachers. (2) He works as a mobilizer of resources for the pupil within the school, involving other teachers as active participants in the counselling process. (3) He is a resource person for his teacher colleagues in the sense that he provides them with relevant information which is helpful to the pupil and passes on some of his skills. (4) He acts as a link between the outside agencies and those actually teaching the pupil.'

Individual attention can be given in the school, in a centre or clinic, in the open air, and in the home. When it requires specialist services it is extremely expensive, but when parents or volunteers can play a part, it is relatively cheap. It is therefore the responsibility of all who work with individual children to use their time to the best possible advantage. Often this means working with an individual child for a relatively short period, and at the same time helping parents and teachers to take on a more supportive role. It does not make sense for teachers or for therapists to use one-to-one sessions for activities which could be carried out just as well in groups or at home.

Small groups of two to five children are familiar to most remedial teachers. With a group of this size it is possible to run completely individual programmes, to pair children off for certain activities, to bring the whole group together for visits, reading games, listening to stories, etc., and to organize project work in which each child plays a distinctive part. Individual attention can be given to one child at a time if the others are kept busy. Audio-visual aids such as film loops and slides can be used individually or as the basis of group discussion. Tape-recorders, teaching machines and automated group-pacing programmes (Morgan, 1971) can also be used in a very flexible manner.

Like Hamblin (1970), the author has found that paired working has several advantages, not least when the children concerned are unused to taking turns and working co-operatively.

Provided that everything is to hand, a teacher can organize individual programmes within larger groups of six to 15 children, but there are certain limitations on what can be done single-handed. For example, individual phonic-articulatory work as described by Sonenberg and Glass (1965) cannot be carried out in groups of this size unless everyone else is quietly occupied; visual-motor training programmes cannot be implemented on an individual basis unless someone is there to give instructions for each sheet or card; ancillary or technical help is required if extensive use is to be made of audio-visual equipment; and an outside observer/consultant is required for the proper execution of a behaviour-modification programme. The competence of the teacher, the children themselves, the space available and the availability of resources (especially self-instructional programmes) have a great effect, but it is asking too much of any teacher to cope unaided with a class of six to 15 children with learning difficulties and/or behaviour problems. There is a need for ancillary help and for the occasional use of other professionals, sometimes in the same room, and sometimes in a room set aside for individual work.

With groups of 16 to 25 children, more constraints are placed on the teacher, and in the author's opinion it is impossible for all but the most highly competent to organize special educational programmes unaided, with the exception of certain kinds of group work in movement and PE. While it is true that a massive investment in teaching machines and programmes can facilitate the organization of group and individual work in groups of this size (Morgan, 1971; Noble and Gray, 1968), the number of classrooms that are equipped in this way is incredibly small. Even if the technology were available, technical and ancillary help would still be needed. In its absence, the need for ancillary and team-teaching support is overwhelming.

If the teacher wishes to use a child's own speech as the basis of reading and writing activities, he will need ancillary or technical help in writing it down (to dictation or from a tape) and in typing it out (with a large-print typewriter). If the teacher wants all the children to read or to write at appropriate levels, he will need at least one extra person available to answer questions and to check the work. Even for hearing reading and for setting up listening points so that children 'read' as they listen to a recorded text, a single person cannot really cope if he has 16 or more children. He may succeed once in a while, but he will be unable to find enough time to do the work thoroughly on a daily basis. The time factor also limits the opportunities for dialogue and for expressive language work. Only the exceptional teacher, like Mrs Pyrah (Moseley, 1972), can develop a true sense of audience for all speakers in classes of this size. The problem of noise can be a serious one with 16 to 25 children, especially in classrooms with poor acoustics. One of the reasons why so many teachers prefer to dominate their classes with a verbal barrage (Flanders, 1970; Wragg, 1973) is that it is difficult to train all children to speak loudly and clearly enough for everyone to hear what they have to say.

In classes of 26 children or more, space as well as time and noise is an additional problem. Most classrooms are too small for the proper organization of group work, the storage of equipment and books, and the building up of class resource units (Merritt, 1972). It is often impractical for additional teachers or ancillaries to work in already over-crowded classrooms, and in these circumstances the only thing to do is to operate a system of withdrawal or class splitting.

Many of the points made in the preceding paragraphs are expressed in rather more detail in Table 23. This table is based on the author's experience and subjective judgement, and is offered as a guide to the kind of thinking that is needed in planning special provision. It is recognized that some teaching situations are much more difficult to handle than others, and that there are bound to be exceptions to the rules.

TABLE 23: *Special programmes and their staffing requirements in groups of different sizes*

TYPE OF PROGRAMME	CLASS OR GROUP SIZE			
	2–5	*6–15*	*16–25*	*26+*
Language-experience (including E2L)	1	1	4	3, 4
Graded reading/writing exercises	1	1	4	4
Self-instructional programmes	1	1	4	4
Teacher-directed phonic/articulatory	1	3	0	0
Visual-motor training	1	4	2, 4	2, 4
Movement programmes	1	1	1	0
Child reads aloud	1	1	3 or 4	3 or 4
Child listens and reads silently	1	1	3 or 4	3 or 4
Audio-visual enrichment	1	4	4	4
Reading games	1	1	4	4
Remedial play, art, drama	1	1	3	3
Talking treatment (e.g. counselling)	1	0	0	0
Behaviour modification	1	2	2	2

Key 0 Cannot be done effectively in a group of this size.
     1 Can be organized at appropriate levels by a single person.
     2 Teacher requires occasional professional assistance.
     3 Teacher requires considerable professional assistance.
     4 Teacher requires ancillary or technical help.

At junior-school level it is obviously unrealistic to expect each school to be able to provide the full range of special programmes listed in Table 23 but it should be possible to arrange this with a peripatetic supportive service, with a remedial teacher/adviser covering four or five schools.[1] At secondary level each school could be largely self-sufficient, except for the services of the educational psychologist, school doctor, speech therapist, welfare officer, and LEA advisory staff.

As we saw in Chapter 4, many secondary schools have grossly inadequate remedial provision, but there are some exceptions. A few schools are moving towards the kind of flexibility and inter-departmental co-operation which is necessary in order to give a sense of purpose to all staff concerned with backward readers. It sometimes happens that an over-all literacy policy is formulated by a school only at the point when large numbers of staff are worried about standards of reading, and writing (especially writing), and feel that something must be done to maintain interest, attendance and discipline. Hopefully, many more schools will see the need to improve and co-ordinate their remedial and pastoral care services before they reach the point of crisis.

Gordon and Wilson (1969) described the work of remedial department at Sidney Smith High School, Hull. They saw three distinct aspects to the job: (a) advising subject teachers about individuals who would be able to cope in normal classes if suitable materials and remedial programmes were available in those classes; (b) giving intensive help in small groups to children who lack certain reading skills (six periods a week in groups of four); (c) providing a secure base with one remedial teacher for children who are unable to meet the demands of school life.

As Dean (1973) pointed out, there are very often more children who need help with their reading in secondary schools than can be coped with by the remedial department alone. Help is needed not only in English lessons but in all subjects where reading and note-taking are involved. Some schools see this as a task for the English department, and in some ways it is. What is really needed is for remedial English and other specialist departments to get together to work out a co-ordinated approach to the problem. This has happened in some schools known to the author, and the result is that a number of teachers have volunteered to give up 'free' periods and lunch-breaks in order to work with individuals and to supervise a scheme in which sixth-form volunteers also spend time with individual children. The sixth-formers are not expected to teach, as such, but they can give help with specific

[1]See Appendix G.

assignments. The idea of using sixth-formers as voluntary tutors for backward readers was successfully adopted by Edwards (1971) who was running an adult education class at Havering Adult Institute. A scheme organized by the Community Service Volunteers whereby sixth-formers visited a nearby school three afternoons a week was described by Vaughan (1972). Here different books, games, and methods are used 'depending on what stage the child is at, and what particular problems he comes to the class with.' A similar scheme was described by Storey (1972):

'Each sixth-former has a "son" or "daughter" whom he (or she) takes under his wing. Using a variety of books, the Talking Page and word and letter games, they tutor these slow or backward children in reading and writing. In addition to this, the sixth forms run a story club, which is held in school during every lunch period. During this time, the younger children are entertained, introduced to books which they themselves might not otherwise enjoy, and are (we hope) educated by the wide variety of stories, plays and poems which are read to them.

'An extension of this scheme has recently been introduced. Each week a group of sixth-formers, preparing for the Cambridge Board Oral English Examination, visits one of our contributing junior schools to work under the direction of the head and remedial staff. These visits have the additional value of introducing children in their final year in the junior school to sixth-formers, with whom they can retain contact when they eventually enter the lower school here.

'These schemes, which have produced a marked improvement in the reading ability of the slower-learning pupils, have also, we feel, been responsible for a decrease in behaviour problems. The very important fact that these for the most part neglected children are being given care and attention by sixth-formers who are to them, demi-gods, has changed their whole attitude to school in general, and reading in particular.'

Parent and other volunteer help is, of course, an alternative to the use of sixth-formers. In one Haringey comprehensive school known to the author, parents have given valuable help in special literacy classes of 12 pupils. The classes worked as a group for some purposes, but also individually, using tape-recorders for the development of listening skills, and receiving individual attention from the teacher and volunteers. In a three-month period, a mean gain of six months in reading accuracy took place, and the majority of puipls were reading much more extensively, both in school and at home, than they had done previously.

If neither parents nor sixth-formers are available, the only thing to do is to assign more teachers to remedial work. Wallbridge (1972) described the work of a Special Reading Department in a streamed ILEA boys' secondary school. Up to eight part-time staff were appointed and trained on the job by Wallbridge. Some of the principles underlying the work done were formulated as follows:

'Reading involves relating to books in a manner closely analogous to relating to people. Boys who cannot relate, usually cannot read effectively either.

'The management of the problem requires a period of individual help which may be short or long.

'The idea that all that is needed is a good relationship between teacher and pupil is inadequate. Many backward readers, while they need a good relationship, also need efficient, appropriate instruction – correctly timed and matched to their particular problem.

'Some of this instruction can take place in groups, but only if the groups are carefully selected.'

Wallbridge emphasizes 'the compensating value for the pupil of learning again to move from dependence on one person through dependence on a group to independence.' It was possible for this to happen, as several teachers worked together in one room, some with individuals and some with groups.

The scheme developed to the point where individual attention was given on a tutorial basis, the number of sessions varying from three tutorials a week to one a month, and four types of group were in being:

(a) reading practice groups – mixed ability groups capable of working independently;

(b) language development groups – graded according to severity of problem (including children who speak very little English);

(c) compensatory experience groups – emphasis on expression work with the emphasis on the talk associated with the activity;

(d) instruction unit groups – each dealing with a specific aspect of reading and lasting for half a term or a term.

This particular project came to an untimely end, before a full range of equipment and resources had been built up, and before it became fully integrated into the life of the school. The trouble seems to have been that there was poor communication between the Special Reading Department which proclaimed itself to be concerned with persons and which became a 'home' or 'sanctuary' within the school for some of the pupils, and the subject-based departments who had little time to consider individual learning difficulties and personal feelings. The Special Reading teachers were mainly young, temporary members of staff, and they were themselves learning the job. It was therefore

difficult, if not impossible, to set up team-teaching situations, to introduce new materials and individualized work into the ordinary classes,
and to establish the new department as a service which extended across
departmental boundaries.

While provision for children with learning difficulties remains a
low-status branch of the teaching profession, without an adequate
system of training and promotion-structure, it will be difficult to
convince other teachers that there is much to be gained by working co-
operatively with specialist staff. Brennan (1971) outlined a policy for
remedial education which has much to commend it, and other progressive ideas have been put forward by Mason (1969), Pumfrey
(1970, 1971), and Adams (1971).

It is probable that schools which introduce mixed-ability teaching
will be among the first to see the need to strengthen their remedial/
pastoral/vocational guidance provision, and to build up a genuine
sense of team-work between departments. At the same time, if more
demands are going to be made on certain members of staff, a great
deal of effort will have to be put into courses of in-service and college-
based training. Booth and others (1974) and the Community Relations
Commission (1974) have argued that these courses should not be too
academic, but should include a strong element of 'learning on the job'.
In-service training in conjunction with colleges, reading units and
clinics, whereby teachers spend part of the time working in their
own schools (freed from many of the constraints of their normal
job) and part of the time at a resource centre, should be greatly
extended.

Resource rooms and centres

When one considers the practical problems involved in organizing
special school- and home-based programmes for children in need of
such help, it becomes obvious that two things are needed: more space,
resources and time within each school, and support from outside the
school. Both for assessment and for effective teaching purposes, a
specially equipped room is really needed in every school. These rooms
need not be big but they should be quiet and comfortably furnished.[1]
Parental involvement can be initiated much more effectively in such a
setting than in a large class, and children can concentrate better.
Present school medical rooms are quite unsuitable for these purposes:
special education resource rooms are needed (Moseley, 1972a).

LEAS can back up preventive, remedial and special programmes in
schools through teams of advisory and peripatetic teachers attached to

[1]The Bullock Committee of Inquiry recommends that schools should be
designed with areas where individual attention can be given.

schools psychological services or to other special and compensatory education departments. Ideally, these teams should be co-ordinated and should operate from area centres, Halsey's concept of a multi-purpose local resource centre has much to commend it. A resource centre can combine advisory, teaching, therapeutic and training functions with curriculum development work. The Croydon Language Centre is apparently developing along these lines (Wolfendale and Bryans, 1972).

In the United States there is a developing network of Instructional Materials Centres for Handicapped Children and Youth. Their functions include information services concerning educational research and instructional materials, conferences and in-service programmes, demonstrations and displays, borrowing facilities, publications, and the preparation, validation and distribution of new materials. These centres clearly meet important needs and a few of the large British LEAs (e.g. Edinburgh and ILEA) now have their own special education centres. But perhaps these would be even more effective if they also provided an ongoing service for children and parents.

Valett (1970) described a multi-purpose Learning Resource Centre which may serve as a model for progressive LEAs. Programmes for individuals as well as special projects and new forms of provision were planned in consultation with teachers and parents. Educational therapy for severely handicapped children was carried out at the centre, with parents modelling their interaction with their children on work done first by the therapist. Parent and pupil counselling services were available, and courses for parents in understanding and managing children's problems proved very successful. Finally, an extensive programme of in-service training and curriculum development was being carried out. Future plans included the extension of demon-stration teacher services to enable periods of a month or more to be spent assisting interested teachers in developing model classrooms.

There are several points in common between Valett's Learning Resource Centre and the NSMHC Centre for Learning Disabilities (which closed in 1971 for financial reasons). Children attended the NSMHC Centre for one-and-a-half-hour periods to follow individualized programmes of various kinds. preferably on a daily basis. Parents were frequently shown what they could do to help their children at home, and advisory work was carried out in schools. Equipment such as the Talking Typewriter (Moseley, 1969b; 1969c; 1971b) and the Hansel Training Machine (Moseley and Sowter, 1972) was evaluated. Field trials were organized for the Frostig and Horne (1964) and Fairbanks–Robinson (1967) perceptual-motor training programmes and for the Autobates and Touch–Tutor reading programmes. In addition, new materials were produced (Moseley, 1971c), conferences were organized and in-service training was carried out.

In 1972 the writer set up a resources room to serve children with learning difficulties in one Haringey school. A peripatetic remedial teacher was responsible for the assessment of learning and behaviour difficulties and worked with children for varying lenghts of time, with the aim of 'weaning' them as soon as possible after the initial 'extended assessment' period was over. The room was equipped with a variety of materials and equipment which were used in such a way as to lead children towards independent working habits. In the early stages of assessment, little follow-up work was done in the ordinary classroom, but as time went on the aim was to involve the class teacher more and more. This was done in three ways:

1 The class teacher would visit the resources room and see his pupils at work. He would be encouraged to use some of the materials in his own classroom.

2 The specialist teacher would visit the classroom, first as an observer and then as a helper. She would discuss with the class teacher possible ways of changing undesirable patterns of interaction and avoidance behaviour which she may have noticed.

The pupils would be given the opportunity to use self-corrective materials in his classroom. In some cases, these were borrowed from the resources room, and in others were purchased for classroom use.

After an initial period in which the pupil developed better work habits and began to make undeniable progress, his visits to the resources room would become less frequent. As he was gradually weaned away from the smaller group, the class teacher would assume full responsibilty for ensuring that he continued to meet with success in reading in the class situation. He would be discharged when he could participate adequately in class activities, as judged not only by attainment testing but also by observation of his work and behaviour.

In this particular case, the resources room ceased to function as intended as soon as the peripatetic teacher was required to spend more time in other schools. Unfortunately, the room came to be seen as a child guidance facility, not as part of the LEA resources available to the school. However, a film was made (Open University, 1973) which illustrates the resources room approach. The author is now continuing with his efforts to help schools set up their own resurces rooms by advising teachers and encouraging those within travelling distance to bring their children to the resources room at the Child Guidance Training Centre as a short-term method of in-service training.

In several parts of the United States the resource room and resource centre approach to special educational provision has been introduced on a large scale,[1,2]. For example, Reger and Koppmann (1971) described a network of 23 school resource rooms set up by the Board of Co-operative Educational Services in Buffalo, New York, in 1969-71. These resource rooms are for any child within the school (*not* from other schools) who is handicapped in any way relevant to his educational needs. No child may be in the resource room for more than half a day at any time, and a resource room teacher sees no more than 20 children in the course of a week. The class teacher is closely involved in the initial assessment at a Child Evaluation Centre. This assessment takes three days and is carried out by teachers with parents present throughout, if this can be achieved. The class teacher then spends a day at the centre going over results and recommendations, and centre staff then spend a day at the referring school. After this, it is largely up to the resource teacher to maintain good relations with the class teacher. Reger and Koppman stated (perhaps rather optimistically) that the classroom teacher is seen as 'the learning coordinator and the resource room teacher is an assistant who helps farther the goals established primarily by the learning coordinator'.

Reger and Koppman saw the resource room and Child Evaluation Centre system as a cheap alternative to special class provision. They quoted an annual cost of $300 per pupil attending a resource room, compared with between $2,000 and $3,000 for each student placed (full time) in a special class. It is interesting to note that the personnel at the Child Evaluation Centre were all teachers – not psychologists, doctors or therapists.

It is not difficult to imagine British child guidance and remedial services developing along these lines. The problem is that very few of them are in a position to influence curriculum development and school provision through intensive work in a small number of schools at any one time. A few LEAs (notably Corydon, Edinburgh, Glamorgan and Staffordshire) have already achieved a great deal, but the majority have not yet brought adequate resources to the task. It is not until a centrally organized service has a teacher serving every school in its area for at least one full day a week that schools can really be helped to organize

[1]The Australian government has recently decided to train enough specialists in learning difficulties to appoint one such teacher in every school. The resource-person approach, with the specialist seen as aiding the class-teacher, is a much-favoured model.

[2]The Schools Council has recently (1975) adopted a policy statement which deals with the curricular needs of children with learning difficulties. The resource-room approach is seen as providing a flexible framework for corrective and remedial programmes.

and improve their own forms of special provision. Even on this basis it may take a year or more before real improvements are seen.

Summary

Instead of thinking of special provision for children with learning difficulties as a series of palliatives and appendages to the education system, LEAs should view their task as one of redesigning the system in order to provide a genuine chance for all children to learn in accordance with age, ability and aptitude. A unified special education service working in conjunction with school and community organizations is one means of achieving the necessary changes in ordinary schools and in special units. Such a service could also provide a much-needed common core of training for the various professions involved.

Instead of waiting until children are seven or eight before giving the slow ones extra help, it is preferable to intervene at nursery or infant level. Both class teachers and specialists have a part to play in the process of assessment and in implementing special programmes. While formal tests have their value, a process of extended assessment which can include additional informal and observational procedures has important advantages. Specialist teachers and educational psychologists are needed for this job, for teaching some individuals and small groups, and for on-going advisory support.

Young children need the experience of a small family group and consistent adult care. Schools can and should provide such an atmosphere, which is a pre-condition of learning. In their learning, beginning readers need an appropriate model, short-term goals, a high degree of feedback, and rewarding experiences. Some need individual attention, and some work well when paired with another child. Audio-visual aids and 'responsive' teaching machines are also helpful at this stage, and their use can facilitate flexibility of group size. Non-professional helpers in the form of parents, older pupils and volunteers should be involved in assisting the class teacher, who in turn should be able to call on a specialist to help resolve problems which might be concerned not only with learning difficulties, but also with interpersonal relationships, the use of resources, and the elements of decision-making.

The same general principles apply when working with older children, but the main purpose should then be to enable the pupil to function in the ordinary class. This may involve number of transitional stages as the pupil progresses towards the goal of independent learning. It is suggested that schools should establish resource rooms for children with special problems in order to provide a stable but flexible setting for this work.

Children of immigrant parents

The special problems arising in boroughs with high proportions of immigrant families deserve a separate description, even if one believes that they will not, in the long term, need a separate solution. The dropping of the official DES definition of an 'immigrant' pupil is a step in this direction. In an attempt to assess the special difficulties of the overseas children within each LEA the DES used to collect information every year on Form 7(i). This was unsatisfactory for reasons which will be discussed, and was not issued after 1973 as a result of a recommendation from the Select Committee on Race Relations and Immigration (1973).

Form 7(i) asked each Chief Education Officer for the numbers within his LEA of immigrant children and for the numbers within these categories whose mastery of the English language was inadequate to enable them to follow a normal school curriculum. The definition of 'immigrant' included:

(i) children born outside the British Isles who have come to this country to join parents or guardians whose countries of origin were abroad, and

(ii) children born in the United Kingdom to parents whose countries of origin were abroad and who came to the United Kingdom on or after 1st January (ten years before).

Both these categories proved unrealistic. The definition of 'immigrant' excluded a large number of children, born in this country of parents living here for more than ten years, who entered school at the age of five with no English whatsoever. The measure of 'adequate English' was entirely subjective and varied enormously from school to school and from borough to borough. These variations were particularly confusing in the case of the largest group of immigrants, the West Indian children. Most West Indians have English as their mother tongue and are therefore considered by many head-teachers and

A co-operative effort in dictating and typing a letter to an absent pupil.

Careful planning, good organization, the use of ancillary help and a respect for individual work are in evidence here.

One of the most distractible pupils at the Centre for Learning Disabilities t
illuminated letters consistently from left to right.

An adult studies the phonic and graphic structure of spoken and written langu
at the Centre for Learning Disabilities.

education officers to be linguistically able to profit from normal schooling. The survey reported in *Schools Council Working Paper 29* (1970) and the high proportion of West Indian children in ESN schools indicate that some special provision is necessary for this group, yet Form 7(i) made no suggestion of this kind. The exact nature of a 'normal school curriculum' gave rise to yet further confusion. According to a DES Education Survey (1972), four out of ten immigrant pupils in streamed secondary modern schools were in lower streams. As this survey was concerned only with pupils who were born overseas (one half of them had arrived in this country after the end of the junior-school period) these figures seem rather encouraging and might offer little justification for the survey's urgent appeal for more special help. However, one should remember that very few of the maintained grammar schools are likely to be included in the sample. In spite of their high academic aspirations, most immigrant pupils tend to find themselves in the least academic secondary schools. Here the normal curriculum might make minimal demands on language skills. The Asian or Cypriot pupil would not be noticeably weak, although he might be unable to express his own intelligent ideas in English and to fulfil his academic potential.

Attainments

It is not only newly-arrived immigrant children and those from a non-English speaking family resident in this country who have difficulty in adjusting to a normal school curriculum. Many children of immigrant parents have difficulty in reading and writing as well as in listening and speaking, and this may last well beyond the period when they are thought to need special *language* help as such. They may continue to be handicapped educationally because of limited opportunity to use and develop spoken language. Some of these children also find reading difficult, because they are unfamiliar with the syntax and vocabulary used in reading schemes. This type of difficulty is also likely to be found in children whose spoken English is a form of West Indian creole.

At the same time, the problems of immigrant groups overlap with those of indigenous groups of children needing special help on account of learning difficulties. There is also an overlap in some of the behaviour disorders associated with poor attainments in both groups, but there are also important differences. Instead of parental indifference or antagonism, one often finds undue reverence for education among the immigrant parents, sometimes associated with quite unrealistic expectations. Differences in the attitudes of parents and teachers towards a child-centred approach to education can also affect a child's progress and adjustment.

F

In order to fill in the changing picture of levels of attainment among the children of immigrant parents, a number of findings from some published and unpublished surveys will now be summarized.

A recent unpublished survey of reading and language standards in 11 infant schools in Haringey is particularly relevant, as Haringey has the highest proportion of immigrant children in the country. Table 24 gives the relevant statistics for 967 children tested at the average age of seven years, two months.

TABLE 24: *Reading standards in 11 infants schools*

GROUP	% OF TOTAL POPULATION	% WITH NEALE ACCURACY SCORES BELOW 7 YRS.
1. Born in UK, indigenous parents	42	34
2. Born in UK, immigrant parents	42	47
3. Born elsewhere, immigrant parents	16	49

It is most interesting that there was no significant difference in the proportion of backward readers in groups 2 and 3. More detailed analysis showed that, among the immigrant subgroups, the highest proportion of backward readers was found among Cypriot children, and the lowest among Indians and Pakistanis. Children born in the West Indies were just as likely to fail in reading as were those whose first language was not a form of English. In fact, those children who entered school speaking no English at all performed just as well as the West Indian immigrants. This suggests that factors other than language difficulties have an important part to play. The whole range of socio-economic factors described in Chapter 3 is of course relevant, but the authors of the *Schools Council Working Paper 29* found that the socio-economic status of immigrant families could not fully account for observed differences in school attainments.

Children of immigrant parents meet with the same problems of classroom communication that are experienced by working-class children who have had little contact with middle-class language and mores, but they suffer to a greater extent because the entire family is involved in adapting to a different culture and educational tradition. In the case of West Indian families, there is the additional problem of colour prejudice.

The ILEA Literacy Survey of 1968 covered all children in the first year of junior school (n=31,308). It was found that 17 per cent obtained standardized scores below 80, compared with 8·6 per cent nationally.

Various factors were shown to be associated with reading standards in this survey. Family size and parental occupation, as well as teacher ratings of parental interest and cultural stimulation, were prominent among these. Children who had changed schools frequently, who had experienced frequent changes of teacher, or who were often absent from school were more likely than others to come within the 'poor reader' category. In addition, immigrants (DES definition) were almost twice as likely to come in this category as non-immigrants. Among the immigrants, Turkish Cypriots presented the biggest problem, as 46 per cent were poor readers. Again, as in Haringey, West Indians[1] (30 per cent of whom were poor readers) performed at very much the same level as those for whom English was a second language. However, the large immigrant population (17 per cent of all children) does not account for the difference between reading standards in London and those obtaining in the rest of the country. Even if we were to double this proportion to include all children born in the United Kingdom of immigrant parents, the expected incidence of backwardness would be about 12 per cent (as compared with the actual incidence of 17 per cent). See also Chapter 3, page 71 for further evidence on this point.

In his survey of spelling ability at second-year junior level (referred to in Chapter 3), the author was able to consider various immigrant subgroups separately, and also to measure their non-verbal ability by means of a new spatial test (POP). It was found that the incidence of poor spelling was highest in those children for whom English was not a first language. There were 88 such children and 56 per cent of the boys and 50 per cent of the girls obtained spelling quotients of 75 or less. The difference between the proportions of backward boys and girls was not significant.

By way of contrast, there were significantly more boys than girls among poor spellers with West Indian parents. Here the proportion of boys to girls was 2·6:1 among children who had received all their education in this country and 1·7:1 among those who had arrived after the age of five. Among the former group, the incidence of backwardness in girls (13 per cent) was no greater than in the indigenous population (12 per cent). In the group of children who arrived after the age of five there was considerably more backwardness, associated with particularly low levels of listening vocabulary. Nevertheless, low EPVT scores did not necessarily mean low reading and spelling scores. Of the 31 West Indian girls who arrived in this country after the age

[1]Pumfrey (1969) was in the rather unusual position of being able to compare samples of West Indian and Irish children. He found that the West Indians (n = 149) obtained a mean reading age only four months below that of the Irish (n = 124). The Irish children were seven months below the English.

of five, only eight (26 per cent) obtained spelling ages of less than seven years, and yet as many as 22 of them (71 per cent) obtained listening vocabulary scores below the seven-year level.

The spelling, listening vocabulary, and spatial test scores of the subgroups described above are given in Table 25.

TABLE 25: *Mean listening vocabulary, spatial ability and spelling ability in subgroups of nine-year-olds*

SUB-GROUP		MEAN EPVT SCORES		MEAN POP SPATIAL	MEAN SPEL-LING AGE
	n	*ss*	*Age Equiv.*	*ss*	*Age Equiv.*
Indigenous pop.	1070	95	8y. 9m.	97	8y. 7m.
Pre-1963 WI	184	86	8y. 0m.	88	8y. 3m.
Post-1963 WI	51	75	6y. 10m.	84	7y. 5m.
English not spoken at home	88	77	7y. 1m.	90	7y. 2m.

The first point of interest is that children of West Indian parents obtained relatively poor scores, even though they had lived in the United Kingdom for more than four years. In vocabulary development they were approximately nine months behind indigenous children, in spatial ability, 15 months, and in spelling five months. It is perhaps surprising that it is in the area of spatial ability, not language, that the greatest difference is apparent. However, Pollak's (1972) research into play habits, mobility, and the use of toys among children of West Indian parents revealed a comparative poverty of experience.

The more recently arrived (post-1963) West Indian children were still more backward; about 23 months in vocabulary, 24 months in spatial ability, and 14 months in spelling behind indigenous children. Here the degree of backwardness was more uniform, suggesting general difficulties in adapting to a different culture. The listening vocabulary of these children was just as restricted as that of the 'foreign language' group. Their spatial ability was also limited.

The 'foreign language' group was made up of 36 Turkish Cypriots, 15 Greek Cypriots, 11 Indians/Pakistanis and 28 others. The highest scores were obtained by the Indian/Pakistani children, who were particularly gifted in spatial ability. There was little difference between Turkish and Greek Cypriots, except in spatial ability, and here the Turks were markedly inferior. In fact, if the Turkish Cypriots were excluded, the mean spatial score of the foreign language group would be 94, which is close to the mean for the indigenous children.

In summary, we may draw certain tentative conclusions from this study of immigrant subgroups:

1 There is little difference between boys and girls in the rate at which non-English speakers learn to write and spell in English.

2 Children learning English as a second language are in general more advanced in spatial ability and non-verbal reasoning than their language skills might lead one to believe. However, Turkish Cypriots are relatively weak in spatial ability and may need considerable experience in practical and constructional activities if their language is to develop fully.

3 Recently arrived West Indian children perform badly on most kinds of tests. It may be years before they adjust to a new way of life and begin to show some improvement in oral and written skills.

4 Children of West Indian parents who have received their education in this country are likely to resemble indigenous children of similar socio-economic status in their school attainments. As with English children, more boys than girls are backward in reading.

5 Many immigrant children of eight-plus have a limited vocabulary but this does not in itself mean that they cannot master basic reading and spelling skills.

Rutter and others (1974) reported on an extensive survey of ten-year-olds in an Inner London borough, in which the reading attainment and school adjustment of 100 children from West Indian families was the focus of attention. As in the author's study, attainment level (on the Neale test) was related to the length of time spent in this country. Those born in the UK were eight months below indigenous children, whereas those who arrived up to the age of eight were a further ten months behind, and those who arrived between the ages of eight and ten were another three months behind. It was found that new arrivals typically had to live in very poor accommodation, and that from the start it was a struggle for survival. As a group, the West Indian fathers had poorer jobs and housing than the fathers of indigenous children. Families tended to be large, wives worked long hours, children were frequently minded (rather than played with) and they were relatively restricted in social activities. The quality of family relations did not, however, differ between the groups, and neither did the child's adjustment in the home. However, conduct problems were more frequently reported by teachers for West Indian children. The possible reasons for this were thought to include 'their often lower educational attainment; the disparity between home and school patterns of discipline; the effects of racial prejudice; and the consequences of their being more likely to attend schools which had high rates of pupil turnover, absenteeism, and children from poor homes.'

At secondary level there are many areas where immigrant children are absorbed into normal schooling with apparently little difficulty, although, as we have seen, they tend to be found in the lower (including the remedial) streams. As Bhatnagar (1971) pointed out, the immigrant pupil 'is likely to be there because of his language problems, bad learning habits acquired earlier, and maladjustment.' Of course, this is also true of many of the indigenous pupils to be found in remedial classes, but it does mean that a different emphasis is needed, and if many of the immigrants do not improve to the point of being able to cope with a normal curriculum, something is clearly amiss. It is mainly in areas with a very high immigrant population that additional special measures are needed. For example, in Haringey (which has large numbers of children of Cypriot origin) 11 per cent of secondary pupils were said to be unable, by reason of language difficulties, to follow a normal curriculum (DES Education Survey, 1972). Something more than conventional remedial provision was clearly needed.

In the 1971 NFER survey of reading standards, the mean reading scores for non-European immigrant children were approximately three and a half years below the national average. The performance of children born to immigrant parents in this country was again considerably better than that of immigrant children born abroad. In all, the proportion of children classified as immigrant by the official Form 7(i) definition was 7·3 per cent and about a quarter of these were born in this country. As the rate of immigration has declined considerably in recent years, it is likely that the problems of severe language and reading difficulties will eventually diminish. On the other hand, while immigrant subgroups continue to fill many of the low-paid jobs in our economy (Field, 1973), a disproportionate number of their children are likely to have difficulty in adjusting both to school and to society at large.

Provision

LEA provision for immigrant pupils has been the subject of a recent full-scale survey sponsored by the DES and carried out by a research team based at the NFER (Townsend, 1971; Townsend and Brittan, 1972). The definition of an immigrant child, the numbers coming from various countries and information about where they have settled and where they are in school in the United Kingdom, all basic factors in the NFER survey, were taken directly from the 1970 Form 7(i) returns. The reservations previously outlined should therefore be born in mind.

Townsend (1971) circulated the 146 English LEAs with a questionnaire investigating special arrangements made for immigrant schoolchildren. 75 authorities including ten with between 500 and 2000 immigrant pupils, had made no provision. Organization varied widely among the 71 authorities who had made special arrangements. All had arranged English language teaching for secondary school children, all but four for junior school children, and all but 12 for infants. However, 22 authorities excluded West Indians from special help at secondary and junior levels, and 19 excluded them from infant language classes. The English language teaching took place either in full- or part-time language centres, or in full- or part-time language classes within the pupils' own schools, and most pupils attended a centre or class for about a year. The teaching of *reading* to children of immigrant parents is normally the responsibility of class, subject and remedial teachers, but this does not apply during an intensive initial period of language teaching.

There are strong educational arguments against isolating immigrant children in full-time special centres. Segregation from indigenous children, lack of provision for subjects such as craft or games, which can be enjoyed with very little English, and lack of contact between the specialist English staff and the subject or class teachers for whose lessons the children are being prepared, are probably the most notable disadvantages. Part-time centres often cater for children either every morning or every afternoon and this means that there is little continuity for the children in the half-day classes they attend back at their parent school. Busy teachers comfort themselves with the thought that Ahmed is getting some education elsewhere, and find it difficult to provide suitable work on the few occasions they see him each week. However, where there are only a few non-English speaking children in each of several schools there are definite advantages in collecting them together for work with a specialist teacher. Some of the Language Centres have become highly professional well-equipped units, used by local teachers as a source of information on all immigrant matters, and for teaching English in the context of the subjects that children are going to need if they are going to fulfil themselves when they return to school. In cases where English is a second language to several children in one school, there are good grounds for appointing a specialist teacher to the staff. Special English lessons can then be dovetailed to fit in with other activities, and pupils who no longer need full-time or even part-time help can still seek advice as they pursue more advanced studies. It is also possible for the English specialist to work with the other teachers and help them to become more sensitive and sympathetic to the problems of children from overseas.

For some time, teachers and administrators alike have felt that the high incidence of immigrants in school was unlikely to be permanent. This has caused considerable staffing problems in special centres and classes. Career prospects in a small, possibly temporary field are not attractive, and the five specialist training courses for teachers of English as a foreign language are all directed at graduates planning to teach overseas. Some centres rely for their teachers on specialists returning from abroad, but conditions in the UK often compare unfavourably with overseas, and the turnover of such staff is high. Twenty LEAs employed a total of 137 teachers from Commonwealth countries (Townsend, 1971), most of whom were working with pupils from their own country of origin. The disadvantages of this arrangement are obvious where the work is designed primarily to prepare children for integration into an English school. In one authority, remedial teachers get a grade A or B allowance and have to have a recognized qualification for their work, while immigrant service teachers have no allowances and are not required to have specialist training. It is not surprising, therefore, that more than half of them are probationers or unqualified. Luckily, this situation is not typical but a sobering number of parallels to it could be found.

With these problems in mind the DES and many of the local authorities have arranged in-service training courses, and Townsend reports that an average of 48 courses attended by 1818 teachers were held each year from 1967-70. He also comments, however, that even this in-service training was patchy and inadequate except in the few authorities where there was a centrally-organized peripatetic team meeting regularly for discussion and preparation.

Since the revision of the immigration laws there have been fewer non-English speakers entering junior and secondary schools in England. The discontinuation of Form 7(i) is indicative of the fact that many educationists no longer feel able to distinguish between 'immigrant' and 'indigenous' pupils. However, attainment scores (discussed on pp. 162–5) verify the opinion that children from different cultural backgrounds are not likely to achieve as much in English schools as their friends whose families have always lived here. Both the DES (1972) and the Parliamentary Select Committee on Race Relations and Immigration (1973) regard this as a matter of grave concern. Segregation for formal English language training no longer seems the answer. Although it is possible that schools with high proportions of overseas children will introduce multi-racial curricula, less than ten per cent of our school population is likely to consider itself other than British. The best answer in the future for these children is likely to be the same as that for any child who finds it hard to fulfil himself and express himself in school – a well-organized network of special services staffed by well-trained, sympathetic teachers, with particular sensitivity in the field of language development.

The responsibilities of the individual teacher: a dilemma

Very few teachers enter the profession, still less specialize in work with backward readers, purely for the financial reward. Many find the work satisfying in itself, and many believe that they are making a positive contribution to society. Underlying political, moral, and philosophical attitudes vary enormously, but education is almost universally thought of as a means of strengthening a child's physical and mental powers and of opening up a wider range of options in adult life than would otherwise be available.

It is because failure to learn to read and write severely limits one's possibilities in life (NARE,[1] 1972) that teachers who are committed to a belief in equality of opportunity come to feel very strongly about the need to give disadvantaged and handicapped children a better deal. After all, how do you approach a child who is making no progress, but would, you are sure, if you had more time, space and resources to offer him? Is it better to do a poor job with 50 children or to make sure that ten backward readers overcome their difficulties and learn to cope with a normal curriculum? What do you do if you are unable to apply some of the progressive ideas learned in college when you find yourself in a formal, authoritarian school? What do you do if there are no suitable books available, if you are not allowed to arrange meetings with parents, or if you disagree with a recommendation about special schooling?

The majority of teachers of backward readers work in isolation, and many of them are part-time. As individuals they are relatively powerless, although, as suggested in Chapter 4, they can achieve better working conditions if they are part of an integrated LEA service. What is lacking is a generally accepted means of identifying need and of ensuring satisfactory standards of provision. While this would not be an easy matter, the Canadian Committee of the Council for Exceptional Children (1971) made a considerable number of practical proposals. The DES Assessment of Performance Unit (House of Commons, 1973) has the appropriate terms of reference.

[1]National Association for Remedial Education.

It is, in general, more effective to work through professional and community pressure-groups of various kinds than to take a lone stand against the system. However, on occasion a teacher may have good reasons for refusing to accept certain conditions, and may be unable to secure professional support for his action. If he is wise he will resign, and one can only speculate about the proportion of teacher-turnover which results from restrictions placed on the initiative of young and energetic teachers.

In a paper submitted to the Bullock Committee of Enquiry into Reading and the Use of English (Booth and others, 1974), the author argued for greater staff and community involvement in decision-making, thereby reducing the overwhelming power of head-teachers regarding the curriculum. It is not only frustrated individual teachers, but also LEA officers, who are in effect powerless when a head-teacher shows little interest in pupils with difficulties, has little experience or expertize in the teaching of reading, and offers no overall policy to the staff. Goodacre (1968) showed that heads of infant schools who had unfavourable attitudes towards the home backgrounds of children from lower working-class areas not only tended to produce lower reading standards, but seemed to influence their teachers to expect less from their pupils. It is important that ways of avoiding this kind of situation should be found, without in any way reducing the beneficial effects of effective leadership.

Of course, teachers in Great Britain have an enormous amount of freedom compared with countries where details of the curriculum are laid down by the state or by local government. They may not always use this freedom wisely; indeed, they may relax standards too much if they are accountable neither to the community nor to their employers. However, contact with class and remedial teachers has convinced the author that the vast majority are capable of taking on greater responsibility regarding special provision for backward readers than they at present enjoy. Goodacre found that class teachers were less satisfied than heads 'in regard to the opportunities their work offered for intellectual growth, independence of action, putting ideals into practice, and the contacts with parents'. The author is currently involved with a project in the London Borough of Barnet (1975) which, through a programme of test development and in-service training, offers such opportunities to all teachers who have a special interest in helping backward readers.

Special projects can serve a useful purpose, and so can many other situations in which interested teachers can share ideas, learn and plan together. If, however, an LEA does nothing to facilitate professional development for teachers of children with learning difficulties, except when forced to take positive steps to avert a crisis, it cannot expect anything but declining standards of work and behaviour. If the individuals in positions of power have elitist political attitudes, teachers of egalitarian persuasion are bound to be frustrated. If LEA officials and committee members have lost touch with the reality of the classroom, the playground and the street corner, their provision for children with learning difficulties is likely to be only a form of window-dressing.

Jonathan Kozol (1967) found himself in an impossible position as a teacher in Boston, Massachusetts. Some would regard his reaction as immature, but his story has highlighted a crisis of conscience which many teachers experience in a less acute form. The circumstances are quite different from those facing British teachers, but the underlying issues are not irrelevant. Is the educational system failing children with special needs? Is talk about remedial and compensatory education anything more than a ritual political gesture?

Extracts from 'Death At An Early Age' by Jonathan Kozol

Perhaps a reader would like to know what it is like to go into a new classroom in the same way that I did and to see before you suddenly, and in terms you cannot avoid recognizing, the dreadful consequences of a year's wastage of real lives.

You walk into a narrow and old wood-smelling classroom and you see before you thirty-five curious, cautious and untrusting children, aged eight to thirteen, of whom about two-thirds are Negro. Three of the children are designated to you as special students. Thirty per cent of the class is reading at the second grade level in a year and in a month in which they should be reading at the height of fourth grade performance or at the beginning of the fifth. Seven children out of the class are up to par. Ten substitutes or teacher changes. Or twelve changes. Or eight. Or eleven. Nobody seems to know how many teachers they have had. Seven of their lifetime records are missing: symptomatic and emblematic at once of the chaos that has been with them all year long. . . .

You check around the classroom. Of forty desks, five have tops with no hinges. You lift a desk-top to fetch a paper and you find that the top has fallen off. There are three windows. One cannot be opened. A sign on it written in the messy scribble of a hurried teacher or some custodial person warns you: DO NOT UNLOCK THIS WINDOW IT IS BROKEN. The general look of the room is as of a bleak-light photograph of a mental hospital. Above the one poor blackboard, grey rather than really black, and hard to write on, hangs from one tack, lopsided, a motto attributed to Benjamin Franklin: '*Well begun is half done*'. . . .

Try to imagine, for a child, how great the gap between the outside world and the world conveyed within this kind of school must seem: a little girl, maybe Negro, comes in from a street that is lined with car-carcasses. Old purple Hudsons and one-wheel-missing Cadillacs represent her horizon and mark the edges of her dreams. In the kitchen of her house roaches creep and large rats crawl. On the way to school a wino totters. Some teenage white boys slow down their car to insult her, and speed on. At school, she stands frozen for fifteen minutes in a yard of cracked cement that overlooks a hillside on which trash has been unloaded and at the bottom of which the New York, New Haven and Hartford Railroad rumbles past. In the basement, she sits upon broken or splintery seats in filthy toilets and she is yelled at in the halls. Upstairs, when something has been stolen, she is told that she is the one who stole it and is called a liar and forced abjectly to apologize before a teacher who has not the slightest idea in the world of who the culprit truly was. The same teacher, behind the child's back, ponders audibly with imagined compassion: 'What can you do with this kind of material? How can you begin to teach this kind of child?'

Gradually going crazy, the child is sent after two years of misery to a pupil adjustment counsellor who arranges for her to have some tests and considers the entire situation and discusses it with the teacher and finally files a long report. She is, some months later, put onto a waiting-list some place for once-a-week therapy but another year passes before she has gotten anywhere near to the front of a long line. By now she is fourteen, has lost whatever innocence she still had in the back seat of the old Cadillac and, within two additional years, she will be ready and eager for dropping out of school.

Once at school, when she was eight or nine, she drew a picture of a rich-looking lady in an evening gown with a handsome man bowing before her but she was told by an insensate and wild-eyed teacher that what she had done was junk and garbage and the picture was torn up and thrown away before her eyes. The rock and roll music that she hears on the Negro station is considered 'primitive' by her teachers but she prefers its insistent rhythms to the dreary monotony of school. Once, in fourth grade, she got excited at school about some writing she had never heard about before. A handsome green book, brand new, was held up before her and then put into her hands. Out of this book her teacher read a poem. The poem was about a Negro – a woman who was a maid in the house of a white person– and she liked it. It remained in her memory. Somehow without meaning to, she found that she had done the impossible for her: she had memorized that poem. Perhaps, horribly, in the heart of her already she was aware that it was telling about her future: fifty dollars a week to scrub floors and bathe little white babies in the suburbs after an hour's street-car ride.

The poem made her want to cry. The white lady, the lady for whom the maid was working, told the maid she loved her. But the maid in the poem wasn't going to tell any lies in return. She knew she didn't feel any love for the white lady and she told the lady so. The poem was shocking to her, but it seemed bitter, strong and true. . . .

Of all the poems of Langston Hughes that I read to my Fourth Graders, the one that the children liked most was a poem that has the title 'Ballad of the Landlord'. . . .

BOSTON PUBLIC SCHOOLS

SCHOOL COMMITTEE

15 BEACON STREET, BOSTON 8, MASSACHUSETTS

ATTORNEY

THOMAS S. EISENSTADT

MEMBER

A careful investigation of the facts pertaining to the discharge of Mr Jonathan Kozol reveal that the administration of the Boston Public Schools were fully justified in terminating his service. . . .

It has been established as a fact that Mr Kozol taught the poem 'Ballad of the Landlord' to his class and later distributed mimeographed copies of it to his pupils for home memorization. It is also true that a parent of one of the pupils registered a strong objection to the poem to the school principal. Miss ——, properly carrying out her responsibility to all of the pupils and to their parents, admonished the neophyte teacher for his persistent deviation from the course of study. She further suggested that the poem 'Ballad of the Landlord' was unsuitable for fourth-graders since it could be interpreted as advocating defiance of authority. At this point Mr Kozol became rude and told Miss —— that he was a better judge of good literature than she.

The confirmation of the above facts is adequate justification for the discharge of a temporary teacher hired on a day-to-day trial basis. It has been stated quite adequately that the curriculum of this particular school, which is saturated with compensatory programmes in an effort to specially assist disadvantaged pupils, does allow for innovation and creative teaching. However, this flexibility does not and should not allow for a teacher to implant in the minds of young children any and all ideas. Obviously, a measure of control over the course of study is essential to protect the 94,000 Boston school children from ideologies and concepts not acceptable to our way of life. Without any restrictions, what guarantees would parents have that their children were not being taught that Adolf Hitler and Nazism were right for Germany and beneficial to mankind? . . .

In conclusion, I must add that Mr Kozol did bring to his pupils an enthusiastic spirit, a high degree of initiative, and other fine qualities found in the best teachers. It is my hope that Mr Kozol will develop his latent talents and concomitantly develop an understanding and respect for the value of working within the acceptable codes of behaviour.

Adults with reading and spelling problems

There has been a steadily growing interest in the problems of adults who wish to improve their standards of literacy, and provision has expanded considerably during the last 10 or 15 years (Haviland, 1973). With the establishment in 1975 of the Adult Illiteracy Resource Agency, the need to investigate needs and to improve services was officially recognized.

We do not know how many adults would benefit from further instruction in basic literacy skills, but there is little doubt that those at present receiving help (approx. 5,200 in 1972 according to Haviland) are a very small proportion of those who would enrol if facilities were readily accessible in all parts of the country. Various authorities have estimated that there are between 1,000,000 and 3,000,000 adults who are able to make little or no effective use of the printed word.

Voluntary agencies (notably the British Association of Settlements and Social Action Schemes) and professional bodies (notably the National Association for Remedial Education) have played an important part in drawing attention to the problem. The Home Office has also taken steps to provide special courses in prisons and borstals. Press, radio, and television have given much-needed publicity to pioneer efforts, and LEAs have begun to respond to all these initiatives. Some have relaxed the common requirement that classes must include at least eleven students, and others have modified their programmes in such a way that real 'non-starters' are no longer deterred by class teaching aimed at potential examination candidates. However, Clyne (1973) found that 48 per cent of the LEAs were still making no provision at all. The BAS Adult Literacy Group (1974) concluded that 'at best we are managing to help around half a per cent of the people in need.'

It is not easy for an LEA to provide adult literacy programmes on a big scale, since by doing so it would be implicitly admitting to deficiencies in its provision for children. Interestingly, the NARE Survey (NARE, 1972) showed that adult students ascribed their difficulties first and foremost to poor teaching. Next they blamed their own truancy, which at the very least, suggests a mismatch between pupil-need and school curriculum.

In a relatively new field there is no consensus about successful methods and types of provision, nor about cost-effectiveness. Another major deterrent to expansion is the shortage of well-trained professionals. Doubts about whether to reduce group size by recruiting and training volunteer tutors are also perplexing LEA administrators and others.

The NARE Survey showed that almost half (46 per cent) of 1,125 adults enrolled in basic literacy programmes were aged 15–20. The ratio of males to females was 4:1. Teachers estimated that about half of the students were average in intelligence and in verbal expression, and that a small proportion (5 per cent) was clearly above average. However, only 9 per cent were in skilled occupations, and 12 per cent were unemployed. This is perhaps not surprising in view of the fact that 46 per cent were said to be below the seven-year level in reading, with a further 30 per cent with RAs between seven and nine years. It is clear that there is a considerable waste of potential here, as well as a great deal of avoidable hardship and personal distress.

Overwhelmingly, the students who completed the NARE questionnaire mentioned vocational reasons and self-improvement as the major reasons for enrolling in courses. A comparison with Haviland's data obtained from teachers shows that, unfortunately, the interests of teachers and students do not always coincide. While everyone hoped to see increased independence, confidence and coping with everyday life (especially tutors working for voluntary agencies), only 5 per cent of the teachers thought of their role primarily in terms of enabling students to obtain better or more satisfying jobs. Only 41 per cent of the teachers used job or skill-related material in their teaching, and only 41 per cent helped students to cope with official forms.

In view of the fact that successful learning is primarily a function of motivation, it would appear that teachers who can respond to the personal and vocational interests of their adult students should be able to achieve excellent results. Admittedly, there are often deeply ingrained feelings of inadequacy, resentment, etc. to be overcome, but this can be achieved in various ways. The formal, if not sinister image of Teacher must be avoided, and somehow the buoyant feeling of a fresh start must be created.

Stevenson (1972) described how this can be regularly and reliably achieved in the rather special context of an Army School of Preliminary Education. Working with men reading below the eight-year level, coming from extremely deprived backgrounds, with a high incidence of interrupted education and truancy, mean gains of four years were achieved during an 11 week intensive course of 20 hours instruction per week. Controlled experiments showed that the use of ITA and the introduction of typewriters as basic tools in the Remedial Centre were the two main factors in helping to create the sense of a new opportunity. The motivation to reach minimal army standards of literacy was also, of course, an important variable.

Others have emphasized personal individual contact as the key to the problem. It may well be significant that schemes which use individual tutorial methods, very often rely on volunteers who can establish an informal friendly contact perhaps more easily than many teachers. As mentioned in Chapter 6, Edwards found that sixth-form volunteers 'hit it off' very successfully with adult students. Yet another approach, which was developed at the NSMHC Centre for Learning Disabilities, is to use a multiplicity of resources including tape-recorded instruction, teachers, volunteers, teaching machines, vocationally orientated programmes, home study assignments, personal counselling and informal club-like activities.

It is clear that individual learning needs have to be met if adults are to overcome their reading and spelling problems. Haviland recommended a broadly-based educational strategy, including the investigation of 'television instruction, programmed learning material and self-instruction lessons.' A REHAB[1] working party (1974) pleaded for the establishment of centres which could serve as foci for in-service training on a multi-disciplinary basis. Booth and others (1974) put forward a similar model, suggesting that these centres should be used both for children and for adults. They also argued that LEAs should set up introductory training courses for 'community tutors' who might then work either on a voluntary or on a paid basis. There is an enormous untapped pool of willing helpers – well-meaning people who are looking for opportunities to exercise a sense of social responsibility.

While much can be done within a purely educational framework, it is important that the problems of adults with reading and spelling difficulties should be considered in a wider context. The policy document prepared by the BAS Adult Literacy Group urged the Government to 'enter into a firm commitment to eradicate adult illiteracy. They also considered that the CBI, the TUC, the media and publishers had important parts to play.' As recommended in the REHAB report, attempts could be made to simplify the text of official documents and public notices. The written element in various examinations could be minimized for certain candidates, and aids such as dictaphones and typewriters could be made available to students and to employees who

[1]British Council for the Rehabilitation of the Disabled.

would otherwise be handicapped. Remedial groups could be set up in industry and in vocational training centres, and careers officers and disablement resettlement officers could be made aware of the special needs of potentially able but dyslexic clients. The involvement of other government departments such as DEP and DHSS would hopefully result in a more practical approach, with programmes closely geared to vocational and social, as well as to educational needs. Much of the long-term cost to the community of inadequate educational provision is at present met by these departments and by the Home Office, who would surely welcome an opportunity to participate in preventive work.

An appraisal of some diagnostic tests for backward readers

Introduction

Many backward readers respond to remedial teaching irrespective of the method used. It is not unknown for a pupil described as handicapped in one or more sensorimotor channels to make remarkable progress simply in response to the emotional climate of a small group. Moreover, there are in ordinary schools many children who do not fail in reading, although they have limited powers of perception. Yet diagnostic testing will invariably show that such pupils have already developed basic skills to such levels as may be thought essential for success in reading. Careful analysis of the decoding and encoding processes involved in reading makes it possible to estimate the critical levels of skill without which a pupil is unlikely to respond to sympathetic teaching and/or psychological treatment. A child may initially fall behind because of perceptual or motor weakness, but when referred for remedial teaching several years later may respond without specialized help, because his skills have developed in the interim. Some backward readers have minor speech defects, some are unable to discriminate between similar-sounding words, and some have a poor command of language structure. These defects can be accentuated when, at the same time, the child is trying to decode a word visually, or when he is *consciously* trying to blend phonemes, while still keeping part of his attention on the sense of the passage. Other children fail to respond to the visual cues for the identification of letters, graphemes, syllables or words, because of perceptual defects or directional confusion. Some fail to grasp concepts of orientation and left-to-right sequence, while others are unable to achieve the perceptual integration of parts within a whole. Here again, failure is most commonly experienced when the reader tries to do everything at once (i.e. visual decoding, visual–auditory–vocal association, auditory–vocal sequencing, and apprehension of meaning).

Diagnostic testing should aim to assess relevant functions, both separately and in combination. A judgement has to be made as to whether observed difficulties are primary or are simply consequences of prolonged failure. Auditory, visual and kinaesthetic tests will show whether phonemes, syllables or words can be handled as units in each sensorimotor channel. An individual learning programme can then be planned, which may be designed either to remedy or to circumvent certain weaknesses, presenting information in such units as the pupil can assimilate. In view of the interaction between the processes involved, it is reasonable to expect that only rarely will tests reveal a single specific defect in an otherwise normal child; and it is most unlikely that a single remedial exercise will overcome a severe learning disability. However, it is usually possible to decide whether perceptual or motor training is worth trying and whether additional props and cues should be supplied. Kirk and Kirk (1971) described some common patterns of disabilities as diagnosed with the Illinois Test of Psycholinguistic Abilities (Kirk and others, 1968), and put forward some useful guidelines for remediation.

Sound and symbol

The average word contains two to three syllables (only about one-sixth of adult speech is monosyllabic). Each syllable is made up of phonemes, varying in number between one and seven. There are many hundreds of different spoken syllables in common use, but in all only 49 phonemes (including diphthongs). In English, there is almost a one-to-one correspondence between sound (phoneme) and written symbol (grapheme) for consonants, but a one-many overlapping correspondence for vowels: about 120 vowel graphemes are used to represent 17 vowel sounds.

The irregularity of English spelling is an important cause of reading difficulty (Lee, 1960). Reading tests were given to 211 normal schoolchildren (CA seven to 13 years). Lee found that 'about one-fifth of the misreadings of isolated words appeared to involve the attribution to letters of sound-values they possessed in other words'. From an analysis of the spelling of nonsense words, Lee was able to conclude that 'on the whole . . . the children had formed no mental association between speech-sounds, if indeed they were aware of these as units into which a word could be analysed and the most frequent ways, from the point of view of a non-positional analysis, of representing them. This was true at least of the vowel sounds. . . . It was not so true of the consonant sounds with several of which there was first and second place correspondence.'

While phonemes are cued by distinctive sound-wave patterns and by manner of articulation, graphemes are cued by the shape, orientation, left–right ordinal position and number of their constituent letters. It would be a mammoth task to devise reliable tests which would assess each of the above aspects of phoneme-grapheme correspondence in isolation. What we have is a mixed bag of largely unreliable measures, some of them dealing with several different skills at once, and others dealing with processes which are related to but are different from reading itself. Some of these are believed to measure 'underlying' cognitive skills, such as spatial ability and memory factors. We shall now consider a selection of published and unpublished tests, together with relevant research findings.

Auditory discrimination

Monroe (1932) and Wepman (1958) have produced short tests of the ability to discriminate between pairs of similar-sounding words spoken by an examiner. Monroe's test is perhaps preferable because the vocabulary level is simpler, especially for English children, and because there are equal numbers of 'same' and 'different' pairs. A poor performance may indicate hearing loss, poor speech habits, or deficient powers of auditory analysis. Reed's Picture Screening Test of Hearing (1960) should be used if deafness is suspected, and children failing on this should be referred for audiometry. Daniels and Diack's Test 6 (1958) is not suitable for this purpose, as it presupposes that the child understands what is meant by the *first* sound in a word, and as the choices of initial consonant sound indicated by the pictures include phonemes which are likely to be confused only by severely deaf children.

A teacher can usually judge whether poor speech habits reflect a child's social milieu, or whether they arise from a motor articulatory disability. If there is any doubt, a speech therapist should be consulted.

Defective auditory discrimination, if not associated with slight deafness of indistinct speech, is usually linked with other symptoms of inaccurate auditory analysis. Crookes and Greene (1963) described a group of backward readers with poor auditory discrimination who were found to have additional problems of auditory sequencing, difficulty in imitating blends and grammatical constructions, poor memory for the names of things and people, and limited digit span.

Monroe's test was one of a large battery administered to five-year-olds by de Hirsch and others (1966). It predicted progress in reading during the first two years of school better than Stanford–Binet IQs. Weiner, Wepman and Morency (1965) gave the Wepman Test of Auditory Discrimination to groups of advanced and retarded readers (CA six to seven years) matched for age and Peabody Picture Vocabulary scores. The good readers obtained significantly higher scores on

Wepman's test (p<0·01). The author gave Monroe's test to 29 children in one junior school, all of whom were more than two years backward in reading (CA eight to nine years, RA (Burt) four to seven years). As many as 15 children made three or more errors each, a level of performance which indicated difficulty *in seven-year-olds* according to Monroe's norms. The test is not designed for older children but clinical experience shows that the norms for seven-year-olds may be used as an index of the level of difficulty likely to prove a real handicap in reading. None of the nine children who made four or more errors each in the above study was able to blend four phonemes reliably, thus betraying additional sequencing problems. The author is at present developing a Discrimination of Phonemes (DOP) test which promises to give a better spread of scores and to be more readily understood by the child than auditory discrimination tests of the Wepman type.

Immediate memory and sequencing skills

Alwitt (1963) compared a group of backward readers with controls on the oral reporting of visually presented digits, both with and without an interval between exposure and report. In both conditions the backward readers had lower mean scores, but there was no evidence to suggest that they had a faster decay rate of immediate memory. The number of items grasped at once was what really mattered. Alwitt's finding adds weight to other reports that a limited digit span and associated sequencing difficulties are symptomatic of reading disability (e.g. Altus, 1956; Kallos and others, 1961; Kass, 1966; Reid and Schoer, 1966; Lyle, 1969; Bakker, 1972; Klasen, 1972; Rugel, 1974). It is worth noting that the three 'sequencing' subtest scores of the Wechsler Intelligence Scale for Children (Digit Span, Coding and Arithmetic) which are most frequently depressed in cases of reading disability are also characteristically low in children diagnosed as 'brain-injured' (Hopkins, 1964), as well as in those described as 'anxious' (Maxwell, 1961). It is also important to observe that Coding subtest scores are not significantly depressed in girls with reading difficulties (Moseley, 1972b; Klasen, 1972).

From the age of seven, the average child is able to repeat five randomly ordered digits, letters, phonemes (if he is familiar with them as pronounced in isolation), or names. If these items are ordered, not randomly but in such a way that they can be grouped into meaningful units (e.g. WIP4AR or co-co-nut), several groups can be retained, and thus many more items can be handled at once. If a child is to learn to read phoneme by phoneme, he needs to be able to blend at least four phonemes reliably in order to group speech sounds into meaningful monosyllables. Syllabic and whole-word recognition methods may be used with pupils unable to blend more than three sounds, provided that their powers of visual discrimination are unimpaired.

Chall and others (1963) found that auditory blending ability at six years was moderately correlated with oral and silent reading two to three years later, and that this ability was quite unrelated to IQ ($r = 0.03$). Similarly, de Hirsch and others found that Monroe's test of phoneme blending (1932) gave some indication of likely progress in reading between the ages of five and seven. The author devised a similar test (Blending of Phonemes – BOP), and gave it to 41 children (CA nine to 12 years) attending a remedial centre. Only 14 children were able to blend five phonemes reliably, when the phonemes in monosyllabic words like 'crisp' were articulated by the examiner at the rate of one per second. A group of nine children who failed to blend four phonemes reliably were individually matched for age and verbal intelligence (Wechsler) with nine others who made no errors on the test. It was found that the poor blenders were significantly more retarded in reading than the competent blenders ($p < 0.01$, Mann-Whitney U Test, 1-tailed). The difference between means was 18 months in word recognition, as measured by the Burt test. The phoneme blending test was also given to the 29 backward second year juniors mentioned above. It was found that none of these children was able to blend five phonemes reliably, and 16 of them were unable to blend three-phoneme words reliably.

If a blending test is intended to measure auditory processes, it must be aurally presented. Schonell's test R5 (1950) involves blending, but is primarily a test of the knowledge of grapheme-phoneme correspondence, in the form of word-recognition. Daniels and Diack's Diagnostic Word Recognition Tests (1958) do have the merit of distinguishing between monosyllables and polysyllables, and between graphically simple and graphically complex words, but it is possible to miss a poor blender with these tests, as many of the words may be recognized on a 'look and say' basis. Ideally, equivalent lists of words should be presented both aurally and visually, for both oral and written response, involving the blending of (a) phonemes within a syllable, (b) syllables within a word. When an oral response is asked for, it is wise to ask the pupil to repeat the sounds himself before blending them, so that the factors of articulation, memory span and closure (blending) can be considered separately. There are some children who can repeat, but cannot close: some of these have had little practice in blending and some translate the spoken phonemes into letters, thus confusing themselves with letter names or with irrelevant visual imagery.

In both reading and writing, a variety of strategies may be used; broadly, auditory, visual or kinaesthetic. After giving a diagnostic test, it is often useful to ask a child whether he 'listened to the sounds and put them together', 'saw the letters in his mind,' or 'imagined himself writing'. There may be a sex difference in decoding and encoding strategy. Beard (1956) found that a representative sample of 15-year-old boys tended to remember digits and sentences, to recognize mutilated words and to complete words and phrases through the use of visual imagery, while girls relied much more upon auditory and verbal skills (n=145).

'Diagnostic' word-recognition tests like those of Daniels and Diack, Williams (1970), Carver (1970), and McLeod and Atkinson (1972) make demands on both auditory and visual memory. Carver reported very satisfactory reliability and validity data for his test, including a factor analysis which identified a specific visual memory factor on which boys performed much better than girls. Some of these tests have a multiple-choice format, which creates an emphasis on correct serial identification of letters and sounds. All are designed to identify several categories of error such as initial letter substitutions, letter rotations and distortions, short vowel confusions, changes of letter order, errors in word-endings, initial and final multiple consonants, vowel digraphs, irregular sight words, etc. The author (1975) has developed a method of scoring Carver's test objectively, so that it is possible to tell whether a child makes a normal or an unusual number of errors of each kind for the particular stage he has reached in learning to read. A factor analysis of nine error categories identified four factors: omission of sounds, auditory confusion, changes in letter order, and visual confusion of single letters and vowel digraphs. McLeod and Atkinson's Domain Test of Phonic Skills is relatively time-consuming, but it is the only test of its kind to include enough examples of each phonic element (st, ar, etc.) to permit diagnostic interpretation at the level of individual graphemes. Williams' Swansea Test of Phonic Skills is decidedly unsatisfactory for diagnostic purposes. For example, in the section testing reading of initial letter blends, 11 of the 24 marks could be scored for reading the initial letter only; in nonsense words like narm and dorn, the 'r' is not treated as part of a vowel digraph; vowel digraphs such as ee and ai are omitted; common consonant confusions such as b/d, g/j, ch/sh are inadequately covered; and at least one item is ambiguous. The Daniels and Diack and Carver tests are not entirely exempt from criticisms of this kind, but as it is left to the teacher to draw up his own error profiles, misinterpretations can be avoided. Of these four tests, only the Domain has the advantage of linking error-profiles to specific remedial exercises. It also enables the factor of word length to be evaluated independently of the vowel graphemes used.

Schonell's Visual Discrimination Test (1950) is a test of immediate visual memory, although word recognition and previously acquired knowledge of spelling can affect the results. This test also draws attention to reversals of letter shape and order which may or may not be side-effects of a limited immediate memory span. Graham and Kendall's Memory for Designs Test (1960) and Benton's Revised Visual Retention Test (1963) measure various aspects of visual perception and memory, as well as visuomotor co-ordination. As the results are often difficult to interpret, a psychologist should be consulted when a disability is suspected in this area. Walters (1961) claimed that Graham and Kendall's test discriminated between groups of good and poor readers (CA seven to nine years), but other studies of visual memory have given equivocal results (e.g. Kendall, 1948; Weiner, Wepman and Morency, 1965). The author gave Wedell's (1960) Light-Tracing Test to 82 educationally subnormal children (CA 12 to 15 years, RA four to 13 years, IQ 45 to 95). No manual response is required in this test, as the subject has to identify on a multiple-choice card the pattern previously traced by a moving point of light. It was found that the only type of error which was significantly correlated with reading quotient (Burt–Vernon) was the poor organization of elements correctly perceived, resulting in a simplified, more symmetrical pattern. It is not unreasonable to believe that those children who rapidly forget the position, orientation and serial order of visual stimuli are likely to be handicapped in learning to read. Hirshoren's (1969) results with the ITPA visual-motor sequential subtest, in which a relatively high predictive validity was established, underline the point.

Visual perception

Ffookes (1965) has produced a useful test of visual acuity which is particularly suitable for non-readers because it does not depend on the discrimination of letter orientation or sequence. As we shall see, some backward readers (especially young ones) find this kind of discrimination difficult and may therefore give unreliable responses on the conventional 'E' test.

Wechsler and Hagin (1964) devised a 'Lamb Chop' test. The child has to identify the orientation of a simple figure (matching or memory task), given a card bearing the same figure in eight different spatial transformations. Susceptibility to all kinds of perceptual rotation (except 90-degrees rotations) was significantly more frequent in the lowest than in the highest quartile of reading ability (n=50, CA six to seven years). The test proved to be too easy for older children. Gibson and others (1962) carried out a valuable developmental study of

H

shape-matching, using letter-like forms. It was found that all types of error studied (orientation, substitution, fragmentation and closure) tended to disappear between the ages of four and seven, and were rarely found in eight-year-olds. These authors point out that rotations and reversals are not distinctive features for object discrimination, so that previous experience with objects does not transfer to the task of identifying the orientation of letters and words. Daniels and Diack (1958) have devised a Visual Discrimination and Orientation Test which measures most of the visuospatial skills essential to letter- and word-recognition. Frostig's Developmental Test of Visual Perception (1961) is supposed to measure five different aspects of visual perception, but this claim is not supported by factor analysis (Corah and Powell, 1963). However, the Position in Space subtest is useful in picking out children who are subject to confusions of orientation (Chapman and Wedell, 1972). The Frostig Test, as a whole, has been shown to have little predictive value so far as reading is concerned (Jacobs and others, 1968).

It has been established that tests of visual similarities and differences, picture completion, shape discrimination and spatial orientation are correlated with reading ability, and can give more specific diagnostic information than intelligence tests (Goins, 1958; Potter, 1949). But are visuo-spatial tests useful with older backward readers who have made a start in reading and spelling? The evidence here is equivocal, but in general it seems that such tests are less useful with older children. However, Whipple and Kodman (1968) have shown that backward readers of junior school age often perform badly on tests involving *difficult* visual discrimination and perceptual learning, compared with controls of the same age and intelligence.

Lovell, Gray and Oliver (1964) found that Block Designs, Weinstein's test of spatial orientation, Shapiro's rotation test and a test of pattern copying failed to discriminate between retarded and non-retarded groups of 14- to 15-year-olds, matched for age and intelligence. There was, however, a significant difference on the Gottschaldt hidden figure tests. The mean reading age of the retarded readers was 9·5 years (Watts–Vernon), so it is not surprising that tests of the precise imitation of shape and position should prove irrelevant. At this level, the reading task involves instant recognition of complex and infrequent graphemes against an ever-changing background, not unlike the Gottschaldt stimulus situation.

Mirror-imaging is a phenomenon which is simple to define, and which for many a teacher and research worker retains the fascination of a discovery first made in childhood. For these reasons (and for others, perhaps more esoteric), mirror images have been given undue significance in the diagnosis of reading disability. Goins (1958) and Wechsler and Hagin (1964) reported that excessive mirror-imaging was associated with poor reading in six-year-olds, as were other orientational errors. However, Wechsler and Hagin found that good readers made almost as many mirror-image reversals as poor readers in the eight to nine age-group. In his study of 82 educationally sub-normal children (yet to be reported in detail), the author found that, although there was a significant age-trend in mirror-imaging between the ages of 12 and 15, there was no correlation between mirror-imaging and reading attainment (r=0·02). The mean reading age of these children was 8·2 years (s.d.=1·9), and at this level the proportion of errors due to the confusion of 'b' and 'd', 'p' and 'q' is small. Many authors have claimed that backward readers (or certain types of back-ward reader) are especially prone to 'reversals', but have, like Witty and Kopel (1936) classed mirror-images together with rotations and sequential errors as types of 'reversal', when they are, in all probability, independent effects. The author knows of no study showing that mirror images *per se* are of diagnostic significance. They are ignored by Graham and Kendall in the assessment of 'brain-damage' with the Memory for Designs Test. However, rotations and impairment of spatial sequencing *are* important diagnostic signs, especially where neurological dysfunction is suspected (Kinsbourne and Warrington, 1963).

Visuomotor co-ordination

It is important to realize that the motor element involved in copying and drawing may be quite unrelated to any perceptual factors involved in object and picture perception. Pencil control lags behind two-dimensional shape perception by several years, and the ability to copy letters and words can lag several years behind reading ability. Heinrich (1968) found that good readers who performed badly on Bender's (1938) Visual Motor Gestalt Test did so because of poor motor control. They had much less difficulty in assembling and matching similar shapes. Zach and Kaufman (1972) found that for 70 normal five- to six-year-olds the tasks of copying the Bender designs and matching them (using a four-choice match-to-sample paradigm) were com-pletely unrelated (r=0·19).

Thweatt (1963) and de Hirsch and others are among those who claim that the Bender Gestalt Test predicts reading progress during the first two years of school. On the other hand, Keogh (1965) found that it did not, when IQ was held constant. If a child cannot copy simple figures accurately, he is likely to have trouble in learning the shapes of letters, especially for writing. Once he has mastered this, however, he will not be unduly handicapped in his reading by an inability to maintain exact proportion and detail when copying. Care should be taken, therefore, in assessing performance in copying complex designs in unstandardized tests such as Daniels and Diack's Test 2. Only grossly inaccurate reproductions suggesting an impairment of visual perception are likely to be significant. Lachmann (1960) found that older retarded readers and controls (CA eight to 12 years) made similar errors on the Bender test, most of which suggested slight difficulties of motor execution. Ninety-degree rotations occurred just as often among the good readers. In the author's sample of 41 children (CA nine to 12 years) attending a remedial centre, only eight achieved a perfect performance in copying the three most difficult Bender figures, but these were not more advanced in reading than the others. In clinical practice one sometimes finds that children whose visuomotor co-ordination is at the six- to seven-year level are able to read and spell at the ten- to eleven-year level. On the other hand, if eye-movement control or visual perception itself is severely impaired, reading and spelling is not likely to progress beyond the stage of simple letter-sound associations, aided by phoneme-blending.

Both Silverman (1962) and Bakker (1972) found that kinaesthetic memory is not significantly weak in poor readers. This suggests that a kinaesthetically-based method is inappropriate in most cases. Unfortunately, there is no simple test which will indicate whether a child with visual impairment is able to learn by a motor-kinaesthetic approach, such as Fernald's tracing technique (1943). There may be some children with this potential who are confused by fragmentary, scrambled or perseverating information from other defective sensory channels. However, in cases of neurological dysfunction, it is not uncommon for fine motor control to be affected and for tactile-kinaesthetic sensations to be confused (Illingworth, 1963; Francis-Williams, 1963; Wedell, 1973). Children who are evidently clumsy or have unusual difficulty in drawing, copying and writing should be referred for full neurological and psychological assessment.

Perceptual integration and associative learning

In learning to decode print, children pass from a stage in which words look like meaningless squiggles to a point at which the apprehension of meaning is virtually immediate. To begin with, unfamiliar words are not perceived as units, and links have to be formed between visual, auditory, kinaesthetic and semantic elements. While these links are being established (an associative learning process), significant demands are made on immediate memory systems. Verbal coding and the grouping of meaningful units are two linguistic skills involved in this learning process. As a child progresses, reading and writing become increasingly integrated with other language skills, and it becomes difficult if not impossible to isolate the parts played by different sensory modalities and memory systems, unless relatively pure (i.e. association-free) stimuli are used.

Katz and Deutsch (1967) carried out an ingenious experiment in which children had to lift a finger whenever they saw a light or heard a tone. They showed that backward readers were much slower to react than good readers only when light unexpectedly followed sound or vice-versa. This difference obtained throughout the age range six to 12 and could not be attributed to IQ differences. In another experiment, they found that backward boys had relatively more difficulty with a visual vigilance task than with an auditory one, when compared with normal readers. These results show that backward readers do have difficulty in maintaining and in switching attention rapidly.

Several experiments have been carried out on the ability to match series of taps, dots, lights, etc. presented in different or with the same sense modality (Birch and Belmont, 1964; Blank and Bridger, 1966; Muehl and Kremenak, 1966; Sterritt, 1966; Cashdan, 1970). Some of these have apparently shown that the inter-modality variable is not an important one with regard to reading. This may be because the tasks involved did not require a rapid inter-modal switching of attention, as in the study of Katz and Deutsch. Moreover, both Blank and Bridger and Cashdan have shown that the differences between backward readers and controls on these can be explained in terms of verbal coding strategies. Cashdan found that backward readers performed better if the series of taps was described to them verbally before being presented. This may be taken to imply that backward readers who are unable to describe the structure of words may learn better if they are taught to identify and name consonants, vowels, digraphs, etc., and to describe their position and function.

Muehl and Kremenak did, however, find that in first grade beginning readers (CA six to seven years) the auditory/auditory test results (using a series of bleeps) were not correlated with reading ability, unlike the auditory/visual and visual/auditory forms. Here there was a substantial correlation both with letter-naming and with reading achievement, even when IQ was controlled.

It is not clear whether poor performance on these tasks results from attentional, memory, or associational deficiencies. Much work remains to be done in this field, and it is probable that educationally relevant tests will eventually be produced.

Measures of learning rate are a promising line of inquiry, but there are at present few suitable tests on the market. Craik (1968) found that associative learning ability was correlated with letter-naming and reading in first-grade children, but that measures of selective (multiple-choice) learning were not. Further evidence that paired-associate and serial learning is a factor in learning to read which is partially independent of IQ has been put forward by Silverman (1962), Katz and Deutsch and Giebink and Goodsell (1968). The Symbols Test described by Evans (1972) requires the child to learn six word/symbol associations and to apply them in a simulated reading task. This test has a short-term test-retest reliability of 0·76, and may well prove to be valuable in remedial work as well as in infant departments.

Laterality

The large-scale surveys of Douglas and others (1967) and Rutter and others (1970) have conclusively shown that handedness, eyedness and crossed laterality have nothing to do with reading attainment. Woody and Phillips (1934), Witty and Kopel (1936), Gates and Bond (1936) and Hillman (1956) also found identical distributions of degrees of left- and right-handedness and eyedness in populations of backward readers and in controls of equivalent intelligence. Other workers who have reported on increased incidence of sinistrality or of ambiguous and mixed laterality among backward readers have failed to control for intelligence level (Dearborn, 1933; Galifret-Granjon and Ajuriaguerra, 1951; Harris, 1957). Gordon (1920) found that left-handedness was more than twice as common among the educationally subnormal (n=4620) as among ordinary children (n=3298). Rutter and others confirmed this finding, and also showed that mixed-handedness and eyedness was more common among subnormals than in the control sample. The slight, but not significant, tendency for there to be an excess of left-handed children among 86 children with specific reading retardation disappeared when the six children with IQs below 70 were eliminated from the group. Naidoo (1961) found that children of ambiguous handedness were significantly inferior in verbal intelligence, often having histories of birth complications and slow speech development.

The author gave a stereoscopic test of eye dominance to 46 children attending a remedial centre. Nineteen were left-eyed, 19 right-eyed and eight gave indeterminate results. Mean reading ages (Burt), verbal IQs (Weschler), mirror-image and letter-order errors (Schonell R6) for strongly left-eyed, indeterminate and strongly right-eyed groups were almost identical.

It will be noted that 50 per cent of this population of backward readers were left-eyed. A stereoscopic test is in no way affected by hand preference, as are conventional sighting tests, and so may be expected to give a larger proportion of left-sided results. Using a sighting test suggested by Asher (personal communication), which minimizes the effects of hand-preference, the author found that 42 per cent of 89 unselected junior-school children (CA ten to 11 years) were left-eyed compared with 45 per cent of 31 pupils at a Remedial Centre.

Keller (1937) found that eye dominance had no effect upon the span of visual apprehension in left or right eyes, nor upon the recall of letters presented on the left or right of a card. Flescher (1960) concluded that no one combination of eyedness and handedness was related to the perception of, or to the ability to read, mirror images, 90-degree rotations, or inversions. Beck (1961) reported that no more reading reversals were made whether words were presented to one eye (dominant or non-dominant) or to both. 'Crossed' laterals made no more reversals than others and neither did those with poor knowledge of left and right.

One can safely conclude that eye dominance is probably a randomly distributed characteristic, quite irrelevant to reading disability. Other aspects of lateral preference, such as direction of visual scanning, left/right visual field differences (McFie, 1952), or left/right direction of strokes in drawing (Shepherd, 1956) may eventually prove to be more relevant, but the *experimentum crucis* has yet to be carried out.

Some practical implications

Children with specific learning disabilities should first be given practice in the basic skills which have not yet been mastered. Some will respond immediately, others will not. After such a trial period, the teacher can decide how best to teach the individual pupil and the child will understand that there are good reasons for the use of special cues, methods or remedial activities.

If a pupil is unable to blend at least four phonemes reliably, he should not be taught by a conventional phonic method unless he is even more severely handicapped in other modalities. He may respond to purely auditory–vocal practice in blending, as described by Moseley (1973). Writing to phonic dictation can be introduced, as long as word-length is kept within the pupil's blending capacity. If he simply *cannot* blend phonemes, he may be able to learn to recognize syllables as units if they are separated in writing and print or cued by bold print or colour.

In cases of limited visual span/memory, a phonic approach may lead to good results and the initial teaching alphabet may be helpful if the additional number of letters for visual discrimination does not prove too much of a burden. If eye-movements or visual perception are seriously impaired, it is necessary to simplify the task of grapheme recognition. Again, this can be achieved through the use of bold print or colour coding.

Slight motor incoordination and dyspraxia are often unrelated to reading disability, as are handedness and eyedness. Children should not be selected for remedial teaching because they are slightly clumsy or because they are not firmly lateralized. A number of backward readers do, of course, have these symptoms and such pupils are unlikely to benefit from a motor-kinaesthetic method of teaching reading. However, if a motor disability manifests itself in faulty articulation, speech training exercises are valuable.

Backward readers are children who have failed to cope with the complexity of the task which faces them. They need to tackle the problem step by step, mastering basic skills first singly and then in combination. They are usually acutely aware of their own deficiencies and prefer to avoid situations in which they are reminded of them. Careful diagnosis can give a child the reassuring feeling that he is not going to be asked to perform tasks which are beyond him, and without a feeling of confidence there can be no panacea.

Table of percentile points and equivalent standard scores

Reference to the table below is meaningful only when test results are expressed as *standard* scores with a mean of 100 and a standard deviation of 15, not as *quotients*. The table gives the percentage of children who will obtain scores up to a given point, *if the population tested is equivalent to the population on which the test was standardized.*

PERCENTILE POINT	STANDARD SCORE	PERCENTILE POINT	STANDARD SCORE
1	65–7	26	90
2	68–70	27	91
3	71–2	28	91
4	73–4	29	92
5	75–6	30	92
6	77	31	93
7	78	32	93
8	79	33	93
9	80	34	94
10	81	35	94
11	82	36	95
12	82	37	95
13	83	38	95
14	84	39	96
15	84	40	96
16	85	41	97
17	86	42	97
18	86	43	97
19	87	44	98
20	87	45	98
21	88	46	98
22	88	47	99
23	89	48	99
24	89	49	100
25	90	50	100

Table continued overleaf

PERCENTILE POINT	STANDARD SCORE	PERCENTILE POINT	STANDARD SCORE
51	100	76	111
52	101	77	111
53	101	78	112
54	102	79	112
55	102	80	113
56	102	81	113
57	103	82	114
58	103	83	114
59	103	84	115
60	104	85	116
61	104	86	116
62	105	87	117
63	105	88	118
64	105	89	118
65	106	90	119
66	106	91	120
67	107	92	121
68	107	93	122
69	107	94	123
70	108	95	124–5
71	108	96	126–7
72	109	97	128–9
73	109	98	130–2
74	110	99	133–5
75	110		

Some practical suggestions for developing perceptual and cognitive skills associated with reading and spelling

---

Teachers often complain that specialists who test and assess children with learning difficulties give them little feedback and no practical advice. They do not know whether this is due to over-work, professional secretiveness, ignorance or malice. Another possibility, less often considered, is caution based on lack of evidence which would justify a detailed prescriptive approach.

Experimental evidence in the field of learning difficulties is slow to accumulate, and tends to focus on precise but relatively unimportant details or else to be too diffuse to support firm conclusions on major issues. In the absence of a few simple prescriptions, it is the responsibility of the individual teacher to adopt a pragmatic, and at times a frankly experimental approach with each pupil. In order to do this, the teacher must be able to select and use reliable methods of assessment, must define his objectives clearly, and must regularly review progress and modify his approach if necessary.

A programme of test-development, assessment, remediation, and in-service training has been set up in the London Borough of Barnet, with the aim of providing skilled help for backward readers in every school. The project began in 1974, when 3,373 top-infants were given the Carver Word Recognition Test, and 405 (12 per cent) of the most backward and retarded were seen individually for further assessment.

A new method of scoring the Carver test was devised, which yielded a profile of different types of error. Teachers were then referred to the following texts for ideas regarding the development of specific reading sub-skills, and for guidance in the selection and use of books and reading schemes: Atkinson and Gains (1973), Bell (1970), Goodacre (1971a), Jackson (1971a), Leevers (1974), Maguire (1974), Mason (1972, 1974), McNicholas and McEntee (1973), Moon (1975), Moyle (1968), Parfit (1974), Raban (1974), Reid (1972), Tansley (1967) and University of Reading Centre for the Teaching of Reading.

Seven other diagnostic tests were given to the children with reading problems and for each of these children a further profile of strengths and weaknesses was drawn up. The tests measure various skills and abilities which underlie or are pre-conditions of learning to read. Three of them were developed especially for this project. All of the tests are intended for use by teachers and yet they cover most of the relevant cognitive and perceptual areas that psychologists normally look at. They are also intended to be of immediate practical value in that the test profile can be translated directly into remedial reading activities. Each of the tests in the battery has an activity sheet or sheets corresponding to it. The titles correspond as follows:

TESTS	ACTIVITY SHEETS
English Picture Vocabulary Test (EPVT)	Language Development Activities
Finding Visual Patterns (POP)	Finding and Making Visual Patterns
Immediate memory for L-R order of pictures (PAWS)	Developing Immediate Visual Memory of Sequentially Perceived Material
Immediate memory for a series of spoken letters (LMS)	Developing Immediate Auditory Memory
Hearing sounds in words (DOP)	Developing the Ability to Discriminate between Sounds
Blending sounds in words (BOP)	Phonic Blending Skills
Learning sights words (WR)	≃ Some Observations on Learning Styles and Strategies

If a child had a weakness on one or more of the tests it was not always suggested that he should be given all (or any) of the activities on the corresponding sheet. It was felt that experience and common sense should be the real guides to action. However, the following tentative generalizations were made:

(1) If a child has no specific difficulties on the tests, his reading failure is likely to be bound up with lack of interest and/or motivation.

(2) If a child has only one or two weak areas, and one or two positive strengths, he may be able to progress if a change of emphasis is made so that he can capitalize on his strengths.

(3) If a child performs badly on the DOP, BOP, and WR tests, this may be because he is unfamiliar with the tasks. A change of method may be appropriate.

(4) If a child has three or more weak areas, it is unlikely that he will progress unless some of the weaknesses are tackled directly and intensively.

(5) If a child performs badly throughout, it is probably best to abandon the use of a reading scheme and to concentrate on pre-reading and other very basic activities. Children who cannot organize their own learning may need regular periods of help, initially at least on a one-to-one basis.

The results of the assessment procedure are to be used by schools as a basis for answering questions such as the following:

(a) should a child be given any extra help with his reading other than that provided by his class teacher?

(b) should the help given consist simply of additional reading practice or should other remedial methods be used?

(c) should the method used have a phonic emphasis?

(d) should the help be on a one-to-one basis or in a group?

(e) should the child be referred for expert remedial help or for other special placement?

Taking the test battery and the Activity Sheets as starting-points for discussion, teachers from more than 30 schools decided to meet regularly in local groups of from two to five schools. They will report on the planning and implementation of individual learning programmes, and will deal with wider issues such as co-operation with parents and class-teachers. Opportunities for making and sharing materials will also undoubtedly arise.

The Activity Sheets are not intended to be a comprehensive guide to the remediation of all kinds of learning difficulty. They do not, for example, say much about motor skills, grammatical accuracy, verbal reasoning or number sense. Throughout, the emphasis is on ways in which the sub-skills of reading and spelling can be developed, so relatively little is said about the possible value of non-linguistic material. The author feels that in both readiness and remedial work this aspect has already received far too much attention. Sabatino and others (1973) confirmed what some would consider to be self-evident: that specific training with abstract shapes or with artificially-created sounds does not transfer to reading whether it is given to 'audiles' or to 'visiles'.

The Activity Sheets are reproduced here so that they can be tried out on a wider scale. It should be understood that they may be revised in the light of experience gained through field-testing.

Language development activities

Language development is a vast teaching area involving the whole curriculum. The following are a small selection of suggestions, chosen because of their direct relevance to reading skills. They fall into three broad areas.

(1) Helping the child to learn specific verbal concepts necessary to the teaching of reading, e.g. next, along, above, below, order, first, last, right, left, after, before.

(2) Helping the child to be aware and make use of the predictability of language, both in grammar and meaning.
Aim: that he be able to 'use context' in reading, applying his expectations of what words are likely to come next and simultaneously evaluating the sense of what he has just read so that he can correct his own mistakes.

(3) Helping the child to extend his vocabulary, to express himself more precisely and to become familiar with the type of language to be found in the books.

As all teachers know, there is no substitute for language development in a context of meaningful experience, where the child is sufficiently interested in his activities to want to communicate and learn new vocabulary and concepts. Nevertheless, there is a place too for more structured language work, for five minutes set aside specifically to learn a new word or skill; the examples here fall into this category.

(1) *Helping the child to learn specific verbal concepts related to reading*
– The vocabulary of order (first, last, next, along, at the end, left, right, after, before, etc.) is particularly important in learning to read. Many children have little understanding of these concepts.
– Left and right: Teach these concepts in relation to actual body movements. A useful start is to stand with your back to the group and ask them to copy your movements: say what you are doing, e.g. touch your head with your left hand, lift your right foot. Slowly phase out your visual model so that the children are just following your verbal instructions.
– Matching a sequence: Using beads or blocks, the teacher stands with her back to the group. She constructs a sequence from left to right and the children copy it. She then makes the sequence again, using words to describe it, e.g. first, next, last, on the right, after. Finally she omits the demonstration and gives the verbal description only; the children listen and make the sequence.
– 'Where is it?' game: Using a sequence of any kind (beads, toy animals, pictures) the teacher asks questions, e.g. Where is the dog?

The child must reply, e.g. at the end of the line, on the left, next to the cat, after the cow. Encourage him to use as many ways as possible to describe the position.

– Following instructions (which may be recorded on tape). Present a series of complex instructions to be followed, e.g. draw first a cross, then a circle, and last a square. On the next line below the cross draw a circle.

– Matching pictures: Find me the picture that shows a brown cat on the left and a black cat next to it.

Published materials[1]

Brake: *Developing Pre-reading Skills, Expressive Language, Spatial Relations*

ILEA: *Language for Learning*, Unit 4: listen, discuss and do. Here a group of four children listen to a tape, and discuss the instructions, riddles, puzzles and stories before responding by drawing and colouring in their books.

Shiach: *Teach Them to Speak*, lessons nos: 1, 3, 17, 19, 25, 26, 37, 41, 54, 56, 68, 72, 79, 80, 92, 97, 99, 109, 113, 129, 131, 141, 145, 150, 175, 180, 189, 192, 197, 198.

(2) *Helping the child to make use of the predictability of language*

– Detecting mistakes in sentences and stories. What's silly about this – the rain poured up from the sky. He ate his milk quickly. The plums grew thick and heavy on the apple tree. Ask the child to make the sentences sound right.

– Completing sentences:

Open-ended: the radio did not work because . . .
             It rained to day so I wore a . . .

Closed: Using grammatical structures: Here is a man, here are two . . .
         A mouse is small, an ant is even . . .

Limited choice: delete (say) every sixth word in a short paragraph, or delete (say) every adjective in a passage. Have the children suggest suitable words for the gaps and discuss their choices.

– Predicting outcomes of stories: Encourage the children to think of as many different endings as possible.

[1]Materials listed here and in later sections of this appendix are not included in the bibliography. For further details please refer to the final section of the appendix: 'Ordering books and materials'.

Published materials
Brake: *Developing Pre-reading Skills, Expressive Language*
Gahagan and Gahagan: *Talk Reform*, pp 34–59
ILEA: *Language for Learning* materials, Unit 2: story telling
Karnes: *Helping Young Children Develop Language Skills*, section VII
Shiach: *Teach them to speak*, lessons nos: 2, 5, 7, *10*, 11, *15*, 18, *20*, 24, *29*, 32, *34*, *39*, 40, 43, *44*, *49*, *55*, 57, *60*, *65*, 66, *67*, *70*, *75*, *76*, *80*, 83, *85*, *88*, *90*, *94*, *98*, *102*, *103*, 104, *108*, 109, *112*, 114, *117*, 118, 119, 120, 121, *122*, *127*, 128, 131, *132*, 134, 136, *137*, 141, *142*, 147, 150, *152*, *153*, *158*, *162*, *167*, 168, *172*, 173, 174, *177*, *182*, 183, *187*, *188*, *193*, 194, 196, 197

NB The lessons in italics are based on stories which may be used for sentence completion activities or for predicting outcomes.

(3) *Putting the child in situations which demand precise and well-ordered expression*

Many children have available a more complex language structure than they find occasion to use. Compare these two classroom situations: in one a pair of children are using Lego. One has made a model and is 'telling' the other how to copy it. The conversation might go like this: 'Put this one here . . . and that one there . . . no, *there*, . . . and that one.' In the second situation there is now a screen between the children, so that the one who has made the model must communicate without the aid of pointing, gesture, helping, etc. This time the conversation might go: 'Make a square, out of five red blocks each side. On top of these put blue blocks . . . leave a gap of one block in the middle of one side for the window.' At the end the children compare their models, to see where the verbal instructions went wrong.

It is clear that it is the second type of situation which the teacher interested in language development wishes to create: situations where children cannot rely on a shared context to convey meaning, but must use words – the right words in the right order. The teacher can work with the child herself, taking turns in communication so that she provides a model of precise speech; alternatively she can pair a verbal with a less verbal child, again providing for imitation. Suggested activities are:

– Pairs of children, communicating through a screen or by telephone. Each pair has two identical sets of materials to be assembled: coloured blocks, peg board and pegs, Lego, toy animals for a farm. One child instructs his partner how to copy his assembly.

or each has paper and pencil: one child does a drawing and instructs the other how to copy it.

or each has an identical road map and a model car. One child marks
out a route and then tells the other child how to follow the same
route.

or each has an identical box of materials, varying in texture, colour,
pattern, shape, size. One child chooses a piece, describes it, and the
other child tries to pick the same piece.

or each child has a set of pictures: one chooses and describes, the
other tries to identify it. Careful choice of highly similar pictures
in the set can force the child to make precise use of tense, adjectives,
propositions, etc. e.g. the girl has drunk some milk/the girl is going
to drink some milk; there is a tall boy with brown hair sitting at a
table/there is a small boy with fair hair sitting under a table.

– Tell me how: ask the child, without using gestures, to tell you
how he brushes his teeth, gets to school, puts on socks.

– My friend: ask a child to choose in his head another class member
and describe him (without using a name) so that the others can guess
who he is. Then ask him to tell one way in which he and his friend are
alike, one way in which they are different.

– Grab bag: items are felt by or shown to the children one at a time
in a covered container. Each child tells what he has in as much detail
as possible e.g. (an orange) – it is round, and juicy. It has seeds. I eat it.
It is a fruit. Others guess what it is. Encourage the child to say what
the object is *not*, as well as what it is, e.g. it has no straight lines, it is
not yellow, it is not a vegetable.

– Riddles: make up riddles about objects which are not there in the
room, so that the child has to think and talk in the abstract.

– Twenty questions: I am thinking of a piece of furniture. What is it?
Child has to ask questions requiring a yes or no answer.

– Oral composition through pictures: Start with a single picture,
and move on to longer sequences (2, 3, 4, 5 pictures). Comic strips are
also a useful source.

– Listening to stories on tape. This can be done with or without
books, and with or without gaps to fill in by reading or speaking. The
reading should be at a slightly slower pace than usual if the child is
expected to follow in his book, but it is more important to make longer
pauses then to slow down the speech. Instructions to look at the next
page should be inserted.

Published materials
Ainsworth: SRA Listening Laboratory 1b (for use with tape-recorder)
Brake: *Developing Pre-reading Skills, Expressive Language*
Gahagan and Gahagan: *Talk Reform*, pp 34-59

Heaton: *Composition Through Pictures*
Karnes: *Helping Young Children Develop Language Skills*, Parts III, V, VI
Remedial Supply Co: Oral Comprehension Tapes.
   Pictures in Sound. Reason and Write (all for use with tape-recorder).
   Picture-Writing Series. Stories without Words.
Shiach: Teach them to Speak: lessons nos: 1, 2, 7, 8, 9, 11, 13, 14, 16, 21, 23, 30, 31, 35, 37, 38, 40, 42, 43, 45, 46, 47, 50, 51, 53, 56, 61, 62, 74, 77, 86, 87, 92, 93, 95, 101, 105, 106, 107, 110, 115, 121, 123, 125, 129, 131, 133, 134, 135, 136, 138, 139, 140, 143, 144, 146, 148, 157, 161, 165, 166, 168, 170, 171, 176, 181, 187, 190, 191, 192, 194, 195, 196, 199, 200. The stories listed in Section 2 may also be found useful.

Finding and making visual patterns

Visual perception is involved in a great many classroom activities, such as painting, learning from pictures, number work and reading. An extreme weakness in visual perception can impair performance in all these activities. To cope with a normal education all children need to be able to draw simple shapes, to see and understand what is happening in pictures, and to count without using their fingers. These are important skills in their own right, and have no direct connection with reading. Yet a child who has extreme difficulty in organizing visually perceived elements (whether lines, surfaces, figures or letters) into a unified picture or pattern is almost certainly going to find reading difficult.

Whenever attempts have been made to train visual perceptual skills using stimuli other than letters and words, there has been little or no transfer to reading. It seems that once a child with a visual perceptual weakness has reached a very low basic level of visual competence, he then needs specific training in the visual analysis of letter and word patterns if his reading is to improve. For this reason it is suggested that children who are still at a pre-reading level (i.e. Carver stages 1–3) should be taught how to form their letters in a consistent manner. Jones' 'From Left to Write' programme is one effective way of doing this. Another idea is to prepare letter and word writing patterns in dots on Polyart sheets. These can be used again and again, practice hopefully making perfect. Once the writing movement becomes standard for each letter, directional confusions such as b/d, p/q, are less likely to occur, and letters of similar shape such as n/r, i/l are less likely to be confused.

In planning a programme of visual perceptual training using non-linguistic stimuli it is essential to evaluate proposed activities in terms of whether the skills involved are of value in themselves, rather than whether they will facilitate learning to read. In some cases, of course, it is possible to apply skills first developed with shapes or pictures, in the decoding of print. For example, exercises in discriminating objects by orientation alone can lean on to b/d, n/u discriminations. But the transfer will not be automatic – the picture or shape activities are not in themselves enough. Indeed, if the ability to match abstract shapes by their orientation is not considered to be a worthwhile skill in itself, these exercises may well be omitted.

Visual perceptual training should not be thought of as a non-verbal activity. Indeed, ways should constantly be sought of linking language with action and arrangement. This is especially important in learning concepts of direction and orientation. Words like 'up', 'down', 'left', 'right,' 'top', 'middle', 'bottom', 'corner', 'across', 'sideways', 'slant', should be used as the child points, builds or draws. Children who ignore the orientation of shapes on the POP test certainly need training of this kind. Those who confuse the following pairs of visually similar letters: a/c, b/g, b/h, c/e, d/h, d/p, f/k, g/p, h/y, h/n, i/l, g/y, l/t, n/w, n/r, n/u, p/q, v/x, u/y, x/z should be taught some verbal description of the letter shape, to be used until they can form the letters consistently.

There are two important principles in selecting appropriate activities for a particular child, (1) the activity should not humiliate the child by being far too simple; (2) artificial difficulties should not be built into the task. Picture, shape, and colour matching and/or sorting activities are very often too simple, even for infants. If children fail at these activities, it may be because artificial difficulties are built in, such as complex or ambiguous verbal instructions, an overcrowded page, or the use of far too many alternatives in a choice situation.

Once a child has mastered initial letter-sounds, training in the serial aspect of work and sentence structure becomes important. Left-to-right ordering habits can be developed by arranging pictures as in a comic strip, but it is much more important to apply these skills to graphemes and to words. Suitable pictorial material can be found in:

Jackson and Reeve: *Look* (Visual Perception Materials)
Learning Development Aids: *Sequencing by Size* – Concept cards
                                       Sequential Thinking – Concept cards
Paul and Haskell: *Training in Basic Motor Skills*, booklets 6–8
                                Training in Basic Cognitive Skills, booklets 17–19
Remedial Supply Co.: *Stories Without Words*
Stott: *Programmed Reading Kit, Make-a-Story Game.*

'Breakthrough to Literacy' word folders are a convenient method of storing known words with which children can both copy and compose their own sentences. Those who have difficulty in keeping to a left-to-right sequence may be helped if the teacher draws a masking card across a model sentence one word at a time. First the teacher and then the child can read the sentence as this is done. In one-to-one work it helps considerably if the words to be arranged in order by the child are taken from the word folders or storage trays by the teacher. More sentences can then be set out in a given time, and greater emphasis can be placed on the left-to-right sequence.

For purposes of word recognition, graphemes, not letters, are the key units. A grapheme is a written symbol corresponding to a single speech sound, such as s, ss, sh, ea, ure, etc. Word-building with grapheme-tiles is a valuable activity which draws attention to the sequence of sound and symbol elements in a word. As there are so many graphemes to consider, it is again best if the teacher selects the particular ones needed for a word, and leaves it to the child to arrange them. This kind of activity is especially recommended for children with high error scores in Carver categories 0 (order), 1 (omissions) and 2 (visual confusions), and for those who neglect parts of the figures in the POP Spatial Test.

Using word and grapheme-tiles, unlike writing, does not require fine hand-eye co-ordination. This is an advantage for children who cannot write neatly and fluently. Young children, and some older backward readers, are usually more competent in visual perception that we would guess by looking at their handwriting or at their drawings. Visual perception and the ability to copy shapes with a pencil do not necessarily go together even in older children and adults. The POP Spatial Test is intended to identify cases of perceptual weakness, not motor difficulty. Children with low scores will benefit from appropriate training, but the form this takes should largely depend on their motor skills. For example, children with clumsy hand movements and illegible writing should not work through a remedial reading programme in which the majority of responses are written ones. Instead it would be better to tackle the pencil-control problem as a separate disability, and to use word and grapheme-tiles and/or a typewriter as an integral part of the reading programme.

As soon as the child can identify single-letter graphemes in any position in a word, he should move on to activities where he has to look for more complex graphemes (especially consonant and vowel digraphs e.g. ch, sh, th, ng, ea, ee, oo, or). He must learn to respond to these as *single visual units* corresponding to sounds, and here a variety of games can be tried. Dominoes, rummy, or other matching games can be prepared using words in which the key part is printed either in colour or in extra **bold** letters. This principle is applied in some commercially available schemes, such as:

Cox: *Choose the Word*
Gibson: *Teenage Twelve*
Kenworthy: *Phonic Rummy*
Lee: *Remedial Refresher Cards*
Moseley: *English Colour Code Programmed Reading Course*
Stott: *Programmed Reading Kit, Colour Sound Cards, Snakes Games.*

Later on, the same principle can be applied to syllable units, and this has been shown to help children spell large words. In preparing work cards, all that is needed is two pens, differing in colour or in size of print. In the ECC Programmed Reading Course, stressed syllables are cued in this way.

The activities given below are suitable for all children with visual perceptual difficulties. Each type of activity can be designed with an emphasis on part–whole relationships or on the orientation of the shapes, according to the type of error a child makes.

Pattern recognition at speed
– Play snap
– Play bingo
– Recognizing silhouettes
– Finding hidden figures
– Identifying dotted outlines
– Odd man out exercises
– Sort cards into categories, emphasizing speed
– Letter game. Type out short rows of letters, missing capital and small letters. The children have to put a circle round the small letters (for example) BBbB CCC DDdD, etc.
– Tricky sight words. A word which a child often misreads (e.g. who, were, they, etc.) can be printed on tracing paper or on a piece of clear plastic. The child then finds examples of the same word in his reading book and reads the sentences in which it occurs.

Published materials
Brake: *Developing Pre-Reading Skills, Visual Discrimination*
Frostig: *Visual Perception Program, Figure-Ground and Position-in-Space Exercises*
Jackson & Reeve: *Look* (Visual Perception Materials)
Karnes: *Helping Young Children Develop Language Skills*, Part X
MacDonald: *Wordmaster Major*
Paul & Haskell: *Training in Basic Cognitive Skills*, booklets 21–28
Remedial Supply Co.: *Visual Perception 1–4*. b:p:d Books, Games and Materials

Root: *Phonic Sets, Family Pairs, More Family Pairs, Match It*
Stott: *Programmed Reading Kit, Post-Boxes, Capitals and Smalls, First-Letter Bingo, Portholes, Pattern Bingo, Which of Two, Brick Wall, Noun Cards, Sentence Cards, Colour Sounds, Cinema Seats.*

Incomplete shapes and jigsaws

- Add missing lines or parts to drawings, patterns, or partially assembled jigsaws.
- Joint up dots to achieve closure.
- Take a simple jigsaw to pieces and then re-assemble it.
- Make your own 2–12 piece jigsaw by cutting up folded pictures or photographs, making straight cuts.
- Identify pictures or words where a wire mesh or hatch marks have been superimposed over the surface.
- Write a word on a card, and cut it horizontally, or cover it up to the centre. Let the child discover that the top half of a word is more useful than the bottom half.
- Use a word screen with window allowing part of a word to be exposed at a time.
- Cut up words, phrases or sentences as jigsaws.

Published materials

Brake: *Developing Pre-Reading Skills, Spatial Relations*
Jackson & Reeve: *Look* (Visual Perception Materials)
Karnes: *Helping Young Children Develop Language Skills,* Part X
Paul & Haskell: *Training in Basic Cognitive Skills,* booklet 12
Stott: *Programmed Reading Kit, Half-moon Cards, Sense-and-Nonsense, Snakes Games, Long Word Jig-Saws.*

Making patterns

(a) *non-repetitive:*
- Build up pictures or a pattern from paper, cellograph, felt or magnetized pieces.
- Ask child to draw what he has seen – house, bedroom, friends, relatives, toys, etc.
- Make a model from a two-dimensional drawing.
- Draw a two-dimensional plan of a model. Add instructions on how to make model, so the child can have other children using his work.

(b) *repetitive:*
- Make patterns with mosaics, from a picture design.
- Make patterns on a pegboard.
  Build with Cuisenaire rods.

– String beads, painted macaroni, drinking straws, etc. in a given order.
Patterns may involve size, colour, shape, and combinations of these.
– Cut out shapes and make paper chains and bunting to a prescribed pattern.

Published materials
Brake: *Developing Pre-Reading Skills, Spatial Relations*
Frostig: *Visual Perception Program, Spatial Relationships Exercises*
Jackson & Reeve: *Look* (Visual Perception Materials)
Karnes: *Helping Young Children Develop Language Skills*, Part X
Learning Development Aids: *Cube and Pegboard Patterns.*

Other sources: The following publishers produce a wealth of material, most of it excellent. As there is too much to itemize, catalogues should be consulted:
E. J. Arnold & Sons Ltd., Butterley Street, Leeds 10
Educational Supply Association, Pinnacles, Harlow, Essex
James Galt & Co. Ltd., 30–1 Great Marlborough Street, London, W1
Invicta Plastics Ltd., Oadby, Leics.
Philip & Tacey Ltd., Northway, Andover, Hants.

Developing immediate visual memory of sequentially perceived material

The ability to remember a series of items after scanning them visually (whether in a left-to-right sequence or in some other way) is very important indeed in the early stages of learning to read. If a child can 'hold in his mind' the letters and the words he perceives for a few seconds, while the effort after sound and meaning is made, he is in a strong position. On the other hand, if he can 'see' nothing but the few letters which are in clear focus at any one time, he will not get very far.

Immediate visual memory is by no means the same thing as long-term visual memory for familiar people, places or things. Some children have good immediate visual memory, but poor long-term memory, because they do not form associations between recently perceived items and other relevant parts of their store of knowledge and impressions. Children who fail to name what they see and who are content to parrot words without understanding are at risk in this respect.

In carrying out the activities suggested below, it is important to check whether children have a systematic method of looking at a visual display or at a word. If not, they can be taught to adopt a left-to-right pattern of scanning where appropriate.

The teacher should always be ready to suggest helpful techniques or strategies, e.g.:

(a) Grouping. Encourage the child to break down the sequences into more easily remembered segments, and to look for meaningfulness or for a mnemonic in the material.

(b) Verbalization. Provide a model, showing how you would perform the task. Verbal labelling is likely to facilitate recall, unless auditory memory is exceptionally weak.

(c) Rehearsal. A review of visual image and/or verbal description before reproduction.

Children with weak visual memory often have difficulty in following and applying a procedure demonstrated largely in visual terms. If they show marked difficulty in carrying out instructions given visually, they may do better if simplified taped instructions are made available, allowing them to check at every stage and to recap if necessary. Children with visual sequencing difficulties need to have complex activities broken down into smaller units. If they are encouraged to keep time records for certain limited tasks, they may well learn to direct their attention more efficiently. The complexity of the task can then be gradually increased.

Activities
– 'Same or different' game, using pairs of relatively complex objects, pictures, words, etc. – some identical, others differing in colour, shape, size, orientation, number, etc. Show one, then the other (having hid the first) and ask whether they are the same or different. Gradually decrease exposure times, and increase the interval between the presentations.
– Put a number of objects on a table. Have the child name them and then close his eyes. Remove one and ask which one has been taken away. Do this with pictures, letters, words, etc. as well.
–Present a visual stimulus consisting of more than one part (e.g. beads, a word). Remove, and have the child select the same item from a selection of up to five similar stimuli.
– As above, but ask the child to reproduce the stimulus from memory.
– Play copy-cat games. Draw a picture part by part, and then have the child copy several parts at once.
– Reproduce body-movement sequences from memory.
– Line up a series of objects, etc. for inspection in left-to-right order. To emphasize the order, draw a masking card across the display, revealing one object at a time. Mix up the objects and then have the child replace them in correct left-to-right order.

- Fernald's finger-tracing method. The teacher writes a word to be learned in large cursive writing. The child then traces over the word with his finger, saying it aloud. He repeats this until he is prepared to attempt to write the word from memory. If incorrect he returns to the finger tracing, practising with his eyes closed if this helps.
- Polyart 'memory trace' method. A plastic-coated paper available from Autobates Learning Systems Ltd. Especially suitable for young children or for those with poor hand–eye co-ordination who cannot manage cursive writing. Words are printed, mirror-wise, on the back of the sheet. The child holds the sheet up to the light to study a word. The words 'disappear' when he puts the sheet down to write on the washable surface, so he has to rely on memory.

Published materials
Brake: *Developing Pre-Reading Skills, Spatial Relations, Visual Memory*
Cratty: *Active Learning: Games to Enhance Academic Abilities*, Ch. 4
Karnes: *Helping Young Children Develop Language Skills*, Part IX
Learning Development Aids: *Shape discrimination cards*
                                            Visual recall cards
                                            Sequential thinking-concept cards
                                            Cube and Pegboard patterns
Remedial Supply Co.: *Stories Without Words*
Stott: *Programmed Reading Kit, Sentence Cards, Sense and Nonsense.*

Developing immediate auditory memory

A child's auditory memory, or the amount of heard information he can retain in proper sequence, is one factor involved in the development of his reading skills. As he reads from the beginning of a story or a sentence, he is using his memory of what has gone before to help him predict what the next word might be, what makes sense and what doesn't. As he tries to blend the sounds of a written word into a whole, he must be able to hold in his mind, or remember, the entire sequence of sounds. More generally, his auditory memory span forms part of his capacity to relate to his ability to understand and use complex language structures or again in reading to the number of simultaneous clues (word shape, sounds, context) he is able to use as he attacks a new word.

Auditory memory span is most commonly tested by asking the child to repeat sequences of letters or digits of increasing length. The span will be a product of several underlying processes: not only memory, but also the child's ability and willingness to listen, to attend exclusively to the task in hand. In training auditory memory we are also training these processes.

The activities suggested here, all oral, may seem very demanding on the teacher's time. Many can be slotted in, however, to odd spare moments with a class or group; none should be extended for too long since they demand a great deal of concentrated effort and attention. It is suggested that children work in pairs or groups for many of the activities. Alternatively exercises can be prepared on tape. The method in all the activities is the presentation of sequences of words or symbols which the child either repeats or acts upon; each child follows a programme which starts with simple material and proceeds to more complex sequences. The progress from simple to complex can be achieved in several ways: by slowly increasing the *number* of items you are asking the child to recall, by varying the *kind* of material used (from meaningful sequences such as sentences to strings of isolated words and then to abstract sequences like telephone numbers and letter sequences), and by increasing the amount of *time* between your presentation of the sequence and the child's response. Immediate recall or action can be followed by asking the child to respond after a delay of several seconds; he will be helped in this if you teach him to 'rehearse', or keep on repeating the sequence to himself, in the interval before responding.

Meaningful material

– Have the children listen for and remember all the sounds they can hear during a 30 second period.

– The suitcase game for words in classes. Child one says, 'I am going on holiday. I will put shoes in my suitcase.' Child two says, 'I am going on holiday. I will put shoes and socks in my suitcase.' Each child repeats the previous list and adds a new item. Variations are many, e.g. 'I went shopping and bought . . .', 'On our way to school we saw . . .' or 'In my fruit salad I put . . .'.

– Increasing sentences. The child repeats after the teacher, 'I see', then 'I see a dog', then 'I see a dog and cat' and so on until perhaps 'I see a black dog and a white cat fighting in the street near my house.'

– Questions on sentences e.g. 'I went to the greengrocer's and bought a melon, 4 apples, and a lettuce.'
Teacher asks: 'What shop did I go to?'
'How many apples did I buy?'

– Word sequences, of unrelated words, e.g. fish, spoon, house, apple. Pictures can be presented with the words as an extra 'aid', then removed before the child repeats the sequence.

– Child has to make sense of a jumbled spoken sentence, putting the words in the correct order.

Abstract material
- Rhythms clapped out or played on a drum. Child repeats the rhythm.
- Match auditory rhythm with its visual equivalent in dots and dashes.
- Child repeats spellings, with a rhythm corresponding to grapheme or syllable structure.
- Which one was missing ? Teacher says a series of letters or digits, then repeats it with one missing.
- Same or different ? 7934, 7394.
- Was there a g ? after teacher says a l g p t.
- Telephone numbers. Each child has a phone number written down. In order for a child to be able to use a toy telephone to phone his friend, he must repeat the friend's telephone number correctly. If he makes a mistake, the 'operator' (teacher) says 'wrong number' and gives him the number to repeat again.
- Imitating and decoding morse messages sent by buzzer.

Following a series of instructions
- Games such as O'Grady says, 'O'Grady says clap your hands', increasing to O'Grady says clap your hands, put one hand on your head and one behind your back.'
- Instructions to the child to draw or mark certain things. For example: 'draw a red circle and inside it a small blue square', or 'put a green cross on the cow and a red circle under the cat', or 'draw this: cross cross dot cross.' If the material is taped the child can replay part if he cannot retain the whole sequence, he can also check his own work.

Recall of story content
This involves recall over a longer period, i.e. long-term as well as short-term memory; it is also highly relevant to reading skills. The child can at first retell a story with the help of the pictures in the book, or answer a series of sequential questions on the story. Later he should be able to recall the story without these aids.

Published materials include:
Ainsworth: *SRA Listening Laboratory 1b*
Brake: *Developing Pre-Reading Skills, Auditory Memory*
Karnes: *Helping Young Children Develop Language Skills*, Parts VII-VIII
Remedial Supply Co.: *Pictures in Sound. Oral Comprehension Tapes. Reason and Write. Spelling Programme* (all for use with tape-recorder)
Schools Council: *Concept 7–9* (Communication Unit, Listening Unit).

Developing the ability to discriminate between sounds

(1) *Listening to non-linguistic sounds*

For young children or older children with extremely poor auditory discrimination, activities to sensitize them to the sounds in their environment, and to distinguish high/low, long/short, loud/soft sounds, e.g.:

– A whistle: child has to stand up for high notes, sit down for low.
– A drum: clap for a loud bang, not for a soft one.
– Matching pictures of animals to the sounds they make (use tape).
– Tape kitchen, classroom, traffic noises, and ask child to identify them.
– Child has his back to you as you crumple tissue paper, tap a glass, tap the table, ring a bell, etc – he turns round to touch the object which made the sound.

(2) *Making and hearing single speech sounds, not embedded in words*

– Ask child to say a sound which can be kept up (e.g. *m, sh, s, l*).
  Tell him to continue the sound while you say others (*r, n, t*) and stop as soon as he hears the one he is producing.
– Ask him to think of a sound he has practised making and clap his hands when he hears it out of a series of sounds you produce.
– Call his attention to the differences between sounds he confuses by asking him to make e.g. *a* and *e* and observe the different positions of his lips and tongue. A mirror can be useful.
– Link speech sounds with other familiar sounds (e.g. c-click, f-foam, g-gurgle, h-laugh, m-humming, p-pop, r-roar, s-hiss, t-tick, ch-sneeze, gr-growl, ow-painful, sh-quiet).

(3) *Discrimination of sounds within words*

Begin with initial sounds, go on to final sounds and then middle sounds.

– Choose a sound, e.g. *m*; ask him to make the sound and then sort out from a set of pictures those which show objects beginning with the *m* sound. There are many commercially produced sets of cards for initial sounds, covering the whole alphabet. Or use worksheets – child puts a cross on all the pictures beginning with *m*. Use similar activities for final and middle sounds, e.g. find all the pictures with *t* at the end of the word.
– Matching pictures which begin (or end) with the same sound. This activity can be presented in game or worksheet form, e.g.:

(a) Dominoes. Child has to join on another picture beginning with the same sound.

(b) Rummy or Happy Families. Make a set of picture cards. Child has to collect three cards which show pictures beginning with the same sound, or ending, or same middle vowel.

(c) Lotto. Each child has a master card with one picture and five blank spaces. From a pile of cards each child picks up a card, names a picture and keeps it if his 'key' picture begins with the same sound.

(d) Worksheets, e.g. have the child draw a line under the pictures that begin with the same sound as a key picture in a box.

– Listening for sounds in words, presented aurally, e.g. the child has to tap every time he hears *t* in a series of words you say.

(a) Make a short tape. Ask child to make a mark on paper every time he hears a given sound. At the end the tape tells him how many he should have found, and goes through the words with that sound in.

(b) Series of questions (as in Moseley's DOP test): Can you hear *t* in seat? Can you hear *or* in soap?

(c) Clap your hands when you hear the odd one out . . . right, fight, light, sit, might.

– Discriminating between two similar sounds, presented orally. The child has to say whether two spoken words are the same or different. The teacher should start with dissimilar words (e.g. wig, dog) and proceed slowly to similar ones (e.g. wig, rig). N.B. If a child seems unable to distinguish between any of the following pairs of sounds, even after repeated practice of this kind, the reason may be an articulatory difficulty or a degree of hearing loss: d/t, e/i, f/s f/v, g/k, l/r, l/y, r/w, s/t.

(4) *Perception of rhyme*

Group oral work: 'Tell me a colour that rhymes with bed.' 'Which of these words rhyme with chair?' 'Can you finish this rhyme . . . ?'

Games, e.g. Happy Families, child has to collect three pictures which rhyme, e.g. Snap for rhyming pictures.

Worksheets, e.g. put a cross on the pictures which rhyme.

(5) *Activities for the child who has learned letter-sound correspondences*

The range of activities can be extended for this child, for example he can be given a series of pictures and asked to put a ring around the initial letter, or the middle sound, in a multiple-choice format.

Most early phonic games and workbooks involve the child in *both* auditory discrimination and practice of letter-sound correspondence.

Published materials
Baldwin: *Patterns of Sound*
Brake: *Developing Pre-Reading Skills, Auditory Discrimination*
Bramley: *Units of Sound* (for use with tape-recorder)
Clift: *Word Study Kit* (for use with Language Master)

Hampson: *Sounds and Rhythm* (rhymes written by a speech therapist)

Karnes: *Helping Young Children Develop Language Skills*, Pt. I, pp. 12–15

Leevers: *Integrated Reading Materials for Adults and Adolescents* (IRMA) (for use with tape-recorder). *Teachers' Manual* (Remedial Package for Secondary Schools)

McLeod and Atkinson: *Domain Phonic Test Kit and Workshop*

Moseley: *English Colour Code Programmed Reading Course* (for use with tape-recorder)

Northern & Sutherland: *Starting Phonics. Phonics Development.*

Remedial Supply Co.: *Listen. Phonics. Sound Discrimination. Letter-Shifting Sequences* (for use with tape-recorder)

Root: *Family Pairs, Match It, I Spy, Pair It*

Sansom, C.: *Acting Rhymes, Speech Rhymes*

Sansom, R.: *Rhythm Rhymes*

Semmel: SOS: *A Developmental Programme of Auditory Perception*

SRA: *Schoolhouse* (Word Attack Skills Kit)

Stott: *Programmed Reading Kit.* Units 1–15

Tansley: *Listening to Sounds* (for use with tape-recorder). *Listening to Sounds Revision Programme* (for use with Synchrofax Audio Page). *Sound Sense Revision Programme* (for use with Synchrofax Audio Page).

Phonic blending skills

An outline of method

Teaching this particular sub-skill should be done as part of the main phonic programme, and kept to short regular sessions to prevent the mechanical nature of the task becoming monotonous. Most exercises require a one-to-one teaching situation, but a tape-recorder, the Language Master or the Synchrofax Audio Page, can also be brought into use.

Acquisition of blending skills is impossible without a basic knowledge of single-letter sounds. However the simple vowel/consonant and consonant/vowel/consonant blends can be introduced at an early stage. Complex consonant blends such as scr, spl, str, thr should not be attempted until the child has mastered the simpler forms.

As well as better blends, syllable blending can also be taught. In fact, this is a useful way of introducing oral phonic work, as syllable units are easier to hear and to speak than are phoneme units. Children can hold a finger below their moving jaw as they say words, counting the number of syllables by chin-bumps. Later, tapping to syllables can be introduced.

The idea that spoken words are made up of sound units is best conveyed by asking children to listen, and to imitate the teacher as she accentuates certain sounds and demonstrates how two or more units fuse together. Children can be confused and can develop a resistance to phonics teaching if they are expected to respond to print at the same time. Auditory-vocal practice, in quiet conditions, is essential to begin with. Later on, grapheme tiles can be introduced, and the child can be asked to point to each sound element in turn. He can then put the tiles together and say the word – a concrete illustration of word-building.

Initial teaching should concentrate on two-phoneme pairs – $a - t$, $i - n$, $d - ay$, $s - ee$. The sounds should be spoken by the teacher rapidly at first – two or three per second. This is almost like saying the word slowly, elongating certain parts. Gradually the gap between sounds can be increased. Three-and four-phoneme blends can later be treated in the same way: $c - a - t$, $s - e - n - d$. Children who cannot blend more than two or three sounds need to be given a method of extending their span. One way of doing this is to begin with a single sound, have the child repeat it, then add a second sound (both repeated), a third and so on. By building up a word cumulatively in this way, the child is less likely to forget the sequence of sounds. With longer words the question arises of whether to work from the initial or final sound. There seem to be arguments for both approaches. By beginning with the final sound (t, $a - t$, $c - a - t$) the child is repeating the new sound first, then adding those he has previously repeated. This method also lends itself more readily to the transition from two- to three-letter words, e.g. from $a - m$ to $h - a - m$. Of course, the backwards approach is suitable for auditory-vocal practice only, and would be most confusing if used in conjunction with grapheme tiles or the printed word. Unless there is extreme difficulty in blending and in repeating a series of sounds, the 'forwards' approach is preferable. The advantage of working from the initial sound is that the child is always working from left to right. As children with blending problems may well have scanning difficulties this can be important.

In all phonic activities it is essential that a clear goal be set for each piece of work. This allows for continued success to be achieved, with its accompanying reinforcement value. Clearly, the size of task will vary from child to child.

Types of activity

Prepare a list of the new words to be encountered by the child in the next few pages of the book he is reading. Give him auditory-vocal practice in blending those that he is likely to be able to work out phonically when he meets them.

Letter tiles provide a useful aid to this process in that the child is able to manipulate the graphemes himself. It is important that digraphs should be available as well as single letters, so that the child is helped to think of pairs of letters like ea ir as a single phonic entity.

Taped programmes can be prepared to assist blending. The Language Master can also be used. The teacher has to prepare the cards, using one word per card. The teacher's voice gives the letter sounds at the appropriate speed. The child must repeat these and blend them into the single word.

Games can be used to help develop blending skills. For example, picture/letter cards can be prepared which join up to make a complete picture plus word. These can be used in several ways, e.g. Happy Families, Rummy, Can-you-go?

The child can be given a series of words each beginning with the same initial consonant, e.g. sat, sad, sip, and be asked to change this initial sound, for instance replacing it with h. More difficult is to change the final consonant or middle vowel sound. This activity must begin with words the child can already read and can be used to introduce new sounds into the blending process. A written response, perhaps after carrying out the operation with grapheme tiles, will help to reinforce learning.

Published materials
Bramley: *Units of Sound* (for use with tape-recorder)
Clift: *Word Study Kit* (for use with Language Master)
Karnes: *Helping Young Children Develop Language Skills*. Part VII, pp. 97–100
Leevers: *Integrated Reading Materials for Adults and Adolescents* (IRMA) (for use with tape-recorder). *Teachers' Manual* (Remedial Package for Secondary Schools)
McLeod and Atkinson: *Domain Phonic Test Kit and Workshop*
Moseley: *English Colour Code Programmed Reading Course* (for use with tape-recorder)
Remedial Supply Co.: *Phonics Blending. Letter-Shifting Sequences. Attacking New Words* (all for use with tape-recorder)
Tansley: *Listening to Sounds* (for use with tape-recorder). *Listening to Sounds Revision Programme* (for use with Synchrofax Audio Page). *Sound Sense Revision Programme* (for use with Synchrofax Audio Page).

Some observations on learning styles and strategies

Learning is involved in all of the activities described on the preceding pages. Additional activities are not described here, but some general guidance is given about ways of presenting learning tasks.

Observation of a child's learning style, both in test situations and in classroom activities, should lead to an individual approach. The Word Retention test, for example, can be used as a guide for learning new sight words.

1. Children who do not verbalize while they are learning and consequently fail can be taught to say the words and/or letters/sounds, as they are trying to learn.

2. Children who apparently learn quickly, but do not retain what they learn, need to *overlearn* (with more repetition) before moving on to new material.

3. Children who master single items but become confused when a second is introduced, need to overlearn the first item and should not be given two similar items in succession.

4. Children who are very slow to learn and who tire or become bored need to practise the same thing in several different ways (e.g. with other materials, in the form of a game, with mechanical aids, etc.)

The way a child approaches a learning task is a function not only of his cognitive strengths and weaknesses, but an expression of his personality. In some cases, faulty or counter-productive habits are picked up because learning situations are not always geared to individual differences in personality, social development, interest and attitude. Children sometimes learn to be dull, or passive, or apparently deaf, or rebellious, or charmingly evasive because they derive some satisfaction from the concern this behaviour produces in adults, compared with no satisfaction at all from repeated failure or neglect when they are sometimes trying hard to learn.

The essence of remedial teaching lies in adjusting the task to the learner in such a way that the activity itself becomes enjoyable, and the child's efforts are rewarded. Encouragement and praise are important, not only from teachers, but from other children in the group and from members of the child's own family.

It is very often necessary for the child and for those in contact with him to modify their expectations of his performance. The teacher should make it clear what she would regard as a good effort in each learning task. If the pupil aims too high or too low and does not accept the teacher's target, even after explanation, he will need very careful handling. The teacher should always work towards the goal of self-evaluation in terms of previous performance, and should avoid the temptation to become authoritarian or to remove from the child all responsibility for his own learning. *Negotiation* of goals and rewards are an important part of remedial work.

I

It is rare to encounter a child with reading difficulties who is creative and independent in his approach to learning. Most become frightened, guilty, defensive, impulsive, or angry when they encounter failure.

A frightened child may appear passive, uninvolved, indecisive, lacking in energy, sad, over-dependent, or excessively worried about details. Such children should be led gradually towards self-evaluation by providing them with individual record cards and graphs. A high level of success (at least 90 per cent), in simple learning tasks should be achieved, and the occasional mistake can then be talked about in a relatively calm atmosphere. Frightened, anxious children need plenty of time to think and to respond – and if they become paralyzed and confused can be encouraged to set themselves time limits. Their responses should always be treated with respect, even if panicky or far-fetched. The teacher should not obtrude too much into the child's field of concentration, and in fact such children aften do well when working alone for short periods, especially if they are able to check their own answers. Again, working with another child can be less threatening than working with an adult.

Children who feel guilty about their failure often adopt an inhibited, defensive attitude. They do not like to talk about their difficulties and many find all kinds of ways of avoiding the challenge of learning. At best, they adopt a fixed mechanical routine of response in order to 'get by'. They usually only take in a limited amount of information at once, and consequently have difficulty in following instructions. For this reason, it is important to require such children to make their own plans, and to state their own objectives. It may help them to think more highly of themselves if they keep a list of things they are able to do independently. Rigid, inhibited children with learning difficulties are usually relieved to find that they are not the only ones with these difficulties, and they can benefit enormously from remedial work in a small group. At the the same time, it is important to try to modify the attitudes of those individuals who may have devalued the child on account of his shortcomings, real or imagined.

Impulsive, restless, distractable behaviour is perhaps the most common pattern among poor readers. This kind of behaviour sometimes reflects a lack of interest, a seeking for instant excitement and fun, and is sometimes a positive form of protest which can develop into active hostility. While it demands great personal resourcefulness from the teacher to meet undisciplined behaviour with equanimity, to look for and to reward behaviour which is incompatible with the disruptive pattern, and to avoid wherever possible a punitive attitude, this is the most effective way of dealing with such children. If the teacher can turn learning into a game, and can create an atmosphere of excitement and success, she will have little need to exert rigid controls. There is always the danger, however, that a remedial teacher who adopts this approach can become idealized in the pupil's eyes, and other teachers can become 'baddies'. In such cases it is important that a consistent approach should be adopted by all teachers concerned, and an attempt should be made by all concerned to present learning tasks in a more attractive manner.

Immediate feedback is important for impulsive children, both in learning and in social situations. When disciplinary constraints have to be imposed, it is important that the child sees them as unavoidable consequences of his own behaviour. Only serious breaches of discipline should be treated in this way: in general, it is much better to ignore undesirable behaviour and to praise wherever possible.

Ordering books and materials

The books listed below can be ordered through booksellers, preferably from a firm specializing in the educational market. Two of the best-known London firms are:

Dillon's University Bookshop,
1 Malet Street, London WC1,
Tel: 01-636 1577.

Foyles Educational Ltd.,
37 Upper Berkeley Street, London W1,
Tel: 01-262 5310, 262 4690, 723 9257.

Books and other materials published in America are not always available in this country, but can be ordered through the:

American Book Service,
Excel House, Whitcomb Street, London WC2,
Tel: 01-839 6745.

Materials other than books referred to in the Activity Sheets are not individually listed. The publisher's address is given here, and in many cases the author's name is also given in the alphabetical list below:

Ainsworth, C. (see SRA),

E. J. Arnold & Son Ltd.,
Butterley Street, Leeds 10.

Autobates Learning Systems Ltd.,
Whitestone House, Lutterworth Road, Nuneaton, Warwicks.

Baldwin, G. (1967) *Patterns of Sound* (5 books),
London, Heinemann.

Bell & Howell Co.,
Alperton House, Bridgewater Road, Wembley, Middlesex.
Local Agent: Commercial Motion Pictures Ltd.,
Vision House, Russell Gardens, London, NW11.

Black, A. and C. Ltd., 4 Soho Square, London W1.

Brake, R. G. (see Holt, Rinehart and Winston, Inc.).

Bramley, W. (see Units of Sound Productions).

Breakthrough to Literacy (see Longman).

Clift, D. (see Bell & Howell).

Cox, D. (see Gibson).

Cratty, B. J. (1971) *Active Learning: Games to Enhance Academic Abilities,*
Englewood Cliffs, NJ: Prentice-Hall.

The Cuisenaire Co., Ltd.,
40 Silver Street, Reading, Berks.

Educational Supply Association (ESA),
Pinnacles, PO Box 22, Harlow, Essex.

Follett Educational Corporation,
Chicago.
London Agents: Media Directions Inc., 41 William 4th Street, London WC2.

Frostig, M. (see Follett).

Gahagan, D. M. and Gahagan, G. A. (1970) *Talk Reform,*
London, Routledge & Kegan Paul.

James Galt & Co. Ltd.,
30/31 Great Marlborough Street, London W1.

Robert Gibson & Sons Ltd.,
2 West Regent Street, Glasgow.

Hampson, N. (1969) *Sounds and Rhythm* (3 books),
Aylesbury, Ginn.

Heaton, J. B. (1966) *Composition through Pictures,*
London, Longman.

Holmes McDougall, Ltd.,
30 Royal Terrace, Edinburgh 7.

Holt, Rinehart and Winston, Inc.,
New York. (120 Golden Lane, London EC1Y 0TU.)

ILEA Media Resources Centre,
Highbury Station Road, London N1.

Invicta Plastics Ltd.,
Oadby, Leicestershire.

Jackson, J. & Reeve, J. (see MacMillan).

Jones, C. H. (see Autobates).

Karnes, M. B., *Helping Young Children Develop Language Skills:* a
   Book of Activities,
Arlington, Virginia,
Council for Exceptional Children (available from: NSMHC Books,
17 Pembridge Square, London W2.

Kenworthy Educational Service Inc.,
Box 3031, Buffalo, New York, 14205.

Language Master (supplied by Bell and Howell).

Learning Development Aids (LDA),
Park Works, Norwich Road, Wisbech, Cambs.

Lee, D. B. (see Gibson).

Leevers, S., *IRMA and Teachers' Manual* (Remedial Package for
   Secondary Schools),
available from: Programmed Learning Centre, College of Further
   Education, Hatfield Road, St Albans, Herts.

Longman Group Ltd.,
Pinnacles, Harlow, Essex.

MacDonald Educational,
49-50 Poland Street, London W1.

Macmillan & Co. Ltd.,
Houndmills, Basingstoke, Hants.

McLeod, J. & Atkinson, J. (see Oliver & Boyd),

Milliken Publishing Co.,
611 Olive Street, St Louis, Missouri, 6310.

Moseley, D. V. (see Senlac).

Northern, M. and Sutherland, L. (see Milliken).

Oliver & Boyd Ltd.,
Tweeddale Court, 14 High Street, Edinburgh 1.

Paul, M. E. and Haskell, S. H. (see ESA).

Philip & Tacey, Ltd.,
North Way, Andover, Hants.

Polyart (supplied by Autobates).

Remedial Supply Co.,
Dixon Street, Wolverhampton.

Sansom, C. (see A. and C. Black).

Sansom, R. (see A. and C. Black).

Schools' Council (see E. J. Arnold [*Concept 7-9*] and Longman [*Breakthrough to Literacy*]).

Science Research Associates (SRA),
Reading Road, Henley-on-Thames, Oxon.

Semmel, E. M. (see Follett).

Senlac Systems (Electronic and Educational) Ltd.,
60 Holland Road, London W14.

Shiach, G. M. (1972), *Teach Them to Speak*,
London, Ward Lock.

Stott, D. H. (see Holmes MacDougall).

Synchofax Audio Page (supplied by E. J. Arnold).

Tansley, A. E. (see E. J. Arnold).

Units of Sound Productions,
23 Pool Green, Neston, Corsham, Wiltshire.

Bullock and after

The title, *A Language for Life* (DES, 1975), has quasi-religious overtones, and there will no doubt be queues to jump on this particular gospel train. The destination appears to be transatlantic, the tickets come at four different prices, and there are special terms for upwardly mobile teachers. Unfortunately, there is a fuel crisis, and Britton doubts whether the children will get out and push.

The Bullock Committee of Inquiry into Reading and the Use of English was set up as a reaction to the NFER survey (Start and Wells, 1972) which suggested that reading standards are declining. The committee has taken the view that new measuring instruments must be devised if reliable evidence is to be obtained, but that in any case reading standards are very much below what might be achieved if teachers were to take substantial courses in language and reading. The report pleads for more and better qualified English teachers and advisers, recommending that every school should have 'a suitably qualified teacher with responsibility for advising and supporting his colleagues in language and the teaching of reading'. This is the American-style reading consultant, concerned with literacy at all levels of the curriculum and necessarily taking a general advisory role rather than concentrating on helping children with learning difficulties.

In evidence submitted to the Bullock Committee, a small group of psychologists (which included the author) argued against centralizing responsibility for the teaching of reading in a single person, whether it be the head or a specialist teacher (Booth and others, 1974). Instead it was suggested that panels of interested staff and parents should bear this responsibility, as in the successful Chicago project described on page 79. Moreover, it was argued that school policy statements on language and reading should be published, so that both parents and children may understand the aims of the curriculum, and so that discussion at LEA level may be conducted in an open and informal atmosphere. Without some degree of democratic staff and community involvement in the curriculum, it is more than likely that teacher-training measures will fail to bear fruit. The Bullock Committee did not point to evidence that more and better courses for teachers would improve their classroom competence and help to improve standards. It did not mention the More Effective School programme in New York which created a teachers' paradise, with extra members of staff, smaller groups, massive advisory support and in-service training, and yet failed to raise levels of attainment (Fox, 1968).

One of the purposes of this book has been to highlight some of the ways in which the attitudes and expectations of teachers affect the progress and adjustment of children with special problems. Those who try to help such children are involved in creating conditions in which personal growth and learning are possible. Many of them develop a sensitivity to individual needs which is only rarely found in class and subject teachers who have not had the opportunity of working closely with slow learners or children with other handicaps. It is therefore important to provide both a learning environment and a personal focus for helping with learning and adjustment problems in the ordinary school. It is not enough for LEAs to appoint a learning difficulties adviser (as Bullock recommends); a special appointment should be made, if not in every school, then on a strictly local basis. The language and reading specialist as envisaged by Bullock has too wide a brief to ensure that the needs of children who find reading difficult will be met.

It is necessary to make these points since it would be most unfortunate if the underlying philosophy and the succinct analysis of language and reading skills in the Report were to remain at a theoretical level. Certain correctives to what some would see as an empire-building document for English teachers are needed, and incentives other than professional advancement need to be built into the scheme if real improvements are to be made. A strong case can be made to support the argument that if children with learning difficulties were given significantly better opportunities for learning to read than their peers, not only would the average child learn more efficiently, but the overall benefit to society would more than justify the expense.

The Committee of Inquiry conducted an extensive survey of provision and practice in 1973. Questionnaires were completed by 1415 primary and 392 secondary schools. Some of the findings which confirm and add to the results of the surveys reported elsewhere in this book are summarized below:

Infant Level:

Approximately 70 per cent of teachers claimed that poor readers read to them every day.

Approximately 40 per cent of teachers claimed to keep records of individual difficulties.

Most teachers allowed between half-an-hour and an hour of class time per week for 'reading practice' and up to half-an-hour for 'individual reading'.

Junior Level:

Approximately 50 per cent of teachers claimed that poor readers aged nine read to them every day. This figure is much higher than that obtained by Morris (1966).

Approximately 45 per cent of teachers claimed to keep records of individual difficulties.

Most teachers allowed up to an hour of class time a week for 'individual reading'.

Eleven per cent of all primary children were receiving extra help with reading, typically on a withdrawal group basis. While the average size of special groups was six, children nine per cent of the schools claimed to provide individual attention.

Twelve per cent of the schools had special classes.

Approximately 70 per cent of the special reading teachers were part-timers and only a quarter of these had attended courses lasting more than six weeks.

Approximately 20 per cent of the schools were visited by peripatetic reading teachers.

Secondary Level:

Although 'remedial' pupils tended to have more 'English' periods than others, the quality of the teaching left much to be desired. Eleven per cent of all the 12-year-olds were receiving remedial help, and five per cent at 14. A further 10 per cent of the 14-year-olds were following non-examination courses.

Mean size of remedial teaching groups was 19 for 12-year-olds and 16 for 14-year-olds. Fewer than two per cent of the groups were for one to five pupils, whereas more than 12 per cent were for 26 or more pupils.

Approximately 60 per cent of head teachers considered that the accommodation for withdrawal groups was partially or wholly unsatisfactory.

Approximately 50 per cent of schools had a senior member of staff with special responsibility for backward readers.

Only 15 per cent of the teachers taking remedial groups or classes had attended relevant courses lasting at least six weeks.

The Committee has made a large number of practical recommendations in the hope of improving present standards. Recognizing the need to relate theory and practice at all levels of training, they have suggested that both initial and in-service training should have on-going work with individuals or small groups as an important focus. Staffs should increasingly determine their own in-service education needs, and should be supported in local action-research projects and in formulating and implementing school policy for language and reading. Head teachers should play a leading part in attending courses, in passing on their skills, and in working alongside their colleagues in the classroom.

One of the important matters to be considered by schools is, of course, the teaching of backward readers. The Committee has recommended that 'LEAs and schools should introduce early screening procedures to prevent cumulative language and reading failure and to guarantee individual diagnosis and treatment.' Systematic observation and an assessment of reading ability should be followed by 'selective diagnostic testing of those pupils about whom detailed and specific information is required.' New diagnostic tests should be developed and 'the teacher should be equipped to determine when a difficulty revealed by a diagnostic test requires further discussion'. Additional help should be given to those who need it, and 'where it is the school's policy to withdraw children from their classes for special help they should continue to receive support at the appropriate level on their return.' It is emphasized that remedial help should 'wherever possible be related to the rest of the pupil's learning' and teachers are urged to 'involve parents and to help them understand the nature of their children's difficulties.'

A number of recommendations are concerned with the special needs of various groups. More teachers in educational priority areas, more home-visiting programmes, more help for children and parents with limited English, more centres for children with severe reading difficulties and the development of counselling and tutoring services for adults with reading problems are some of the more important examples. The Committee made the point that no child 'should be expected to cast off the language and culture of the home as he crosses the school threshold, and the curriculum should reflect those aspects of his life'. Implement that, as part of a democratically-based school policy, and all the rest will follow.

Bibliography

ABLEWHITE, R. C. (1967) *The Slow Reader*. London: Heinemann.

ADAMS, A. (1971) 'Some implications of the organization of secondary schools', *Remedial Education*, **6, 3,** 9-13.

ALTUS, G. T. (1956) 'A WISC profile for retarded readers', *J. Consult. Psychol.*, **20,** 155-6.

ALWITT, L. F. (1963) 'Decay of immediate memory of visually presented digits among non-readers and readers', *J. Educ. Psychol.*, **54,** 144-6.

ASCHER, M. A. (1970) 'The attainments of children in ESN schools and remedia departments', *Educ. Res.*, **12,** 215-9.

ATKINSON, E. J. and GAINS, G. W. (1973) *An A-Z List of Reading and Subject Books*. National Association for Remedial Education, 9 Cranleigh Rise, Eaton, Norwich.

BAILEY, L. (1974) 'Parents as partners in entry-level psycho-educational process'. Paper presented at IFLD conference, Amsterdam.

BAKKER, D. J. (1972) *Temporal Order in Disturbed Reading*. Rotterdam: University of Rotterdam Press.

BANKS, E. M. (1970) 'The identification of children with potential learning disabilities', *Slow Learning Child*, **17,** 27-38.

BARKER LUNN, J. C. (1970) *Streaming in the Primary School*. Slough: NFER.

BARNETT, B. R. (1972) 'Backwardness in reading, social adjustment and family attitudes'. PH.D. thesis, University of London.

BAS (1974) *A Right to Read*. London: British Association of Settlements.

BATEMAN, B. (1969) 'Reading: a controversial view – research and rationale', in TARNAPOL, L. (ed). *Learning Disabilities*. Springfield, Illinois: Charles C. Thomas.

BAYMUR, F. B. and PATTERSON, C. H. (1960) 'A comparison of three methods of assisting underachieving high school students', *J. Counselling Psychol.*, **7,** 83-9.

BBC/OPEN UNIVERSITY (1973) *Using Special Resources*. TV10 of Course PE261. Milton Keynes: Open University Press.

BEARD, R. M. (1956) 'The structure of perception: a factorial study', *Brit. J. Educ. Psychol.*, **35,** 210-22.

BECK, H. S. (1961) 'An experimental investigation of the relationship of hand-eye dominance and reversals in reading', *Diss. Abstr.*, **21,** 2375.

BELL, P. (1970) *Basic Teaching for Slow Learners*. London: Muller.

BELMONT, L. and BIRCH, H. G. (1966) 'The intellectual profile of backward readers', *Perceptual and Motor Skills*, **22,** 787-816.

BENDER, L. (1938) *A Visual Motor Gestalt Test and its Clinical Use*. New York: American Orthopsychiat. Assoc.

BENTON, A. L. (1963) *The Revised Visual Retention Test*. New York: Psychological Corporation.

BEREITER, C. and ENGELMANN, S. (1966) *Teaching Disadvantaged Children in the Preschool*. Englewood Cliffs: Prentice-Hall.

BERGER, M., YULE, W. and RUTTER, M. (1975) 'Attainment and adjustment in two geographical areas: the prevalence of specific reading retardation', *Brit. J. Psychiat.*, **126**, 510-9.

BERNSTEIN, B. (1958) 'Some sociological determinants of perception: an inquiry into sub-cultural differences', *Brit. J. Sociol.*, **9**, 159-74.

BERNSTEIN, B. (1960) 'Language and social class', *Brit. J. Sociol.*, **11**, 271-6.

BHATNAGAR, J. (1971) 'The remedial teacher and the immigrant child', *Remedial Education*, **6, 1**, 14-5.

BILLS, R. E. (1950) 'Non-directive play-therapy with retarded readers', *J. Consult. Psychol.*, **14**, 40-9.

BIRCH, H. and BELMONT, L. (1964) 'Auditory-visual integration in normal and retarded readers', *American J. Orthopsychiat.*, **34**, 851-61.

BLACKSTONE, T. (1973) *Education and Day Care for Young Children in Need: The American Experience*. London: Centre for Studies in Social Policy.

BLANK, M. and BRIDGER, W. H. (1966) 'Deficiencies in verbal labelling in retarded readers', *American J. Orthopsychiat.*, **36**, 840-7.

BLANK, M. and SOLOMON, F. (1969) 'How shall the disadvantaged child be taught?', *Child Development*, **40**, 47-61.

BOND, G. L. (1935) *The Auditory and Speech Characteristics of Poor Readers*. Teachers' College Contrib. to Educ., No. 657. New York: Teachers' College.

BOOTH, A., MOSELEY, D. V. and ROBERTSON, J. (1974) 'Learning to communicate', *AEP Journal*, **3, 6**, 37-53.

BOSHES, B. and MYKLEBUST, H. R. (1964) 'A neurological and behavioural study of children with learning disorders', *Neurology*, **14**, 7-12.

BOXALL, M. (1973) 'Multiple deprivation: an experiment in nurture', *DECP Occ. Pub.*, **2**, 91-113. London: Brit. Psychol. Soc.

BRENNAN, W. K. (1971) 'A policy for remedial education', *Remedial Education*, **6, 1**, 7-11.

BRIMER, M. A. and DUNN, L. M. (1962) *English Picture Vocabulary Tests*. Bristol: Educational Evaluation Enterprises.

BRITISH PSYCHOLOGICAL SOCIETY (1973) 'Memorandum on assessment centres for handicapped children', *Bull. Brit. Psychol. Soc.*, **26**, 235-42.

BROEDEL, J., OHLSEN, M., PROFF, F. and SOUTHARD, C. (1960) 'The effects of group counselling on gifted underachieving adolescents', *J. Counselling Psychol.*, **7**, 163-70.

BRUININKS, R. H. (1970) 'Teaching word recognition to disadvantaged boys', *J. Learning Disabilities*, **3**, 28-37.

BRUININKS, R. H., RYNDERS, J. E. and GROSS, J. C. (1974) 'Social acceptance of mildly retarded pupils in resource rooms and regular classes', *Amer. J. Ment. Defic.*, **78**, 377-83.

BRYAN, T. S. (1974) 'An observational analysis of classroom behaviours of children with learning disabilities', *J. Learning Disabilities*, **7**, 26-34.

BURKHOLDER, R. B. (1968) 'The improvement in reading ability through the development of specific underlying or associated mental abilities', *Diss. Abstr.*, **29a**, 1157.

BURT, C. and LEWIS, R. B. (1946) 'Teaching backward readers', *Brit. J. Educ. Psychol.*, **16**, 116-32.

CANADIAN COMMITTEE, COUNCIL FOR EXCEPTIONAL CHILDREN (1971) *Standards for Educators of Exceptional Children in Canada*. Toronto: Crainford.

CANE, B. and SMITHERS, J. (1971) *The Roots of Reading*. Slough: NFER.

CARROLL, H. C. M. (1972) 'The remedial teaching of reading: an evaluation', *Remedial Education*, **7**, **1**, 10-5.

CARVER, C. (1970) *Word Recognition Test and Manual*. London: University of London Press.

CASHDAN, A. (1970) 'Backward readers – research on auditory-visual integration', in GARDNER, W. K. (ed). *Reading Skills: Theory and Practice*. London: Ward Lock.

CASHDAN, A., PUMFREY, P. D. and LUNZER, E. A. (1971) 'Children receiving remedial teaching in reading', *Educ. Res.*, **13**, 98-105.

CHALL, J., ROSWELL, F. G. and BLUMENTHAL, S. H. (1963) 'Auditory blending ability: a factor in success in beginning reading', *The Reading Teacher*, **17**, 113-8.

CHAPMAN, J. and WEDELL, K. (1972) 'Perceptual-motor abilities and reversal errors in children's handwriting', *J. Learning Disabilities*, **5**, 321-5.

CHARTERED INSTITUTE OF PUBLIC FINANCE AND ACCOUNTANCY AND SOCIETY OF COUNTY TREASURERS (1974) *Education Statistics*, 1972-3. London (joint publication).

CHAZAN, M. (1967) 'The effects of remedial teaching in reading: a review of research', *Remedial Education*, **2**, **1**, 4-12.

CHAZAN, M. and JACKSON, S. (1971) 'Behaviour problems in the infant school', *J. Child Psychol. Psychiat.*, **11**, 191-210.

CHAZAN, M., COX, T., JACKSON, A., LAING, A. and LLOYD, G. (1975) *Studies of Infant School Children, 1 Deprivation and School Progress, 2 Deprivation and Development*. Oxford: Blackwell (in press).

CHEATHAM, R. B. (1968) 'A study of the effects of group counselling on the self-concept and on the reading efficiency of low-achieving readers in a public-intermediate school', *Diss. Abstr.*, **29b**, 2200.

CHESHIRE EDUCATION COMMITTEE (1956) *The Education of Dull Children at the Primary Stage*. London: University of London Press.

CLARK, M. M. (1970) *Reading Difficulties in Schools*. Harmondsworth: Penguin.

CLARKE, A. D. B. (1969) 'Intelligence', Ch. 1 in MORRIS, J. F. and LUNZER, E. A. (eds.) *Contexts of Education*. London: Staples.

CLIFT, P. J. (1970) 'Factors affecting the growth of reading skills in children aged 8-9 years who are backward in reading', MEd. thesis, University of Manchester.

CLYNE, P. (1973) *The Disadvantaged Adult: Educational and Social Needs of Minority Groups*. London: Longman.

COLEMAN, J. S., CAMPBELL, E. Q., HOLSON, C. J., McPARTLAND, J., MOOD, A. M., WEINFELD, F. D. and YORK, R. L. (1966) *Equality of Educational Opportunity*. Washington, DC: Govt. Printing Office.

COLLINS, J. E. (1961) *The Effects of Remedial Education*. Edinburgh: Oliver and Boyd (for University of Birmingham Inst. Educ.).

COMMUNITY RELATIONS COMMISSION (1974) *In-Service Education of Teachers in Multi-Racial Areas*. London: CRC.

CORAH, N. L. and POWELL, B. J. (1963) 'A factor analytic study of the Frostig Development Test of Visual Perception', *Perceptual and Motor Skills*, **16**, 59-63.

COWEN, E. L., ZAX, M., IZZO, L. D. and TROST, M. A. (1966) 'Prevention of emotional disorders in the school setting: a further investigation', *J. Consult. Psychol.*, **30**, 381-7.

CRAIK, M. B. (1968) 'Associative learning and selective learning as stages in the development of reading', *Diss. Abstr.*, **29a**, 3868.

CRAWFORD, A. (1968) Unpublished study (mimeo). Abstract in *Bull. Brit. Psychol. Soc.*, **21**, 124.

CRITCHLEY, M. (1970) *The Dyslexic Child*. London: Heinemann.

CROOKES, T. G. and GREENE, M. C. L. (1963) 'Some characteristics of children with two types of speech disorder', *Brit. J. Educ. Psychol.*, **33**, 31-40.

CRUICKSHANK, W. M., BENTZEN, F. A., RATZEBURG, F. H. and TANNHAUSER, M. T. (1961) *A Teaching Method for Brain-injured and Hyperactive Children*. Syracuse: Syracuse University Press.

CULLEN, K. (1969) *School and Family*. Dublin: Gill and Macmillan.

DANIELS, J. C. and DIACK, H. (1958) *The Standard Reading Tests*. London: Chatto and Windus.

DAVIE, R., BUTLER, N. and GOLDSTEIN, H. (1972) *From Birth to Seven*. London: Longman.

DAVIES, P. and WILLIAMS, P. (1975) *Aspects of Early Reading Growth*. Oxford: Blackwell.

DEAN, D. (1973) 'An easy fit', *Times Educational Supplement*, 19/10/73.

DEARBORN, W. F. (1933) 'Structural factors which condition special disability in reading', *Proc. 57th Ann. Sess., Amer. Assoc. Ment. Def.*, **38**, 268-83.

DE HIRSCH, K., JANSKY, J. J. and LANGFORD, W. S. (1966) *Predicting Reading Failure*. New York: Harper and Row.

DEUTSCH, M. P. (1969) 'Happenings on the way back to the forum: social science, IQ, and race differences revisited', *Harvard Educational Review*, **39**, 523-57.

DE ZUTTER, P. (1973) 'The moulding of an inner city teacher', *Amer. Educ.*, **9, 5**, 22-7.

DOUGLAS, J. W. B., ROSS, J. M. and COOPER, J. E. (1967) 'The relationship between handedness, attainment and adjustment in a national sample of school children', *Educ. Res.*, **9**, 223-32.

DOWNING, J. and THACKRAY, D. V. (1971) *Reading Readiness*. London: University of London Press.

DUNHAM, J. (1960) 'The effects of remedial education on young children's reading ability and attitude to reading', *Brit. J. Educ. Psychol.*, **30**, 173-4.

DUNN, L. M. (1968) 'Special education for the mildly retarded – is much of it justifiable?' *Exceptional Children*, **35**, 5-22.

DUNN-RANKIN, P. (1968) 'The similarity of lower case letters of the English alphabet', *J. Verbal Learning and Verbal Behaviour*, **7**, 990-5.

DURRELL, D. D. and MURPHY, H. A. (1953) 'The auditory discrimination factor in reading readiness and reading disability', *J. Educ.* (University of Boston), **73**, 556-60.

DYKSTRA, R. (1966) 'Auditory discrimination abilities and beginning reading achievement', *Reading Research Quarterly*, **1**, 5-34.

EBBUTT, C. M., KASTELLANIDES, A., PRYTYS, C. and SCOTT, C. (1974) 'Small scale study of teaching backward readers in a secondary school'. (Mimeo.)

EDUCATION, MINISTRY OF (1950) *Reading Ability: Some Suggestions for Helping the Backward* (Pamphlet No. 18). London: HMSO.

EDUCATION AND SCIENCE, DEPARTMENT OF (1964) *Slow Learners at School* (Pamphlet No. 46). London: HMSO.

EDUCATION AND SCIENCE, DEPARTMENT OF (1967) *Children and their Primary Schools* (2 vols.). London: HMSO.

EDUCATION AND SCIENCE, DEPARTMENT OF (1971) *Slow Learners in Secondary Schools* (Education Survey 15). London: HMSO.

EDUCATION AND SCIENCE, DEPARTMENT OF (1972) *Children with Specific Reading Difficulties* (Report of the Advisory Committee on Handicapped Children). London: HMSO.

EDUCATION AND SCIENCE, DEPARTMENT OF (1972) *The Continuing Needs of Immigrants* (Education Survey 14). London: HMSO.

EDUCATION AND SCIENCE, DEPARTMENT OF (1973) 'Educational arrangements for immigrant children who may need special education', Circular letter to CEO's 1/11/73.

EDUCATION AND SCIENCE, DEPARTMENT OF (1975) *A Language for Life.* London: HMSO. (The Bullock Report.)

EDWARDS, C. (1971) 'Good looks and learning', *Remedial Education*, **6**, **1**, 18-9.

ELLIOTT, C. D. and PUMFREY, P. D. (1972) 'The effects of non-directive play therapy on some maladjusted boys', *Educ. Res.*, **14**, 157-61.

ELLSON, D. G., HARRIS, P. and BARBER, L. (1968) 'A field test of programmed and directed tutoring', *Reading Research Quarterly*, **3**, 307-67.

EVANS, R. (1972) *Swansea Evaluation Profiles: School Entrants. Technical Manual* (Report to Schools Council). University Coll., Swansea. (Mimeo.).

FAIRBANKS, J. and ROBINSON, J. (1967) 'Programme of Perceptual-Motor Development'. Boston: Teaching Resources, New York Times.

FAIRMAN, I. E. (1972) 'Tackling the cumulative reading handicap', *London Educational Review*, **1**, 75-80.

FERGUSON, N., DAVIES, P., EVANS, R. and WILLIAMS, P. (1971) 'The Plowden Report's recommendations for identifying children in need of extra help', *Educ. Res.*, **12**, 210-3.

FERNALD, G. M. (1943) *Remedial Techniques in the Basic School Subjects.* New York and London: McGraw-Hill.

FFOOKES, O. (1965) *The Ffookes Symbol Test.* London: Clement Clarke.

FIELD, F. (ed.) (1973) *Low Pay.* London: Arrow.

FINLAYSON, H. (1964) 'A study of maladjustment among the schoolchildren of an industrial small town'. Unpublished thesis, University of Glasgow.

FISHER, B. (1953) 'Group therapy and retarded readers', *J. Educ. Psychol.*, **44**, 354-60.

FLANDERS, N. A. (1970) *Analysing Teaching Behaviour.* New York: Addison-Wesley.

FLESCHER, I. (1960) 'Ocular-manual laterality and perceptual rotation of literal symbols', *Diss. Abstr.*, **21**, 681.

FOX, D. J. (1968) 'Evaluating the "More Effective Schools" ', *Phi Delta Kappan*, **49**, 593-7.

FRANCIS-WILLIAMS, J. (1963) 'Problems of development in children with "minimal brain damage" ', *Little Club Clinics in Developmental Medicine*, **10**, 39-45. London: Heinemann.

FRASER, E. D. (1959) *Home Environment and the School.* London: University of London Press. Revised edition 1974.

FROSTIG, M. and HORNE, D. (1964) *The Frostig Programme for the Development of Visual Perception.* Chicago: Follett.

FROSTIG, M., LEFEVER, D. W. and WHITTLESEY, I. R. (1961) *Developmental Test of Visual Perception.* Palo Alto: Consulting Psychologists Press.

FRYER, K. (1973) 'Parental involvement scheme', *Remedial Education*, **8**, **2**, 35-6.

GALIFRET-GRANJON, N. and AJURIAGUERRA, J. (1951) 'Troubles de l'appren-
tissage de la lecture et dominance latérale', *Encéphale*, **3**, 385-98.
GATES, A. I. and BOND, G. L. (1936) 'Relation of handedness, eye-sighting and
acuity dominance to reading', *J. Educ. Psychol.*, **27**, 450-6.
GATES, A. I., BOND, G. L. and RUSSELL, D. H. (1938) 'Relative meaning and
pronunciation difficulties of the Thorndike 20,000 words', *J. Educ. Res.*,
32, 161-7.
GEORGIADES, N. J. (1967) 'An experiment with i.t.a. in remedial reading', *New
Education* (Sept.), 11-2.
GIBSON, E. J., GIBSON, J. J., PICK, A. D. and OSSER, H. (1962) 'A develop-
mental study of the discrimination of letter-like forms', *J. Comp. Child
Psychol.*, **55**, 897-906.
GIEBINK, J. W. and GOODSELL, L. L. (1968) 'Reading ability and associative
learning for children with a visuomotor deficit', *Amer. Educ. Res. J.*,
5, 412-20.
GILLAM, P. (1974) *An Investigation into the self-concepts of 1st year secondary
school boys*. London: Child Guidance Training Centre. (Mimeo.)
GOINS, J. T. (1958) *Visual Perceptual Abilities and Early Reading Progress*,
Suppl. Educ. Monogr. No. 87. Chicago: University Chicago Press.
GOLDSTEIN, H. (1972) 'Home and school – Plowden re-examined', *Times
Educ. Suppl.*, 5/5/72.
GOLDSTEIN, H., MOSS, J. W. and JORDAN, L. J. (1965) *The Efficacy of Special
Class Training on the Development of Mentally Retarded Children*, Co-
operative Res. Proj. 619. Washington, DC: Dept. Health, Education and
Welfare, Office of Education.
GOODACRE, E. J. (1967) *Reading in Infant Classes*. Slough: NFER.
GOODACRE, E. J. (1968) *Teachers and their Pupils' Home Background*. Slough: NFER.
GOODACRE, E. J. (1971a) *Children and Learning to Read*. London: Routledge
and Kegan Paul.
GOODACRE, E. J. (1971b) *Provision for Reading*. University of Reading Centre
for the Teaching of Reading. Revised edition 1974.
GOODMAN, P. (1962) *Compulsory Miseducation*. Brooklyn: Horizon (also
[1971] in Penguin Books).
GOODWIN, C. (1974) 'Leicestershire: Countesthorpe College', contribution to
symposium, *Remedial Education*, **9**, 16-8.
GORDON, H. (1920) 'Left-handedness and mirror writing, especially among
defective children', *Brain*, **43**, 313-68.
GORDON, I. J. (1967) *A Parent Education Approach to Provision of Early Stimu-
lation for the Culturally Disadvantaged*. Final report to the Fund for the
Advancement of Education of the Ford Foundation.
GORDON, M. and WILSON, M. (1969) 'Helping the inadequate – a flexible
approach', *Remedial Education*, **4**, 76-8.
GRAHAM, F. K. and KENDALL, B. S. (1960) *Memory for Designs Test*. Missoula:
Psychol. Test Specialists.
GRAHAM, P. and RUTTER, M. (1970) 'Selection of children with psychiatric
disorder', Ch. 10 in RUTTER, M., TIZARD, J. and WHITMORE, K. (eds.).
Education Health and Behaviour. London: Longman.
GRAY, S. W., KLAUS, R. A., MILLER, J. O. and FORRESTER, B. J. (1966) *Before
First Grade: the Early Training Project for Culturally Deprived Children*.
New York: Teachers' College.
GREGORY, R. E. (1965) 'Unsettledness, maladjustment and reading failure: a
village study', *Brit. J. Educ. Psychol.*, **35**, 63-8.

GROSS, J. (1974) *Good and Poor Achievers in a Secondary School Remedial Reading Situation: a Pilot Study*. London: Child Guidance Training Centre. (Mimeo.)

HALSEY, A. H. (ed.) (1972) *Educational Priority Vol. 1*. London: HMSO.

HALSEY, A. H., MOSELEY, C., PAYNE, J., SMITH, G., SMITH, T. and WIDLAKE, P. (1973) 'Reading standards in educational priority areas', *Remedial Education*, **8, 2,** 16-23.

HAMBLIN, D. H. (1973) 'A model of counselling for the British secondary school' (abstract), *Bull. Brit. Psychol. Soc.*, **26,** 264-5.

HAMBLIN, J. A. (1970) 'Peer tutoring, token exchange effect on reading'. PHD thesis, University St Louis (summarized in HAMBLIN, R. L. and others, 1971).

HAMBLIN, R. L., BUCKHOLDT, D., FERRITOR, D., KOZLOFF, M. and BLACK-WELL, L. (1971) *The Humanization Processes: A Social, Behavioural Analysis of Children's Problems*. New York: Wiley.

HAMMILL, D. D. (1971) 'Evaluating children for instructional purposes', *Academic Therapy*, **6,** 341-53.

HAMMOND, D. (1967) 'Reading attainment in the primary schools of Brighton', *Educ. Res.*, **10,** 57-64.

HANNAM, C., SMYTH, C. and STEPHENSON, N. (1971) *Young Teachers and Reluctant Learners*. Harmondsworth: Penguin.

Hansard (1973) Written answer to question asked by Mr Parkinson, 25/10/73. London: HMSO.

HARRIS, A. J. (1957) 'Lateral dominance, directional confusion and reading disability', *J. Psychol.*, **44,** 283-94.

HARRIS, P. and TROTTA, F. (1962) 'An experiment with under-achievers', *Education*, **82,** 347-9.

HAVILAND, R. M. (1973) *Survey of Provision for Adult Illiteracy in England*. Reading: School of Education Centre for the Teaching of Reading.

HAWKRIDGE, D. G., CHALUPSKY, A. B. and ROBERTS, A. O. H. (1968) *A Study of Selected Exemplary Programmes for the Education of Disadvantaged Children* (2 vols.). Washington, DC: Dept. Health, Education and Welfare.

HEBRON, M. E. (1957) 'The mental and scholastic status of pupils in various streams of secondary modern schools', University of Hull Inst. Educ. *Studies in Education*, **2, 5,** 400-19.

HEINRICH, M. J. (1968) 'Sources of visual-motor dysfunctions associated with some cases of reading disorder', *Diss. Abstr.*, **29b,** 370.

HESS, R. D. (1968) 'Maternal behaviour and the development of reading readiness in urban negro children', in DOUGLASS, M. P. (ed.) *Claremont: Reading Conference, 32nd Yearbook*. Claremont: Claremont University Centre.

HEWETT, F. M., TAYLOR, E. D. and ARTUSO, A. A. (1969) 'The Santa Monica Project: an evaluation of an engineered classroom design with emotionally disturbed children', *Exceptional Children*, **35,** 523-9.

HILL, B. and MOOREHEAD, C. (1971) 'The making of adult illiterates', *Times Educ. Suppl.*, 1/10/71.

HILLMAN, H. H. (1956) 'The effect of laterality on reading disability', *Durham Research Review*, **7,** 86-96.

HIRSHOREN, A. (1969) 'A comparison of the predictive validity of the revised Stanford-Binet Intelligence Scale and the Illinois Test of Psycholinguistic Abilities', *Exceptional Children*, **35,** 517-21.

HIRST, W. B. (1970) *Prediction of Reading Success*, ERIC abstract of Amer. Educ. Res. Assoc. Conf., Minneapolis.

HODGE, H. P. R. and BAIN, L. D. (1971) *Report of a Preliminary Survey of 12 Secondary Special Schools in Glasgow.* Glasgow: Jordanhill College of Education.

HOLT, J. (1964) *How Children Fail.* New York: Pitman (also [1969] in Pelican Books).

HOPKINS, K. D. (1964) 'An empirical analysis of the efficacy of the WISC in the diagnosis of organicity in children of normal intelligence', *J. Genet. Psychol.*, **105**, 163-72.

HORTON, T. R. (1973) *The Reading Standards of Children in Wales.* Slough: NFER.

HOUSE OF COMMONS (1973) *Report of the Select Committee on Race Relations and Immigration. Education Vol. 1.* London: HMSO.

HUGHES, J. (1967) ' A review of electroencephalography in learning disabilities', in MYKELEBUST, H. (ed.). *Progress in Learning Disabilities.* New York: Grune and Stratton.

ILG, F. L. and AMES, L. B. (1950) 'Developmental trends in reading behaviour', *J. Genet. Psychol.*, **76**, 291-312.

ILLINGWORTH, R. S. (1963) 'The clumsy child', *Little Club Clinics in Developmental Medicine*, **10**, 26-7. London: Heinemann.

INNER LONDON EDUCATION AUTHORITY (1969) *Literacy Survey: Summary of Interim Results of the Study of Pupils' Reading Standards.*

INNER LONDON EDUCATION AUTHORITY (1971a) *Literacy Survey.*

INNER LONDON EDUCATION AUTHORITY (1971b) *Children with Special Difficulties.* Report to Education Schools Sub-Committee, 8/7/71.

INNER LONDON EDUCATION AUTHORITY (1974) *Children with Special Difficulties Scheme.* Report to Education Schools Sub-Committee, 16/7/74.

JACKSON, S. (1971a) *Get Reading Right.* Glasgow: Gibson.

JACKSON, S. (1971b) *A Teacher's Guide to Tests and Testing.* London: Longman.

JACOBS, J. N., WIRTHLIN, L. D. and MILLER, C. B. (1968) 'A follow-up evaluation of the Frostig visual perceptual training programme', *Educ. Leadership*, **26**, 169-75.

JACOBSON, L. I. and GREESON, L. E. (1972) 'Effects of systematic conceptual learning on the intellectual development of preschool children from poverty backgrounds: a follow-up study', *Child Dev.*, **43**, 1111-5.

JENCKS, C. (1973) *Inequality: a Reassessment of the Effect of Family and Schooling in America.* London: Allen Lane.

JENNINGS, S. (1973) *Remedial Drama.* London: Pitman.

JENSEN, A. R. (1968) 'Patterns of mental ability and socioeconomic status', *Proc. Nat. Acad. Sci.*, **60**, 1330-7.

JENSEN, A. R. (1973) *Educability and Group Differences.* London: Methuen.

JOHNSON, D. F. and MIHAL, W. L. (1973) 'Performance of blacks and whites in computerized versus manual testing environments', *Amer. Psychol.*, **28**, 694-9.

JOHNSON, M. S. and KRESS, R. A. (1964) 'Individual reading inventories', in *Proc. 21st Annual Reading Institute.* Newark: Internat. Reading Assoc.

JONES, H. (1969) 'Remedial approaches', *Remedial Education*, **4**, 108-12.

KALLOS, G. L., GRABOW, J. M. and GUARINO, E. A. (1961) 'The WISC profile of disabled readers', *Personnel and Guid. J.*, **39**, 46-8.

KASS, C. E. (1966) 'Psycholinguistic disabilities of children with reading problems', *Exceptional Children*, **32**, 533-9.

KATZ, P. A. and DEUTSCH, M. P. (1967) 'The relationship of auditory and visual functioning to reading achievement in disadvantaged children', in *The Disadvantaged Child.* New York: Basic Books.

KEDDIE, N. (ed.) (1973) *Tinker-Tailor . . . The Myth of Cultural Deprivation*. Harmondsworth: Penguin.

KELLER, M. (1937) 'Ocular dominance and the range of visual apprehension', *J. Exper. Psychol.*, **21**, 545-53.

KELLNER, R. (1967) 'The evidence in favour of psychotherapy', *Brit. J. Med. Psychol.*, **40**, 341-58.

KELSALL, R. K. and KELSALL, H. M. (1971) *Social Disadvantages and Educational Opportunity*. London: Holt, Rinehart and Winston.

KEMP, L. C. D. (1955) 'Environmental and other characteristics determining attainment in primary schools', *Brit. J. Educ. Psychol.*, **25**, 66-77.

KENDALL, B. S. (1948) 'A note on the relation of retardation in reading to a performance on a Memory-for-Designs test', *J. Educ. Psychol.*, **39**, 370-3.

KEOGH, B. K. (1965) 'The Bender Gestalt as a predictive and diagnostic test of reading performance', *J. Consult. Psychol.*, **29**, 83-4.

KINSBOURNE, M. and WARRINGTON, E. K. (1963) 'Developmental factors in reading and writing backwardness', *Brit. J. Psychol.*, 145-56.

KIRK, S. A. (1969) 'Learning disabilities: the view from here', paper given at 6th Ann. Conf. of Assoc. for Children with Learning Disabilities, reprinted in HAMMILL, D. D. and BARTEL, N. R. (eds.) (1971) *Educational Perspectives in Learning Disabilities*. New York: Wiley.

KIRK, S. A. and KIRK, W. D. (1971) *Psycholinguistic Learning Disabilities*. Urbana: University of Illinois Press.

KIRK, S. A., McCARTHY, J. J. and KIRK, W. D. (1968) *The Illinois Test of Psycholinguistic Abilities*, rev. ed. Urbana: University of Illinois Press.

KLASEN, E. (1972) *The Syndrome of Specific Dyslexia*. Baltimore: University Park Press.

KOZOL, J. (1967) *Death at an Early Age*. Boston: Houghton Mifflin (also [1968] in Penguin Books).

LACHMANN, F. M. (1960) 'Perceptual-motor development in children retarded in reading ability', *J. Consult. Psychol.*, **24**, 427-31.

LASKY, E. Z. and TOBIN, H. (1973) 'Linguistic and non-linguistic competing message effects', *J. Learning Disabilities*, **6**, 243-50.

LATHAM, D. (1971) *Six Reading Schemes: Their Emphases and Their Interchangeability*. Cambridge: Institute of Education.

LAWRENCE, D. (1971) 'The effects of counselling on retarded readers', *Educ. Res.*, **13**, 119-24.

LAWRENCE, D. (1972) 'Counselling of retarded readers by non-professionals', *Educ. Res.*, **15**, 48-51.

LAWRENCE, D. and BLAGG, N. (1974) 'Improved reading through self-initiated learning and counselling', *Remedial Education*, **9**, 61-3.

LAWSON, L. (1967) 'Opthalmological factors in learning disabilities', in MYKLEBUST, H. (ed.) *Progress in Learning Disabilities*. New York: Grune and Stratton.

LEE, W. R. (1960) 'Spelling Irregularity and Reading Difficulty in English, *Occ. Pub. No. 2*. Slough: NFER.

LEEVERS, S. (1974) *Teachers' Manual* (Remedial Package for Secondary Schools) St Albans: Programmed Learning Centre.

LEVINE, E., FINEMAN, C. and DONLON, G. (1972) *Prescriptive Profile Procedure for Children with Learning Disabilities*. Miami: Dade County Public Schools.

LEVITT, E. E. (1963) 'Psychotherapy with children: a further evaluation', *Behav. Res. and Therapy*, **1**, 45-51.

236 SPECIAL PROVISION FOR READING

LEWIS, A. (1972) 'The self-concepts of adolescent educational subnormal boys', Educ Res., 15, 16-20.
LITTLE, A. and SMITH, G. A. N. (1971) Strategies of Compensation: a Review of Educational Projects for the Socially Disadvantaged in the United States. Paris: OECD.
LITTLE, A., MABEY, C. and RUSSELL, J. (1972) 'Class size, pupil characteristics and reading attainment', in SOUTHGATE, V. (ed.) Literacy at All Levels. London: Ward Lock.
LOVELL, K., BYRNE, C. and RICHARDSON, B. (1963) 'A further study of the educational progress of children who had received remedial education', Brit. J. Educ. Psychol., 33, 3-9.
LOVELL, K., GRAY, E. A. and OLIVER, D. E. (1964) 'A further study of some cognitive and other disabilities in backward readers of average non-verbal reasoning scores', Brit. J. Educ. Psychol., 34, 275-9.
LOVELL, K., JOHNSON, E. and PLATTS, D. (1962) 'A summary of a study of the reading ages of children who had been given remedial teaching', Brit. J. Educ. Psychol., 32, 66-71.
LOVELL, K., SHAPTON, D. and WARREN, N. S. (1964) 'A study of some cognitive and other disabilities in backward readers of average intelligence as assessed by a non-verbal test', Brit. J. Educ. Psychol., 34, 58-64.
LYLE, J. G. (1969) 'Reading retardation and reversal tendency: a factorial study', Child Development, 40, 833-43.
LYTTON, H. (1961) 'An experiment in selection for remedial education', Brit. J. Educ., 31, 79-94.
LYTTON, H. (1966) 'Some psychological and sociological characteristics of "good" and "poor" achievers in remedial reading groups: clinical case studies', Human Development, 11, 260-76.
LYTTON, H. (1967) 'Follow-up of an experiment in selection for remedial education', Brit. J. Educ. Psychol., 37, 1-9.
MACBEATH, J. (1974) 'Breaking up the egg crates', Times Educ. Suppl., 11/1/74.
MAGUIRE, J. (1974) Preparing Reading Materials. National Association for Remedial Education, 9 Cranleigh Rise, Eaton, Norwich.
MALMQUIST, E. (1958) Factors Related to Reading Disabilities in the First Grade of the Elementary School. Stockholm: Almquist and Wiksell.
MALMQUIST, E. (1969) Lassvarigheter pa grundskolans lagstadium. Res. Report No. 13, Nat. Soc. for Educ. Res. Stockholm: Kungl.
MALMQUISTE, E. (197?) 'The teaching of reading in Sweden and provisions made for children who have difficulties in reading'. (Mimeo.)
MARJORIBANKS, K. (ed.) (1974) Environments for Learning. Slough: NFER.
MASON, D. (1972) Fun With Stones. Hove: Magic Steps Publications.
MASON, D. (1974) How to Help the Non-Reader. Hove: Magic Steps Publications.
MASON, E. (1969) 'Broadening the role of remedial teachers', Remedial Educ., 4, 23-6.
MAXWELL, A. E. (1961) 'Discrepancies between the pattern of abilities for normal and neurotic children', J. Ment. Science, 107, 300-7.
McCOLLUM, P. S. and ANDERSON, R. P. (1974) 'Group counselling with reading disabled children, J. Counselling Psychol., 21, 150-5.
McFIE (1952) 'Cerebral dominance in cases of reading disability', J. Neuro. Neurosurg. Psychiat., 15, 194-9.
McLEOD, J. (1969) Dyslexia Schedule and School Entrance Check List. Brisbane: University of Queensland Press.

McLeod, J. and Atkinson, J. (1972) *Domain Phonic Test Kit and Workshop*. Edinburgh: Oliver and Boyd.

McNeil, J. D. (1964) 'Programmed instruction versus usual classroom procedure in teaching boys to read', *Amer. Educ. Res. J.*, **14**, 113-9.

McNicholas, J. and McEntee, J. (1973) *Games to Develop Reading Skills*. National Association for Remedial Education, 9 Cranleigh Rise, Eaton, Norwich.

Merritt, J. E. (1969) 'Reading skills re-examined', *Special Education*, **58**, 1, 18-22.

Merritt, J. E. (1972) 'The Individual Student Resource Unit: reading and the curriculum?' Paper presented at 17th Annual Convention International Reading Association, Detroit.

Meyerowitz, J. H. (1962) 'Self-derogations in young retardates and special class placement', *Child Development*, **33**, 443-51.

Meyerowitz, J. H. (1967a) 'Peer groups and special classes', *Mental Retardation*, **5**, 5, 23-6.

Meyerowitz, J. H. (1967b) 'Parental awareness of mental retardation', *Amer. J. Ment. Defic.*, **71**, 637-43.

Modarressi, T. (1974) 'The effect of system transaction on children's perceptual and learning functions'. Paper given at IFLD Conf., Amsterdam.

Monroe, M. (1932) *Children who Cannot Read*. Chicago: University of Chicago Press.

Moon, C. (1975) *Individualized Reading*. University of Reading Centre for the Teaching of Reading.

Moore, T. (1966) 'Difficulties of the ordinary child in adjusting to primary school', *J. Child Psychol. Psychiat.*, **7**, 17-38.

Morgan, J. H. (1971) 'DIY at Dinsdale Park School', *Special Education*, **60**, 21-3.

Morley, M. E. (1972) *The Development and Disorders of Speech in Childhood* (3rd edition). Edinburgh: Livingstone.

Morris, J. M. (1966) *Standards and Progress in Reading*. Slough: NFER.

Morse, W. C., Cutler, R. L. and Fink, A. M. (1964) *Public School Classes for the Emotionally Handicapped: a Research Analysis*. Washington, DC: Council for Exceptional Children.

Moseley, C. E. G. (1972) *Communication in Schools*. York: University of York Lang. Teaching Centre.

Moseley, D. V. (1969a) 'Graphic cues for spelling', *Education*, **133**, 171-3.

Moseley, D. V. (1969b) 'The Talking Typewriter and remedial teaching in a secondary school: a comparative study of a basic literacy programme', *Remedial Education*, **4**, 196-202.

Moseley, D. V. (1969c) *The Value of the Talking Typewriter in the Teaching of Letter Recognition and Reading to Severely Retarded Handicapped Children*. Report to ILEA Research Comm. (Mimeo.) London: NSMHC.

Moseley, D. V. (1971a) *Verbal, Spatial and Spelling Abilities in 16 Hackney Junior Schools*. Report to ILEA. (Mimeo.)

Moseley, D. V. (1971b) 'A remedial programme for severely subnormal pupils with and without the Talking Typewriter', in Packham, D., Cleary, A. and Mayes, T. (eds.) *Aspects of Educational Technology V*. London: Pitman.

Moseley, D. V. (1971c) *The English Colour Code Programmed Reading Course*. London: Senlac.

Moseley, D. V. (1972a) 'What is special education?', *Parents Voice*, **22**, 1, 8-9.

Moseley, D. V. (1972b) 'Children who find reading and spelling difficult', in Brennan, W. K. (ed.) *Aspects of Remedial Education*. London: Longman.

MOSELEY, D. V. (1973) *Special Problems in Reading. Option 5, Units 15-16,* Open Univ. Course PE 261. Milton Keynes: Open University Press.

MOSELEY, D. V. (1974) 'Some cognitive and perceptual correlates of spelling ability', in WADE, B. and WEDELL, K. (eds.) 'Spelling: Task and Learner' (*Educational Review,* Occ. Pub. 5). Birmingham: Institute of Education.

MOSELEY, D. V. (1975) 'Applying diagnostic test results in individual learning programmes: a field project', paper given at IFLD Conf., Brussels.

MOSELEY, D. V. and SOWTER, D. (1972) 'The Hansel Training Machine, a new aid to (over) learning', in AUSTWICK, K. and HARRIS, N. D. C. (eds.) *Aspects of Educational Technology VI.* London: Pitman.

MOYLE, D. (1968) *The Teaching of Reading.* London: Ward Lock.

MUEHL, S. and KREMENAK, S. (1966) 'Ability to match information within and between auditory and visual sense modalities and subsequent reading achievement', *J. Educ. Psychol.,* **57,** 230-9.

MUGFORD, L. (1970) 'A new way of predicting readability', *Reading,* **4, 2,** 31-5.

NAIDOO, S. (1961) 'An investigation into some aspects of ambiguous handedness'. MA thesis, University of London.

NAIDOO, S. (1972) *Specific Dyslexia.* London: Pitman.

NARE, (1972) *Adult Illiteracy.* National Association for Remedial Education, 9 Cranleigh Rise, Eaton, Norwich.

NASH, R. (1973) *Classrooms Observed.* London: Routledge and Kegan Paul.

NEALE, M. D. (1958) *Analysis of Reading Ability.* London: MacMillan.

NELSON, H. E. and WARRINGTON, E. K. (1974) 'Developmental spelling retardation and its relation to other cognitive abilities', *Brit. J. Psychol.,* **65,** 265-74.

NICHOLSON, A. (1958) 'Background abilities related to reading success in the first grade', *J. Education, Univ. of Boston,* **140,** 7-24.

NISBET, J., WATT, J. and WELSH, J. (1972) *Reading Standards in Aberdeen 1962-1972.* University of Aberdeen.

NOBLE, G. and GRAY, K. (1968) 'The impact of programmed instruction: a longitudinal attitude study', *Prog. Learning and Educ. Technology,* **5,** 271-82.

OLSON, M. N. (1971) *Identifying Quality in School Classrooms: Some Problems and Some Answers.* MSSC Exchange, **29, 5,** New York: Metrop. School Study Council, Inst. Admin. Res., Teachers' College.

PARFIT, C. (ed.) (1974) *Scrapbooks 1, 2, and 3.* ILEA Media Resources Centre.

PASSOW, A. H., GOLDBERG, M. and JUSTMAN, J. (1966) *The Effects of Ability Grouping.* New York: Teachers' College.

PAYNE, J. (1974) *Educational Priority Vol. 2.* London: HMSO.

PEAKER, G. F. (1971) *The Plowden Children Four Years Later.* Slough: NFER.

PETERS, M. L. (1970) *Success in Spelling.* Cambridge: Institute of Education.

PINNINGTON, J. (1971) 'A follow-up study of the children given remedial teaching in reading at the remedial teaching centre, Huyton', DipTR Diss., Edge Hill College of Education.

PITMAN, J. (1970) *Let's Clear the Clutter.* London: i.t.a. Foundation.

POLLAK, M. (1972) *Today's Three-Year-Olds in London.* London: Heinemann.

POTTER, M. C. (1949) *Perception of Symbol Orientation and Early Reading Success.* Teachers' College Contrib. to Educ., No. 939. New York: Teachers' College.

PRIESTLEY, P. H. (1971) 'Bringing together services for special needs', *Times Educ. Suppl.,* 9/7/71.

PRINGLE, M. L. K. (1962) 'The long term effects of remedial education: a follow-up study', *Vita Humana,* **5,** 10-33.

PRINGLE, M. L. K. (1970) *Able Misfits*. London: Longman.

PRINGLE, M. L. K., BUTLER, N. and DAVIE, R. (1966) *11,000 Seven-year-olds*. London: Longman.

PRINGLE, M. L. K. and SUTCLIFFE, B. (1960) *Remedial Education – an Experiment*. Birmingham: Caldicott Community and Dept. of Child Study Institute of Education.

PUMFREY, P. D. (1969) 'Reading failure in an industrial city', *Remedial Education*, **4**, 149-53.

PUMFREY, P. D. (1970) 'Change in remedial education', *Remedial Education*, **5**, 1, 24-5.

PUMFREY, P. D. (1971) 'The extension of the peripatetic remedial teachers' professional expertise', *Remedial Education*, **6**, 2, 140-2.

PUMFREY, P. D. (1974) *Reading Tests and Assessment Techniques*. London: Univ. of London Press.

PUMFREY, P. D. and ELLIOTT, C. D. (1970) 'Play therapy, social adjustment and reading attainment', *Educ. Res.*, **12**, 183-93.

RABAN, B. (1974) *Reading Skill Acquisition*. University of Reading Centre for the Teaching of Reading.

RALPHSON, H. (1973) 'Absenteeism in a remedial department', *Remedial Education*, **8**, 3, 29-32.

REED, M. (1960) *Hearing Test Cards*. London: RNID.

REGER, R. and KOPPMANN, M. (1971) 'The child-orientated resource room programme', *Exceptional Children*, **37**, 460-2.

REID, J. F. (ed.) (1972) *Reading: Problems and Practices*. London: Ward Lock.

REHAB WORKING PARTY (1974) *People with Dyslexia*. London: British Council for the Rehabilitation of the Disabled.

REID, W. R. and SCHOER, L. (1966) 'Reading achievement, social class and subtest pattern on the WISC', *J. Educ. Res.*, **59**, 469-72.

REIMER, E. (1971) *School is Dead*. Harmondsworth: Penguin.

REYNOLDS, D. (1974) 'Some do, some don't', *Times Educ. Suppl.*, 10/5/74.

RIBICH, I. T. (1968) *Education and Poverty*. Washington, DC: Brookings Inst.

RIGLEY, L. (1968) 'Reading backwardness', *Isle of Wight Educ. and Med-Survey, Res. Bull.*, No. 9. (Mimeo.)

ROSENBERG, C. (1973) *Education and Society*. London: Rank and File.

RUBOWITS, P. C. and MAEHR, M. L. (1973) 'Pygmalion black and white', *J. Pers. Soc. Psychol.*, **25**, 210-18.

RUGEL, R. P. (1974) 'WISC subtest scores of disabled readers: a review with respect to Bannatyne's recategorization', *J. Learning Disabilities*, **7**, 48-55.

RUSHWORTH, F. D. (1974) 'Helping backward readers', *Times Educ. Suppl.*, 20/9/74.

RUSSELL, D. H. (1943) 'A diagnostic study of spelling readiness', *J. Educ. Res.* **37**, 276-83.

RUTTER, M. and GRAHAM, P. (1970) 'Psychiatric aspects of intellectual and educational retardation', Ch. 7 in RUTTER, M., TIZARD, J. and WHITMORE, K. (eds.) *Education, Health and Behaviour*. London: Longman.

RUTTER, M., TIZARD, J. and WHITMORE, K. (eds.) (1970) *Education, Health and Behaviour*. London: Longman.

RUTTER, M., YULE, W. and BERGER, M. (1974) 'The children of West Indian migrants', *New Society*, 14/3/74.

SABATINO, D. A. and HAYDEN, D. L. (1970) 'Information processing behaviours related to learning disabilities and educable mental retardation', *Exceptional Children*, **37**, 21-8.

SABATINO, D. A. and STREISSGUTH, H. W. O. (1972) 'Word form configuration. Training of visual perceptual strengths with learning disabled children', *J. Learning Disabilities*, **5**, 62-8.

SABATINO, D. A., YSSELDYKE, J. E. and WOOLSTON, J. (1973) 'Diagnostic – prescriptive perceptual training with mentally retarded children', *Amer. J. Ment. Defic.*, **78**, 7-14.

SAMPSON, O. C. (1969) 'Remedial education services: report on an enquiry', *Remedial Education*, **4**, 3-8, 61-5.

SAMPSON, O. C. and PUMFREY, P. D. (1970) 'A study of remedial education in the secondary stage of schooling', *Remedial Education*, **5**, 102-11.

SCHONELL, F. J. (1948) *Backwardness in the Basic Subjects* (4th edition). Edinburgh: Oliver and Boyd.

SCHONELL, F. J. and SCHONELL, F. E. (1950) *Diagnostic and Attainment Testing*. Edinburgh: Oliver and Boyd.

SCHOOL OF BARBIANA (1970) *Letter to a Teacher*. Harmondsworth: Penguin.

SCHOOLS COUNCIL (1970) *Teaching English to West Indian Children*, Working Paper 29. London: Evans/Methuen.

SCOTT, G. (1973) 'Chaos behind staff shortage', *Times Educ. Suppl.*, 26/10/73.

SHEARER, E. (1967) 'The long-term effects of remedial education', *Educ. Res.*, **9**, 219-22.

SHEPHERD, E. M. (1956) 'Reading efficiency of 809 average school-children', *Amer. J. Ophthal.*, **41**, 1029-39.

SHOUKSMITH, G. and TAYLOR, J. W. (1964) 'The effect of counselling on the achievement of high-ability pupils', *Brit. J. Educ. Psychol.*, **34**, 51-7.

SILBERBERG, N. E., IVERSEN, I. A. and GOINS, J. T. (1973) 'Which remedial method works best ?', *J. Learning Disabilities*, **6**, 547-57.

SILVERMAN, H. (1962) 'Correlates of reading disability in children', PhD thesis, University of London.

SMITH, G. A. N. (ed.) (1975) *Educational Priority, Vol. 4*. London: HMSO.

SMITH, M. E. (1926) 'An investigation of the development of the sentence and the extent of vocabulary in young children', *Studies in Child Welfare III*, No. 5. Iowa City: University of Iowa.

SONENBERG, C. and GLASS, G. (1965) 'Reading and speech: an incidence and treatment study', *The Reading Teacher*, **19**, 197-201.

STANLEY, J. C. (ed.) (1973) *Compensatory Education for Children Ages 2 to 8*. Baltimore: Johns Hopkins University Press.

START, K. B. and WELLS, B. K. (1972) *The Trend of Reading Standards*. Slough: NFER.

STENNER, A. J. and MUELLER, S. G. (1974) 'A successful compensatory education model', *Phi Delta Kappan*, **55**, 246-8.

STERRITT, G. M. (1966) 'Auditory and visual rhythm perception in relation to reading ability in 4th grade boys', *Perceptual and Motor Skills*, **22**, 859-64.

STEVENSON, C. (1972) *i.t.a. with Adult Backward Readers: a Survey of a Five-Year Experiment in the British Army*, evidence submitted to REHAB working party. (Mimeo.)

STOREY, E. (1972) 'Sixth form reading tutors', *Times Educ. Suppl.*, 22/12/72.

STOTT, D. H. (1971a) *The Social Adjustment of Children. Manual to the Bristol Social Adjustment Guides*. London: University of London Press.

STOTT, D. H. (1971b) *Flying Start Learning-to-Learn Manual*. Guelph: Brook; Glasgow: Holmes McDougall.

STOTT, D. H. (1974) *The Parent as Teacher: a Guide for Parents of Children with Learning Difficulties*. London: University of London Press.

STOTT, D. H., MARSTON, N. C. and BOUCHARD, S. J. (1970) 'Behaviour disturbance in children – classification, epidemiology, etiology' (mimeo.) Pending publication, available from University of Guelph.

TANSLEY, A. E. (1967) *Reading and Remedial Reading*. London: Routledge and Kegan Paul.

TAYLOR, E. A. (1957) 'The spans: perception, apprehensive and recognition', *Amer. J. Opthal.*, **44**, 501-7.

TAYLOR, G. and AYRES, N. (1969) *Born and Bred Unequal*. London: Longman.

THACKRAY, D. V. (1971) *Readiness to Read with i.t.a. and t.o.* London: Geoffrey Chapman.

THACKRAY, D. V. and THACKRAY, L. (1974) *Thackray Reading Readiness Profiles*. London: ULP.

THWEATT, R. C. (1963) 'Prediction of school learning disabilities through the use of the Bender Gestalt test', *J. Clin. Psychol.*, 216-7.

TORDRUP, S. A. (1966) 'Reversals in reading and spelling', *Slow Learning Child*, **12**, 173-83.

TOWNSEND, H. E. R. (1971) *Immigrant Pupils in England: the LEA Response*. Slough: NFER.

TOWNSEND, H. E. R. and BRITTAN, E. M. (1972) *Organization in Multiracial Schools*. Slough: NFER.

TURNER, E. W. (1972) 'The effect of long summer holidays on children's literacy', *Educ. Res.*, **14**, 182-6.

UNIVERSITY OF READING CENTRE FOR THE TEACHING OF READING. *Information Leaflets: Learning to Read*; *Reading Resources*.

US COMMISSION ON CIVIL RIGHTS (1967) *Racial Isolation in the Public Schools* (2 vols.). Washington, DC: Govt. Printing Office.

US NATIONAL ADVISORY COMMITTEE ON HANDICAPPED CHILDREN (1968) *First Annual Report, Special Education for Handicapped Children*. Washington, DC: Dept. Health, Education and Welfare, Office of Education.

VALETT, R. E. (1970) 'The learning resource centre for exceptional children', *Exceptional Children*, **36**, 527-30.

VAUGHAN, M. (1972) 'Each one teach one', *Times Educ. Suppl.*, 7/4/72.

VERNON, P. E. (1968) 'What is potential ability?', *Bull. Brit. Psychol. Soc.*, **21**, 211-9.

WALLBRIDGE, J. M. (1972) ' "his own rede" An essay in the teaching of reading' (Mimeo.)

WALTERS, C. E. (1961) 'Reading ability and visual-motor function in second grade children', *Perceptual and Motor Skills*, **13**, 370.

WECHSLER, D. and HAGIN, R. A. (1964) 'The problems of axial rotation in reading disability', *Perceptual and Motor Skills*, **19**, 319-26.

WEDELL, K. (1960) 'The visual perception of cerebral palsied children', *Child Psychol. and Psychiat.*, **1**, 215-27.

WEDELL, K. (1973) *Learning and Perceptuo-motor Disabilities in Children*, London: Wiley.

WEIKART, D. P. (1970) 'A comparative study of three preschool curricula', Ypsilanti Public Schools. (Mimeo)

WEINER, L. H. (1969) 'An investigation of the effectiveness of resource rooms for children with specific learning disabilities', *J. Learning Disabilities*, **2**, 223-29.

WEINER, P. S., WEPMAN, J. M. and MORENCY, A. S. (1965) 'A test of visual discrimination', *Elementary School J.*, **65**, 330-7.

WEPMAN, J. M. (1958) *Auditory Discrimination Test*. Chicago: Lang. Res. Assoc.

WESTINGHOUSE LEARNING CORPORATION AND OHIO UNIVERSITY (1969) *The Impact of Headstart: an Evaluation of the Effects of Headstart on Children's Cognitive and Affective Development* (2 vols.). New York: Westinghouse Learning Corporation.

WHETNALL, E. and FRY, D. B. (1964) *The Deaf Child*. London: Heinemann.

WHIPPLE, C. I. and KODMAN, F. (1969) 'A study of discrimination and perceptual learning with retarded readers', *J. Educ. Psychol.*, **60**, 1-5.

WILLIAMS, K. (1969) 'The role of the remedial department in a comprehensive school', *Remedial Education*, **4, 2**, 69-72.

WILLIAMS, P. (1961) 'The growth of reading vocabulary and some of its implications', *Brit. J. Educ. Psychol.*, **31**, 104-5.

WILLIAMS, P. (1970) *Swansea Test of Phonic Skills*. Oxford: Blackwell.

WILLIAMS, P. and GRUBER, E. (1967) *Response to Special Schooling*. London: Longman.

WILSON, J. A. (1971) *Environment and Primary Education in Northern Ireland*. Belfast: NICER.

WINKLER, R. C., TEIGLAND, J. J., MUNGER, P. F. and KRANZLER, G. D. (1965) 'The effects of selected counselling and remedial techniques on underachieving elementary school students', *J. Counselling Psychol.*, **12**, 384-7.

WISEMAN, S. (1967) 'The Manchester Survey', App. 9, Vol. 2 of DES report, *Children and their Primary Schools*. London: HMSO.

WITTY, P. A. and KOPEL, D. (1936) 'Sinistral and mixed manual ocular behaviour in reading disability', *J. Educ. Psychol.*, **27**, 119-34.

WOLFENDALE, S. and BRYANS, T. (1972) 'Identification and follow-up of slow readers in the primary school', *AEP Journal*, **3, 2**, 77-80.

WOODY, C. and PHILLIPS, A. J. (1934) 'The effects of handedness on reversals in reading', *J. Educ. Res.*, 651-62.

WRAGG, E. C. (1973) 'A study of student teachers in the classroom', in CHANAN, G. (ed.) *Towards a Science of Teaching*. Slough: NFER.

YOUNG, D. (1964) *Non-Readers Intelligence Test*. London: University of London Press.

YOUNG, D. and STIRTON, M. E. (1971) 'GWR test equivalences and reading ages', *Remedial Education*, **6, 3**, 7-8.

YULE, W. (1973) 'Differential prognosis of reading backwardness and specific reading retardation', *Brit. J. Educ. Psychol.*, **43**, 244-8.

YULE, W. and RUTTER, M. (1970) 'Selection of children with intellectual or educational retardation', Ch. 3 in RUTTER, M., TIZARD, J. and WHITMORE, K. (eds.) *Education, Health and Behaviour*. London: Longman.

ZACH, L. and KAUFMAN, J. (1972) 'How adequate is the concept of perceptual deficit for education ?', *J. Learning Disabilities*, **5**, 351-6.

Index of authors